Bridie's Boy

Sean Brennan

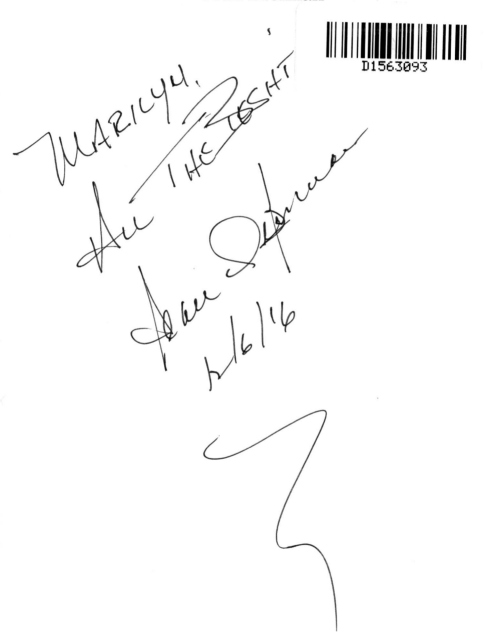

MARILYN,

ALL THE BEST

Sean Brennan

7/6/16

Bridie's Boy

Published By

Kiltimagh Press

Sean Brennan's other published works:
The Altar Boy

AUTHOR'S NOTE

I have tried to recreate events, locales and conversations from my memories of them. In order to maintain their anonymity I have changed the names of individuals and places and in some cases altered identifying characteristics.

Library of Congress Catalog Card Number: 2014908542

ISBN-13 978-1495345135

10 1495345130

www.bridiesboy.com

Dedicated to
Bridie and Tom Brennan
and the *Spirit* that is Cloonmore

Table of Contents

Part I

Part II

Epilogue

Bridie's Boy

By

Sean Brennan

Prologue

The seasonal time change must have occurred that day. "Set your clocks. Fall back." We were caught in the dark outdoors. We would never have been out in the pitch black like that but the unexpected night fell as we were walking home from reciting a Novena at the well-named Our Lady of Sorrows, our parish church.

Most Friday nights were spent like this one – clutching our rosary beads and reciting "Hail Mary's" to the mournful statue of Our Lady in that cavernous Basilica. Novena means "nine" in Latin, the language they would try to teach us in high school. Way back when, Mary, mother of Jesus, convened with the Apostles and waited for a little dove to descend upon them and inject them with the *Holy Spirit*. The dove lost his bearings and didn't arrive for nine days but when he did, Mary and the Apostles had the Spirit. And that's why we were here… to get it too.

To finish a Novena, all we needed was to know the whole prayer, "Hail Mary, Mother of God…" and have the ability to say it ten times. Getting to ten was the hard part because you always lost your count.

"That's number nine."

"No, it's number ten."

"Nine!"

"Ten!"

"Just say an extra one. God will have the count."

"Hail Mary Mother of… done, got the Spirit."

Outside the Basilica, as dusk fell, there was always some time for the ladies to kibitz and exchange the week's events. A good piece of gossip was always a pleasant nightcap to the lengthy Novena. And Bridie wasn't above that. The stories were always

1

made juicy even if they weren't. And as one story ended, the next one began, "Did you hear about...?" It was easy to forget the time

Tonight it was just Bridie and the three youngest lads: Boroimhe (Ba-roo), Phelim and I. "Oh, BeJasus, it's getting dark," Bridie said, remembering that walking home in the dark had its dangers. Daylight saving had changed the weekend before and we still weren't used to it. But we had the Spirit now, after another successful Novena and who would be nuts enough to challenge that?

"Come on lads, let's pick it up," she said as both the darkness and silence descended. All you could hear were our footsteps, and all you could see were the shadows of Mozart Lane slowly growing darker and longer with each step. And then...

"We'll have your purse, lady."

Two teenage punks had jumped out from around the next corner. Well, if you've ever seen a bear protect her cubs or a duck guard her ducklings, you'll get the picture. Bridie stepped forward, and with her powerful arms swept all three of us behind her and looked around for some kind of help.

"Oh no, you won't." Bridie yelled back trying to buy some time. Both the bad guys jumped back. Above us, a second floor window opened and for an instant, I imagined it was a neighbor who would help us.

"Call the police," Bridie hollered.

A woman appeared at the window and called down, "You're on your own, lady," and started to laugh. Bridie wasn't one to ever need much help. She looked around and spotted a rusted can in the gutter. She sidestepped over to the curb, holding us behind her and grabbed the can.

"All right lads. The odds have evened a bit and I'm wondering which of yee will be first?" Bridie held the can up and the jagged edge caught the rays of the street light and sent a ray of Spirit toward the bad guys. They blinked and threw up their arms to fend off the ray.

"You'll pay a price to get my loot. You might want to reconsider. I don't give change." Bridie's bravado grew and she jabbed forward with the can. The bad guys were in a slight retreat now. By now we were peeking around Bridie's side, a bit braver too.

"Well…," she said, "I'm running out of patience." The two bad guys turned to each other, thought better of their heist…and ran off.

"Thanks for nothing," she called up to the lady and pegged the can at the window. The lady ducked, the can bounced off the window sill and came crashing down to the sidewalk and spun like a top.

"Come on lads." And we scurried home.

When we were clear of the muggers and safe at home, Bridie soothed us with her most favorite treat—lightly grilled cheese sandwiches. All trauma was treated in the kitchen with a special something. It wasn't the treat that made you feel special, it was who it came from, and there was no one better than Bridie. She gave the Sorrowful Mother and the Novenas a plug as we noshed our treat. "Did you see that ray of light when I picked up the can?"

"Oh, yeah, Ma, but how come there are bad guys in the first…"

"No questions tonight. We'll savor our good graces without thought."

I was five and that was my first memory of my mother, Bridie, and all that she was. Bridie's magic could turn one harrowing moment into a comforting one. In one brief evening she taught me how to count, how to say the "Hail Mary", how to recognize guidance from above, how to not question it, how to stand up to wrong and finally, how to soothe any sore like it was a blessing.

She wasn't all bows and ribbons either. You see, Bridie knew how to drop the hatchet too. And she did often, but that will come later.

For now, Bridie is the heroine, and not just for me. You see, she and Tom Brennan brought eleven children into the world. Five lasses were born first, followed by six *"bys"* as she sometimes referred to us in her lilting Irish brogue. All thirteen of us became celebrities in Chicago because Tom Brennan found time to design and tailor Easter outfits for the whole clan and parade us around Chicago. On Easter Sunday we would find a Chicago landmark, pose like generals after a great victory, and get photographed by the Chicago newspapers. The photos would travel the world and with them the lore of the "Oak Park Brennans" grew.

"Hey, Tom, how was it that all the girls came first and the boys followed?"

"I remember flipping the mattress once," Tom replied, as proud of his brood as a rooster in a barnyard.

From 1939 to '53, Bridie was never barefoot and mostly pregnant. Back then when the Pope still had sway and mandated having as many children as possible there was no such thing as birth control, only rhythm. Bridie and Tom Brennan wanted to have lots of children but they wanted them spaced out a bit so Bridie engaged in circling the calendar and counting the days.

"Ma, how come you're circling the calendar?"

"Counting the days till Christmas," she'd say.

The calendar went missing often, usually a tool for some school project and would return with missing days, weeks and months. "Ah, it's no blessed use." And Mother Nature would take back the reins and Bridie would be blessed with another of her precious children. And the homework was done too. So rhythm stayed in the dance halls and Bridie and Tom had another angel to christen. I'm grateful because now I have a tale to tell.

I was the tenth child and the fifth son, and a prize at that because St. Anne's, the Catholic hospital (a Protestant one would never do) brought me into the world for free, a "ten for one" deal. My mother went on to have one more lad, the caboose, my brother, Phelim.

Bridie was one of ten (four girls and six boys) and was reared on a dairy farm in Cloonmore, Eire. She emigrated when she was seventeen, fleeing the abject poverty of Ireland for the promise of economic opportunity in America. Landing in Chicago, just two weeks before the 1929 stock market crash, she was following her oldest sister Anne's lead. The Irish faced the usual prejudice, being the new ones on the block and the lowest on the totem pole, and could only find servants' work.

"Bridget, we'll call you Bridie and tone down the Gaelic." Anne had said.

"What about the brogue?"

"Never thought of that...only speak when spoken to."

A plan to tone down the Irishness of an Irishman has little chance of success. There's a pride that glows like the isle itself. Conversation is what they live for. And spirit? Nary a bird is needed and their own brand seeps from the grit in their gut. Bridie already had enough of her own. She must have, because prejudice, poverty and hardship never got her down and only served to make a great girl better. Within a few years she met Tom Brennan and the two of them brought eleven of us into the world and injected us with the values that we all cherish and adore...appreciation, respect, humility, hard work...and our own brand of spirit. And with Bridie's nest, arms and heart full, our story begins.

Cloonmore

"I think it's time," Daddy said, time for the Brennan family to move, to flee Chicago's West Side. We'd had too many close calls. Bridie had surprised an intruder in her own closet. She ran to the kitchen, grabbed her heaviest cast iron frying pan, opened the back door, ran to the front and opened it and ordered the bugger to depart.

"I'm giving you a choice lad, front or back." And then she raised the pan, cocked her head, curled her lip; a look that she used when the receiver had no options…and waited. Not for long, the intruder raced from the house. There had been other incidents, but the attack of the muggers and the flash of that jagged tin can cut the last tie. As much as Tom and Bridie loved the old neighborhood and Our Lady of Sorrows parish, they couldn't risk the safety of their family anymore, especially if Bridie's boys were in danger. Bridie had been through the search for a new world before, leaving Ireland and her family, so it was old hat now, and when Daddy announced a new house in the suburbs, excitement reigned. For all thirteen of us, five lasses and six lads, there would be grass and bikes and alleys and new schools and new friends and a house that could fit us all…or almost.

"You're going to love it," Daddy crowed after he had sealed the deal on the old Victorian wood frame on Euclid Avenue in Oak Park. "It needs a little work, but we're more than capable,"… was our first clue.

On the historic day of the move, Daddy rounded up the regular Irish crew of uncles and brothers-in-law, the usual bottle of poteen, and loaded all of our prized possessions onto a trailer and directed the crew west. Then, after the old sod crew had departed, it was time for a final moment in front of the old two-flat gray stone on Mozart Lane. All of us stood on the curb and peered up like it was an altar. Reverence, remembrance, respect and then tears for the home that had housed so much of us for so long. It was empty and hollow now… except for the memories. They would never go away.

"Time!" Daddy belted out, snapping us from the somber mood.

We all piled into Pop's '48 Cadillac limousine. The "Caddy" was the one, single, luxurious-looking thing we owned and an incongruous vehicle for our crew. The limousine had a movie star/or kingpin aura, with running boards that made the lads feel like Eliot Ness searching for bootleggers. The long, navy blue limo had coasted into our world only because it was already ten-years-old, cheap enough to buy, and could cram all thirteen of us inside. It needed an engine when Daddy bought it. The grand Cadillac had sleek flanks and a silver goddess ornament on its hood. Her metal hair blown back by a permanent wind, her lithe body flattened in aerodynamic grace, her sculptured beauty, leading as if on the prow of a ship. "Forge the trail and bring us luck, honey."

The "Caddy" was cavernous…until we showed up. Window seats were a premium especially on a hot summer day. So were the seats that folded out from the floor. You felt like a movie star when you were lucky enough to get one of those. Every time there was an outing there was a mad dash to claim some perceived plum station. The usual fights ensued, "You always get that one…" And then Bridie put in, "Share! Take turns!"

But today, for some reason, the battles were limited, maybe because everyone was so lethargic from being sad about leaving Mozart Lane. In neat order, the five lasses, Anne, Bantry, Riley, Kaitlin and Megan sat down in the double, back plush rows. Boroimhe and Michael found a lap. Phelim and I (the little boys) wedged ourselves between Tom and Bridie in front, and Tommy and Padraig, the movie stars, got the pop-ups.

Most times, the two of us who sat in the front between Ma and Pa were adjudged "sissies" for avoiding the battles in the back. But not today, as the somber mood outweighed the need for mischief, and the big navy blue Caddy pulled from the curb and edged its way down Mozart Lane toward Jackson Boulevard.

As Daddy hit the gas, as if on cue, we all craned our necks, trying to get one last glimpse at what would soon be our "old neighborhood." Tom Brennan took it slow, knowing that an Irishman needs time to say good-bye. The car listed as we all leaned toward the right, looking back, caressing the last few moments that we had in front of the old manse. With each turn of the wheels the old gray stone diminished and finally disappeared when Daddy made a hard left and headed west down Jackson Boulevard. Westward-ho! The houses started to pass faster as Daddy built-up speed sending fresh breezes over the hood goddess' hair and our open windows. "Ahhh, that feels good!" With each gust our catharsis grew more complete and then the first stop light. We hated the stop lights when the fresh air stalled and inside the squirming began again …

"Move over!"

"Your elbow!"

"Who's the sissy in front?"

"Are we there yet?"

The catharsis was now complete, as the battles renewed.

As we traveled west and left the old neighborhood behind, the houses grew bigger and were better kept; each house had more and more grass. It was early autumn and the great leafy trees tinged with gold hovered over the sturdy homes. We were getting close; we could sense it.

"It's supposed to be around here somewhere."

Ridgeland, Scoville, East, Wesley...We passed a big gray mansion perched on a hilltop.

"Oh, look at the haunted house." I said. It stood erect and... well...haunted, windows blank, empty-socketed, elegant but abandoned. I instantly vowed to explore it someday. My instinct told me treasure and adventure lay within...

Our excitement grew as the promise of our new world neared; our own grand new house with a lawn, trees, a place where we could have bikes, play outdoors, and have more ROOM, that's what we wanted most. ROOM-everywhere, just make it roomy, in the bedroom, in the yard, in the ...

"What's our new street called?" Padraig called out from the back seat.

"Euclid," Daddy answered.

"Oh, the astronomer," Michael bellowed.

"Classy, Pa," Tommy added, "from Mozart to Euclid."

Tom Brennan loved when you displayed anything that you had learned, so we fed him "culture" regularly. He had a smile on his face.

"Just passed Euclid," Anne noted.

"Goddamn...mmm," Daddy's smile was gone. Tom Brennan rarely swore but let one fly every now and then. He always caught himself in the middle of his expletive and let the final syllable die without finish. It was his way of keeping the curse an arguable event. Maybe he didn't.

He pulled a hard right down the alley just after the missed turn and slowed as we passed the neatly kept garages.

"Hey, a hoop. Look!" Tommy screamed from the back. A mad scramble to the side windows ensued in the back, making the Caddy list, this time to the right.

"Yahoo!" came the next howl.

"Got to make friends over there," Michael called out. We finally made it around the corner and pulled up in front of our new home, 321 S. Euclid. The tires stopped groaning as we tipped back to the left.

"Cloonmore!" someone yelled.

Cloonmore stood before us, as big as a church and with the same emptiness. The grass was six inches high, the shutters askew, and the paint chipped, but no matter… there was room and lots of it. The three-story house with its pointed gables looked huge. Gracing the porch were bridal veil hedges and a tall blue spruce that shielded ole Cloonmore from the north winds.

Above the front steps, hanging from the eaves and swinging in the breeze was a shingle, painted yellow and green that read "Cloonmore" in a beautiful calligraphic style. Tom Brennan was at it again, gracing our new manse with his usual artistry in honor of Bridie's hometown in the old sod.

Bridie caught her breath and looked to Tom. He looked back and clutched her around the waist and pulled her closer. They kissed. Embarrassed at any act of intimacy, we looked away.

"What's Cloonmore?" one of us asked. We knew Daddy loved questions.

"Your mother's home village and our new home," he said. "Tara is way too ordinary."

Everyone hushed from the sentiment. No one got the quip. We were too excited, busy taking in the look of our new home and the possibilities it offered us: the wraparound veranda that would later serve as our hockey rink, and below the porch the lattice covered "secret" space that would soon become our hidden club house.

We started toward Cloonmore, the grass thick round our legs… "How long since anyone lived here?"

"Her name was Mrs. Mole," Daddy said. "She was ninety-five and she croaked in the side bedroom where the girls are going to sleep."

The girls screamed in unison: "EEEEEK! We're switching with the lads."

"One play, Ma?" Tommy asked Bridie.

"Just one, there's work to do."

Tom, the oldest boy and our captain took the ball he had been clutching since we had left…waiting, just waiting for the new grass.

"Line it up boys," he called out, "Just like on Mozart."

We dutifully complied, two on one side, three on the other, Tommy in the back waiting for the snap. "Hup, Hup," and we broke into motion, the defense charging and the receivers wading through the knee high grass, one on a slant, one on an out pattern and then Tom's perfect spiral, a catch on the neighbor's lawn and our first "Touchdown!" We all yelled, "Yahoo!" "Daddy," "We got grass!"

"Have."

Pell mell, we raced in to explore the house that was filled with silent, empty chambers. The old sod crew with our furniture was lost… or somewhere refilling their brown paper bags. Everywhere, we found dust, more dust, cobwebs and lots of old radiator covers. Coughing, we took the stairs.

"Where's the haunted room, where old lady Mole croaked?"

"Mrs. Mole," from Bridie.

We ran upstairs seeking the haunted room, then slowed and started to tiptoe and then stopped, suddenly realizing that the ghost of Mrs. Mole was at hand. Curiosity got the better of us like it always did and we started again, one behind the other clutching the guy in front of you, inching closer to the bedroom door and peeked around the corner only to discover an empty rocking chair in an empty room, slowly rocking back and forth. The window was open and a soft breeze was blowing the sheer curtains as if a ghost was inside them. "EEEEK!" someone yelled just as Bridie barged into the room, slammed the window shut, stopped the chair from rocking and declared, "Mole is dead and buried ...in the ground."

Upstairs, there were four bedrooms and the house's single bathroom. For the thirteen of us, there was the obvious need for some division. The ladies would get two rooms, Mom and Pops one bedroom, and the six lads the last one, the front bedroom with three beds, and told to divvy things up. It was another dilemma of not enough to go around and the foundation of our greatest attribute...sharing. "Divvy it up," Bridie would say when selflessness was needed. That front bedroom was actually as large as two bedrooms, twelve feet by twenty-four feet, but had only a single closet and a lone, scarred dresser.

Within a few days, with all of us working, we had the place swept out and clean. The old sod crew had arrived a little late and a little unsteady (the brown bags were empty) and moved in what furniture we had. It was mostly a scarred lot of utilitarian bureaus and old beds. There was one heirloom in the house, a genuine antique: Bridie's china cabinet, filled with sentiment and the fine china and silverware that came from her wedding and was used only at Thanksgiving and Christmas. Faded photos of Eire, a tress of her sister Anne's hair who had died in childbirth, her ticket that brought her to America...it had to be priceless to find a home here.

The brown baggers set down the cabinet in the exact place where Bridie directed, in the dining room, our first one. It would become the essay room, the sewing room, the meeting room, the room where all of us could sit at one table, together. And there the cabinet sat for the next thirty years, safe and secure right where Bridie could find it as she turned from the kitchen into the dining room. Safe from foul balls and sliced golf shots, secure as Bridie's legacy and her most prized possession... save her kids.

Making Do

Not much at Cloonmore was mainstream or would ever be. Our relocation dropped us into the middle of lily white, modernized, suburbia where some assimilation was needed. Being the new kids on the block opened a few doors for us and revealed what we were up against. The neighborhood was already colonized by Irish Catholic families who were earlier emigrants. All the neighbor families had escaped some old neighborhood somewhere in the city and found a home in Oak Park.

Our block had lots of kids. The Maloney's had nine, the Curran's eleven, the McHugh's nine, the Newton's eleven, and the Kennedys, one of the smaller troupes, "only seven." There was a reason for the large families: Catholicism. There was no such thing as birth control so the family numbers were just plain old fates in the wind. Abstinence was no option, only when you had to give something up for Lent...and Lent lasted six long weeks.

I was grateful for all of the fertility because I ended up being the tenth of eleven children and got to be a part of all the madness.

Bridie's brood was complete... but not much else. Her kids were as different as the furniture in her house and the instruments we all played around the piano on Sunday nights. There was an accordion and a clarinet, and trombone, and violin, and trumpet and Padraig on the drums and the rest of the lads belting out the latest standard from "Oklahoma". And how do you think that all sounded? Every Sunday night after dinner the Brennan Symphony and Choir went at it. And Daddy couldn't have been prouder.

We had moved to the "Land of Great Appliances" where the earlier Irish immigrants had already succumbed to the temptations of modernity and owned whirrling blenders, rythmic washers and humming dryers. It gave us distinction, at least in our own minds not having them. For us it was still "the old fashioned way," good old reliable, elbow grease. We were lucky to have so many hands because there was not much in the way of modern conveniences, and what we did have didn't work the way it was supposed to.

Only one side of the toaster ever toasted and the broken timer required attention when using. When one of us wanted toast, we'd stand sentry at the tired relic while trying to oversee the browning bread. All too often, we'd become distracted. Invariably, the plumes of smoke would send us into a mad dash to save what was left. The sound of toast scraping was a constant in the mornings. A few passes with a butter knife on the blackened bread surface over the garbage usually salvaged the toast. The unsalvageable pieces would leave the back porch like a Frisbee and land where the birds could have something to eat, out by Bridie's garden. Everyone at Cloonmore needed care, and got it, even the wild sparrows, jays, and pigeons. We could've bought a new toaster but then the birds wouldn't have eaten.

Bridie's garden was just off of the back porch and consisted mostly of green onions, tomato plants and her solitary rose bush that bloomed as a symbol of her homeland.

There was one sprig of wayward ivy that she had plucked from George Washington's Mount Vernon. "Jasus, the poor thing needs a home," she reasoned as she wrested the wayward plant from George's garden, away from the watchful eye of the guard, wrapped it in a damp napkin and tucked it inside her purse. Bridie was always giving someone a home. The sprig is still there…in Bridie's garden…and has its own family.

Bridie's washer was the double ring sort and stubborn stains met the ribbed washboard. We had some catching up to do, but that could wait, it wasn't until the mid- 1980's, that Bridie had a clothes dryer. Until then, our wet clothes waved on the clothes line strung across the backyard like sad flags. In the winter Bridie strung the clothes line in the basement giving us an arena to play ghost. The refrigerator grew frost like a Chicago winter so Bridie was constantly defrosting it. The cold room off the kitchen served as a larder and was usually…cold. It was one of those rooms that you didn't know what to do with. Too small for a bedroom, too big for a closet but always just cold enough to keep anything growing on the food supply, so it became a backup for the defrosting frig…which was often. The handle on the frig was broken from constant use (every time you went by it you looked inside to see if there were any new arrivals) and mandated a vise grip to open and close. I see the same set-up in the upscale antique shops today. Daddy needed the vise grip for a project one day and fixed the broken handle with a hasp and padlock. In an effort to modernize our routines and get us to eat only at meal time he gave the key to Bridie with the instructions, "Lock after meals." His plan was doomed form the very start because Bridie would never let us be hungry… which was always. At first we stashed some soda bread in our pockets but then resorted to begging, "Ma, could we have some…" We were so active (we didn't have a "tellie") that hunger was a constant and Bridie dutifully succumbed to our entreaties, unlocked the frig and threw some kind of concoction together.

Our assimilation into the neighborhood gained speed after we cleaned up Cloonmore and got situated in our new Catholic school. Going to a public school was completely out of the question because that's where all the "Prods" went and they were all pagans. The Catholic school was for the chosen ones, like us.

After a brief period when we met all the kids on the block and somehow convinced them that there was limited danger in inviting us into their homes, we got in. Each time, it was like walking into a museum. There was a sense of awe and amazement when you entered… door knobs turned and doors closed; there was carpeting and curtains and order and two-sided toasters and blenders and washing machines with windows and napkins and matching dishes, full sets of silverware and glasses without jelly labels, and that's not all: McCarthy had peanut butter and sixteen ounce bottles of coke lining the door of his refrigerator. O'Brian had potato chips and cookies; Curran, muffins and maple syrup. It was a wonderland of discovery compared to our fare of mostly potatoes, oatmeal and cheese sandwiches. To see two slices of golden toast pop up from a silver-lined toaster was magical and out of reach. Is that how it works? When we visited our neighbors' houses we noted their nicer furniture sets that matched and stood on all their proper legs – cushy sofas and plush carpets. There was a kind of hush that went with the well-appointed homes of Oak Park.

It became painfully obvious that we were *different*. One day I overheard my buddy Lurch crack that Cloonmore had, "that lived-in look." I popped him one and he cried.

Most of our furniture was of the used variety and the good stuff that we had was constantly under attack. The buffet that matched Bridie's prized China cabinet had a leg taken out when I came spinning around the corner on a dash to the end zone and slipped on the wet floor that Bridie was mopping.

"Blessed Jasus!" she cried as her attention went to the bruised buffet, caught herself and remembered her wounded lad. "Are you all right, Sean?" We wedged the severed limb back under the buffet and remembered not to lean on that corner. Bridie chipped some of the ice from the frig for my bruised head.

The sofa was another story, and when Bridie wasn't looking, served as a backdrop for our goal line plays. The front right leg became a victim of a sweep play one night and we quickly propped the old relic up with a copy of the Bible. Nobody ever read it anyway.

Few chairs matched and when all thirteen of us showed up for a meal, a mad dash went out to find the strays. But there were never enough. As we were sometimes three to a bed, we were sometimes two to a chair. The slenderest of arses got to share a seat and that meant the youngest lads who were able to wiggle their way onto the narrowest of seats, still others rested on the radiator covers, a warm-up in winter. The silverware and plates were like everything else: incongruent. No knife had a brother, or fork a sister; spoons were scarred from chipping the freezer and the tines on the forks were bent from loosening gym shoe knots. The plates were orphaned as well, clashing in color and shape; cups were handle-less and glasses were old jelly jars with the Smuckers' label long washed away. The plates bore chips and offered an endless variety of designs. All to the good, as no one ever fretted when they broke. None of that ever mattered to us because there was always a plate and a knife and a fork and oodles of Bridie's home spun goodness.

"Don't judge the book by its cover," she would say.

And then there was the grass that had been our first pleasure when we descended upon Cloonmore. Although it struggled to stay alive, it was no match for the football games or Kitchen-Klenzer that we used for yard-line markers.

And so it went at Cloonmore – our lives and our selfless, sharing method stood out along with Daddy's and the brown baggers yellow and green paint job on Cloonmore: materialism was far down the priority list, as Bridie taught. Nothing was precious, but...us.

A Day in the Life of Cloonmore

The six of us boys shared a big bedroom with three beds: a single and two doubles. "Divvy it up," Bridie had said, and we had. Boroimhe, Phelim and I were a unit and a "shkittery" one at that, Bridie's word for the slender. We shared one of the bigger beds, sometimes with three heads at one end but mostly with two at one end and another at the other, the straddle look, and still had room to spare. Each morning at five, the church bells of St. Edmund's rang and next came Bridie's wake-up call. It was always a mad scramble to the single closet in the cavernous bedroom or the stock box at the end of the hallway and first grab for wardrobe selection. Rolling over for an extra wink always cost you the good stuff…and there wasn't much of that. No one "owned" a personal set of clothes or even socks. Whatever someone else wasn't wearing was yours. We had the share-all approach that taught us consideration and how to make do. Selfishness didn't work because sooner or later you needed what someone else had or they needed what you had and we always made it work because Bridie wouldn't have it any other way.

Every morning Bridie would rise sometime before the fifth bell and get the oatmeal bubbling and the teapot steaming. The soda bread had been baked the afternoon before. The whistle on the teapot had long ago died and the only way we knew the water was ready for the leaves were the droplets that the steam sent sliding down the wall in search of an easy path. It was like most things in our house, imperfect but functional. Bridie's life was spent mostly in the kitchen, preparing meals, bandaging scarred knees, extricating embedded slivers, wiping away sad tears. It was a small room with a wide reach, where comfort was always… a part of the fare. While we were in school, she baked her Irish soda bread, rich with buttermilk and studded with raisins. It was our one true and unique luxury. And the rest of the blocks too, drop-ins just to snag a piece were common.

Breakfast tea was more than a beverage as Bridie had the gift of reading the leaves and prophesizing by their foreboding design. She brewed her Barry's Gold (there was never a tea bag), studied the leaf pattern in the bottom of the cup, and uttered her predictions which were almost always positive. "I see good fortune today," but occasionally, the leaves were muddled and ominous. Bridie kept it that way just to teach you that there was misfortune as well as danger. "I see a … be careful." Bridie sometimes got nun-like and used the leaves as a detection tool. "Have you got something to tell me? The leaves were askew…"

"Oh no, Ma, everything went fine."

And she'd look deep into your eyes and let you know she knew there was something, because there usually was and it was just a matter of time until you were discovered.

"Who's going to be calling, the Monsignor, the sergeant or the principal?" And you'd spill your guts because you just couldn't take the torment. She was good; she could read your eyes like she read the leaves.

The droplets started to form on the wall just above the kettle. "Tea time!"

And breakfast was just moments away as Bridie dumped a handful of the loose tea leaves in her porcelain tea pot that had the Connemara Mountains etched across its rounded belly. The teapot, buried deep inside Bridie's grip, had safely made its way across the Atlantic when she had emigrated from Kiltimagh, Eire. By now there were enough cracks and chips to justify a leak, but somehow the tea only found its way out through the spout. Each cup of tea that she poured from her heirloom embraced all of the grace that she brought with her and now was able to share with all those that stopped in.

Bridie would spoon the bubbling oatmeal into your bowl and dribble some homemade syrup on top or a slab of Kerry's Gold butter. Bridie would melt some brown sugar and water; the bottled syrup wouldn't do. Before we dug in we'd wait for the one last lava bubble to pop in the oatmeal, a sure signal that it was time to eat. Every morning was the same routine and the same line-up: bubbling oatmeal, buttered soda bread and hot tea. We're all still alive and we often credit our health to the morning's goodness. You see, it wasn't a matter of money, Bridie knew the dangers of processed foods long before anyone else did. She was as natural as a soft rain in April. And what she fed her crew was going to be too.

"If it didn't come out of the earth and the package has fancy colors, I'm not feeding it to you."

After slurping the oatmeal, munching the soda bread and sipping our tea, and we always sipped our tea, it was time to head out into the world and bring yesterday's news to the masses. We left the dishes in Bridie's tin bucket, filled with steaming water and a bar of American Family and the table orts were dumped off of the back porch for the birdies. The only dishwasher was her lads and most times it took Daddy's directive to get us to the sink. That was usually after dinner when there were no excuses and he could lean back in his chair and enjoy the pain he was inflicting on us. Irish mothers were a bit soft on their lads and Bridie was no exception often letting us off the hook when it came to performing our duties...but not Tom Brennan.

In the winter, Daddy would always cook dinner on Sunday night. He fashioned himself as the great creator and would try anything. After he was done with his latest creation, whether chicken pot pie, homemade pizza, or stew, the kitchen looked like a junkyard after a wind storm and that's when he would exact his payback. "All right boys." Sometimes I think he made the mess on purpose just to watch us squirm, and other times to play the great artist, unconcerned with the order of his atelier, in love only with his masterpiece. His creations were mostly delicious, but the joy of eating was always tempered by the clean-up that awaited.

It wasn't long until the other kids on the block wanted to be inside Cloonmore more than we wanted to be inside their house. It's funny how that works…no, our grass wasn't greener. Maybe it was the chickens that Tom was secretly raising in the attic, or the steam room he built with a baby pool, some plastic, and a hose that ran to the basement hot water faucet. Or the weight set that he built from pipes and the counter-balance plates that he had borrowed from the el-train gates. Or Padraig's drum set, crammed inside the front closet so he could spare the world his practice sessions. Or maybe the basketball hoop that we made by cutting the seat out of a chair, taping a net to the rim and hanging it in the front bedroom from our fine oak woodwork. In the garage there was the boxing ring and one of Pop's broken down service trucks that became lover's lane. There was the club house under the front porch that you had to crawl through a tunnel to get to. Membership was free…especially if you were a girl. It's where we smoked the cigarette butts we found at the curb.

Tom had his chicken ranch until one of the chicks got caught in the duct work and started acting like Mrs. Mole's ghost. One of the chickens somehow turned into a rooster and grew to full size. The rooster loved it at Cloonmore especially the pieces of burnt toast. Daddy was proud of "Ole Brewster's" early morning cackle even though the poor thing needed some voice lessons. After continual complaints from the neighbors, the rooster disappeared and went missing for a couple of days.

"Must have flown away," we all thought, until Daddy went down in the basement and found poor Brewster beheaded in the wash bin. The search for the perpetrator ended right there because most of us knew that a certain farm girl from Kiltimagh was the only one in the house who had the will and know-how to end it for an off-key rooster who didn't know dawn from dusk. It was Bridie that had to listen to him all day. Daddy, in order to assert his love for Brewster and to exact some justice for the deceased capon, plucked and prepped him for Sunday night dinner. Word got out that Tom Brennan would be serving up Brewster that evening and the house emptied. No one was going to be caught dead dining on the dearly departed Brewster. There would have been hell to pay if Daddy had to dine alone after his all day effort, so Phelim and I took one for the team and plunked ourselves at the table as Tom proudly placed the now golden and crisp Brewster in front of us. That day the two of us learned how to look like we were eating without really eating.

"Where is everybody?" Tom Brennan asked, as he sliced into Brewster's tender and moist breast. We squirmed thinking there might be one more cackle as Daddy sliced, ignorant of Brewster's feelings, but both of us feeling Brewster's pain.

"Tastes a little smokey," Pops offered as he sampled poor ol' Brewster.

"Must be the burnt toast that he loved so much, Pops," I said.

"Where is everyone," he reiterated.

"Oh, they were disappointed when they heard we were having Roos…err… I mean chicken, cause we usually have roast beef."
"Just means more for us," I said.

"It's too goddamn good for them," Daddy barked (he didn't try to hide this curse) which is what he always said when someone rejected one of his creations. And the tale of Brewster the rooster was over.

Every month Daddy would visit Market Street on Chicago's west side and buy bulk goods. He'd come home with hundred pound burlap sacks of Idaho potatoes, gallon jars of mayonnaise and relish, quart cans of tomatoes and beans, boxes of oatmeal and dozens of eggs, rolls of liver sausage, bologna and salami and for an occasional Sunday treat, massive cuts of roast beef. And for the daily incidentals, every morning Pops left a fiver on the kitchen table for Bridie's daily trip to the food store. Three blocks away was Krupa's, an old family-style grocery store that had two main aisles and a meat counter with a butcher who had missing fingers.

"Wonder where they ended up?" one of the lads wanted to know when his hamburger was chewy one day.

These were the days before supermarkets and big box stores but that didn't really matter because Bridie wouldn't have gone to them anyway. You see, Bridie loved the personal touch and having someone to talk to. Each day her jaunt to the grocery store was a break from the madness and an outing all wrapped into one.

"Good morning, Father," as she passed the church.

"Beautiful flowers," as she passed the gardener.

"Anything new?" as she passed the newsstand.

"Anything fresh today?" when she got to the meat counter and the missing fingered butcher.

With the fiver that Daddy had left her, Bridie would load up two brown bags of groceries, three if there was a sale, and tote them back to Cloonmore in her powerful Irish arms. Bridie didn't have a food cart and wouldn't have been caught dead with one anyway. Food carts were for old ladies and Bridie was never going to be one of those.

When Bridie got home it was time for lunch and her hungry lads. After a morning of being tortured by the nuns, we'd burst through the screen door, with appetites like hungry bears. Most days there was a refugee or two or three: the abandoned Turk was always around and Lurch would stop in if the menu agreed with him and Pete, whose mother treated him like a red-headed step child.

Bridie could make a sandwich like nobody else. We never knew why. Someone else could make the same sandwich with the same ingredients…but they never tasted like Bridie's. There were regular old cheese sandwiches, and on special days Bridie would grill them and serve them up with some tomato soup. Certain days had bologna, or ham and cheese, but our favorite day was Friday with Bridie's tuna salad and cream of mushroom soup. The Church banned eating meat on Fridays and that left only fish. It had something to do with giving something up for Jesus, but the real truth was the Church owned a lot of fisheries. Whatever Bridie made was delicious and rejuvenating. Along with our now full bellies and some great fun and camaraderie around the table, it was the only reason we could muster up some energy, have a quick game in the alley and go back to school and take more abuse from the nuns. Afternoons were always easier than the mornings because they lasted just three hours which was just about all the time you could spend with a nun without some kind of break. After school we'd explode from the school doors, jubilant that the torture was over until the next day. We'd head over to the "Age" (Tom's term for the news 'agency' that supplied our papers) for our afternoon routes. Each of us had a bike that was an amalgamation of used parts. No one ever got a new bike and no one would ever get a new bike. Daddy would bring home old broken relics from John Perri's Trading Post and we would immediately set out tearing them apart and patching the new parts into the old bikes.

Fenders were passé and the only accessory we had was the wire basket for our newspapers that we attached to the front of the bike. If you had a broken spoke, and who didn't, you wrapped it around one that wasn't broken. My brother Patdraig was the mechanic and he would sit on a little three-legged stool just outside the basement door and mend and bend the mismatched bike parts until they worked. The wheels were never straight, the chains were always loose, the spokes a bit looser, but somehow Paddy could splice them all together and send us on our way.

After the route and a few games in the alley it was dinnertime and another session with Bridie in the kitchen. Boy, was it comforting to get back there. Tired, hungry and waiting for one of Bridie's dinners, and that meant some of her wonderful mashed potatoes with a slab of butter pushed into the center like a small lake at the top of a hill. After your first bite the melted butter would stream down the hillside and gently mix with the steamed carrots.

Tom Brennan was home by now, the girls were at their part-time jobs and would get warmed-up leftovers later, so all Bridie had in front of her were her lads, and she couldn't have been happier. You see, to an Irish mother there is something special about her lads. There's no explanation except, "They're my bys."

After dinner and Daddy putting the squeeze on us to do the dishes, there was always a little homework and an essay or two if Tom felt like extracting a cost, and then bedtime and one of Bridie's stories...

Nighttime at Cloonmore

It had been a long hot summer's day filled with baseball, paper routes and mischief and by the time bedtime came there was little energy for a bath. Cloonmore still didn't have a shower...well we had a shower stall but water didn't come out of the pipe that stuck out of the tiles. Daddy had promised to get the brown bag crew out to fix it but was nervous especially when the brown baggers got near a plumbing project and running water. So it was either three men in a tub or a quick sponge bath from Bridie.

"We're too tired to get up and take turns at the tub, Ma," the three of us chorused, "Can we have a sponge bath?"

"Only if I can dunk you good tomorrow."

"Sure Ma." We would have agreed to anything.

Bridie filled one of her cooking pots with warm water and a worn bar of Ivory soap and dabbed away the spoils of the day. "There's half the blessed yard in the pot," she'd say when she got done.

"Had to slide today, Ma."

With each swath of the old towel that was ending its life as a wash cloth, there was another *ooohhh* or *ahhhh* from the comforted combatants. In minutes our sparkle had returned and the excitement over what story Bridie might tell brought on a chorus of requests:

"The ghost story!"

"No, the murder!"

"No, Nora Corrigan and the leprechaun."

"Once upon a time in a small village in Ireland there was an old lady who would play her fiddle atop a small hill just under God's starlit sky."

We all recognized her ritual retelling of one of our great favorites: *Nora Corrigan and the Leprechaun.*

Bridie nestled into the double bed with two lads on one side and another on her other flank. There was hardly room for a deep breath.

"Nora lived alone in a thatched roof shack that had dirt floors. Her husband had died years ago, a victim of those evil English mercenaries, the Black and Tans." Bridie seldom forgot her manners but often let one fly when it came to the English and how they had treated the Irish.

"Who were the Black and Tans?"

"Rotten bastards that the English brought to Ireland to kill the Irish rebels who were fighting for independence."

"What's independence?"

"Freedom!" she'd bark.

"You see the English came over to Ireland and stole our land and made us grow crops that we had to sell to pay the rent."

"How come you let them do that?"

"They had bigger guns and more bullets."

"Anyway, Nora's husband, Tom Corrigan, was one of the rebels and he used to hide in the forest and when the English soldiers would walk by, he'd take a shot at them with his rifle."

He seldom hit anyone because the rifle had a slight bend in it and the bullet would always come out crooked. The only way Tom could hit anything is if he aimed a little to the left of the target and hoped the curving bullet found its mark. Most of the time he forgot to do that because he used to carry a little brown bag with him."

"What was in the bag?

"His lunch and a bit of poteen."

"What's Poteen?"

"A bit of brown nectar to wash down the lunch."

"One day when he was hiding behind a tree he saw what he thought was a rebel coming up the road. The rebel was dressed just like Tom, himself.

He came out from behind the tree to greet his comrade and when he got close enough, the rebel tore off his coat and underneath was an English soldier's uniform."

"You're under arrest," the soldier yelled and Tom Corrigan had been captured.

"Isn't that cheating?"

"Yes, the English were very good at that and never too worried about playing by the rules."

"Anyway, they took ole' Tom and tied him to the back of a horse and dragged him up and down the road and when they got to the railroad tracks they cut the rope and left poor Tom, unconscious laying across the railroad tracks.

Soon the horn from the oncoming train started blowing away, trying to get whatever was lying on the tracks to move. But the poor, comatose Tom couldn't hear anything because the soldiers had beat him so badly and the train turned one Tom Corrigan into three."

"Oh, Mom, oh, Mom."

"Well, when Nora got the news and the rebels brought back the divided Tom for burial, she decided to dig a hole in the back yard and give ole' Tom a final resting place right under the stars and right where poor Tom could hear Nora playing her fiddle.

Her songs became sad and entrancing and because you could hear Nora's violin roll over the heather covered hills, the villagers would stop whatever they were doing, listen to the tunes and shed a tear in remembrance of poor ole' Tom. There were three lads from the village, Sean, Phelim and Boroimhe who especially liked Nora's songs."

"I named you lads after them."

A wry, proud, comforting smile would radiate from us. "Every time they heard the violin they would stop whatever mischief they were in and run and hide behind a nearby hedgerow and listen to the songs and playfully plot how they would get even with the English soldiers if they ever got the chance.

When Nora finished a tune you could hear her say, "The sons a bitches, the sons a bitches."

"What's a 'sons a bitches,' Mom?"

"I think Nora was talking about the Black and Tans. You know… the bad guys."

"So a 'sons a bitches' is a bad guy? Sometimes I hear Dad say that about the neighbor."

"BeJasus, keep that to yourselves."

"Well, as kind as Nora was, she wasn't one to not fight back. But all she had was her violin.

Each night her songs got sadder and more beseeching, until one night when she was hitting a crescendo, a leprechaun appeared out of nowhere."

"What's a crescendo?"

"That's the high point or when something is as good as it gets."

"Will we ever be a crescendo?"

"If you try hard enough."

"What happened next, Ma?"

"Well the leprechaun asked the now teary-eyed Nora if he could grant her a wish.

In deep gasps, between tears, she could only utter, "The sons a bitches, the sons a bitches."

Well the three lads, hiding behind the heather, knew what she meant but the leprechaun seemed a bit confused."

And when the leprechaun walked away scratching his head, the three lads jumped out from behind the heather and said, "The

Black and Tans are the 'sons a bitches' and they killed Tom Corrigan and we know where they hide."

"You see the three lads would wander through the fields and forests and play army, hiding behind the bushes and hedges just hoping they could see a real Black and Tan.

And one day they finally did. There were three of them and every day thereafter the 'sons a bitches' would stop and rest under the same tree.

This got the leprechaun's attention and he said, "Can you take me there?"

"We'll meet you here tomorrow," replied the lads.

The next day the lads got to the meeting spot but there was no leprechaun. They couldn't have been more disappointed and when they were about to give up, they heard Nora start to play her violin and when she got to her crescendo, out popped the leprechaun."

"C'mon boys, let's go get 'em," he said.

"Well, the leprechaun didn't have any rifles, only his guile."

"What's guile?"

"That's when you try to outsmart someone, like when you lads sneak out before the dishes are done."

"OHHHH," the three of us replied in unison.

"And it works a lot better than using a rifle."

"So the four of them headed out, traipsing through the forest and finally found the Black and Tans tree and then hid behind the heather and waited for the three "sons a bitches' to show up for their lunch.

When the bad guys showed up and were eating their sandwiches and laughing about how dumb the rebels were and how they had caught that one guy with the uniform trick, the leprechaun jumped out from behind the heather and said, "This is your lucky day, lads."

"The Black and Tans raised their rifles."

"There's no need for those, boys," the leprechaun said."

The bad guys lowered their rifles. They couldn't believe their eyes because they had never seen a real leprechaun, only heard about them in folk tales. And they said as they started to rub their hands together, "Will we get a wish?"

"Sure and Begorrah" the leprechaun said."

"The three sons a bitches started dancing up and down and rubbing their hands together in delight. You could see the greed start to ooze through their every vein because they had heard how the leprechauns in Ireland were so magical and could grant any wish."

"Each of you gets to make a wish but it has to be at the wishing well."

"And suddenly in the nearby distance you could see the roof of a small wishing well."

"Over here," the leprechaun said."

"And the greedy, 'sons a bitches' marched over to the well."

"Think very hard and make your wish, because you only get one," the leprechaun said."

"One wished for gold coins, another for silver and the last wished for diamonds."

"It'll be easy to carry," they reasoned."

"Each of your wishes is at the bottom of the well, so I'll just go down inside and get them for you," the leprechaun said."

"The leprechaun jumped over the well wall and acted like he was walking into the well like you'd go down your basement stairs and disappeared.

The 'sons a bitches' started dancing around again in a fit of greed and dancing and dancing and suddenly stopped because the leprechaun wasn't coming back.

"Where is that bugger?" one of the Black and Tans said."

There wasn't a sound and with each new moment the bad guys got antsier and a bit more fidgety waiting for the leprechaun to return with their gifts and finally couldn't wait any longer and all three climbed over the wishing well wall, only now there wasn't any steps and all three of the 'sons a bitches' fell all the way to the bottom of the well and drowned."

"AHHHHH, eeeeek," splash, splash, splash.

"From behind the bushes, all alone, the three lads stood in stunned silence and gasped. They couldn't believe what had just happened. There was only stillness…and no leprechaun."

"Where is he…? They were panicked."

"And just then they heard the sound of Nora's melodic violin in the distance. It reached a crescendo and out popped the leprechaun."

"Whew…the lads breathe a sigh of relief."

"How come you're not wet?" one of the lads asked.

"I'll not be giving my secrets away. Let's just call it guile."

"Oh, we know what that means."

"This one is between me and you lads … get it."

"Oh, yes sir," they all answered.

"But will we ever see you again?"

"I can never tell," he said. "But you must know that I love music …you know the strings."

"And poof! he disappeared."

"Ma, does he ever return? Ma, does he ever return?"

"The leprechaunzzzzzzzz…….

All we could hear was the gentle breath of Bridie slipping into slumber.

"Ma," "Ma."

Like most of Bridie's stories at bedtime, the rest was left to our imaginations.

All three of us laid back and smiled, so proud that there could have been three lads in Ireland with the same names who had righted the score with the 'sons a bitches,' if even for only one day. And with a proud and content smile on our faces, we looked up at the ceiling and had to wonder again how this one ended... and how the next story would end... or if any of them ever would?

Smooches and the Great TV Wars

And then there was the issue of smooching or non-issue because it was always well buried. It was never discussed but always hanging in the air like the scent of Bridie's soda bread. Daddy was uninvolved but Bridie wasn't. She never said anything directly only made subtle references.

"Don't embarrass the family."

"Keep your hands to yourself."

"You're not doing anything to be ashamed of, are you?"

There were two worlds at Cloonmore: the strict Catholic teachings that Daddy espoused and the pragmatic approach of Bridie. Catholicism ignored the reality of a household full of hormones and intrigue, and applied a dictate of abstinence until you were married and legitimate. The Church was deathly afraid of smooching and the intimacy that went with it. It was confusing to have a celibate hierarchy dictate the rules of something they weren't supposed to have ever engaged in. Most of it reached back to the fourth century and a guy named Augustine who had done a good deal of prancing about before he decided that he should tame his dingy and rewrite the sex rules. Since then, sex was all about procreation and not enjoying it because it was a sin of the flesh. But it was the only thing that we had that was free and felt good and could get you a friend if you were good at it. The rules confused our sexual psyches because they denied an ageless instinct, one that wasn't going away with a cursory promise or religious oath. You were made to feel dirty and guilty if you even harbored a thought about it. Smooching was never discussed, only forbidden, and the dreaded curse of pursuing it would be an unwanted child. Bastards could curse a family for generations.

Despite knowing that most of Catholicism was spectacularized just to put it above other religions, Bridie kowtowed to the *status quo* and played the game. She was a pragmatist and didn't much believe in all of the miracles and pageantry that tried to elevate Catholics above everyone else. She just went about her business trying to make everyone feel as good about themselves as she possibly could. It was her only guiding principle. She was however, very cautious of the boys meeting the girls or vice versa and was deathly afraid of an early grandchild because of the social stigma that an unwanted pregnancy would bring. If it did happen…and for others it did, the disgrace was more than most could bear. Either the besmirched was rushed up the aisle in a girdle that was too small, or the mother was exiled to bear her baby, put it up for adoption, and return like nothing had happened.

It was worse for the lasses than it was for the lads because a girl that thought about or engaged in smooching was not only offending the Church and the Lord above, she was ignoring the influence of Mary, the Blessed Virgin. And that meant that on her wedding day, garbed stately in her white wedding dress, she would have to parade to the statue of Mary appearing as virtuous as the fallen snow and say a prayer even though she had a few reservations. Never mind getting caught, having impure thoughts was just as bad because Jesus always knew what you were thinking. And you always had to worry about being seen because there was always a set of eyes watching…from above. If it wasn't Jesus it was an angel that had been assigned to keeping you on a straight path. A girl that wanted to smooch someone had to hope that Jesus was too busy or that the angel had the day off. For us lads none of it mattered yet because we were still wet behind the ears. Even then, going 'all the way' was a long way away because we were just as afraid of the girls as we were of the Catholic rules.

Daddy ruled the roost as he had been raised; Irish fathers were set in a mold to be prickly autocrats. As such, Pops would lay down the law and insist on his way but he didn't have the brutal nature of some other Dads who, like the nuns and priests, applied corporal punishment. Daddy never gave you more than a slap on the wrist or a belt across the arse. Bridie wouldn't allow anything more and most times not even that. Although well opposed, as the years passed, Bridie's way and Tom's way seemed to complement each other. Bridie's soft touch when Tom was away and Tom's hard hand when Bridie wasn't looking, molded us all into pretty good kids.

When we ogled our neighbors' more upscale homes, we found the appliances fascinating and the food enticing, but they paled in comparison to our discovery of television. Our introduction was complete seduction. Once exposed to *"The Three Stooges"* and *"The Untouchables?"* we were completely hooked. We were skeptical that someone inside a box looking out of a window would be there to entertain us. The first time I saw a TV, I checked the back to see who was in there.

At Cloonmore all we had was one of those wooden radios with netting on the front and two knobs, one that raised the volume and the other to turn Dick Tracy into Burns and Gracie. During the mystery shows, at the good parts, we often bumped heads getting closer to the speaker because it had a constant crackle. The radio was like everything else in our lives, there was a flaw somewhere…the stray spoke on your bike… the missing handle on the frig…the frozen knob on the toaster…the broken leg on the buffet…the frozen sink in January…the removable finial on the railing. And those voices inside the radio… where did they come from? After the radio show was over, the bad guy in jail, and next week's broadcast a dream, Daddy would order up an essay on what we learned. That was always his way. If you ever got a treat there was always a cost. And we paid with our essays.

After weeks and months of mooching this thing called the "tellie" at the neighbors' houses, we couldn't take it anymore and hatched a plan to get our own. We were tired of always having to imagine the scene on the radio and wanted some visual reality. We knew it was a long shot because Pop's mantra was "doing" and "creating." We'd hear him say that society was decaying because of television and that people would get fat, lazy and stupid if they ever got one and watched it. Daddy knew without ever having to see one.

"TV is passive; doing is doing." I can still hear him.

"There'll never be one in my house," he'd tell anyone who would listen. We knew we were up against it. Finally, we mustered up enough guts to ask and designated my sister Megan to do the dirty work. Megan, the youngest of the girls, was in high school and could play the piano like Liberace; not that we knew who he was. She got straight A's, worked hard as a cashier at the food store and helped the lads with their math when they were overmatched, which was often. Daddy loved music, straight A's and hard work. He would find it hardest to say no to Megan. Megan was the whole package. Saying no to us was easy and habitual. We hatched the plan: Megan would be our agent.

One night, at the end of dinner and when Daddy' belly was filled with Bridie's slowly simmered corned beef and boiled potatoes, Megan stammered once and then let him have it. "Daddy, can we get a TV?"

"When I'm dead and gone," Daddy answered and he meant it.

"But, everyone else has one."

"Everyone else is not the Brennans and there won't be the devil's tool in my house."

At least it was a start, but not a very good one. Daddy's abrupt response made Megan surrender… at least for the time being.

We tried breaking him down over time but nothing worked.

"How about that TV you promised?" we'd say. And he'd harrumph and walk on. "We're missing a lot of education on TV," one of us would protest and Daddy responded, "There's a lot of that in books."

Daddy was dead against the "devil of modern America" ever coming into his home. "It's a passive pursuit and will melt your minds," he'd say. "Read a book," or "Do a crossword puzzle," or "Drill a hole in the wall," not worried that Cloonmore would be draftier than it already was.

Meanwhile, Bridie was hoping for a "tellie", thinking that it might settle us down a bit. There'd be fewer basketball games in the bedrooms and fewer football games in the living room, she reasoned.

It was tough going to school every day and hearing the other kids kibitz about the shows they'd watched.

"Yeah, I loved that part," I'd lie when I was thrust into a conversation about the previous night's schedule. We were stuck and we knew it.

And then – divine intervention, straight from the Fathers at the rectory. Our prayers and supplications were answered. It was like a bolt of lightning on a sunny day, right out of nowhere. All the prayers and catechism and donations and served masses had finally paid off. We hadn't discovered the saint who was behind it, but knew that he was out there somewhere. We'd thank him later. All that mattered now was that we were finally getting a "tellie".

Everyone knew by now that we didn't have one and coincidentally, the priests at the rectory were getting a new one. There was panic and excitement and dread and confusion all rolled into one afternoon when Fr. Kelly called with the offer. Bridie took the call and accepted his grace.

"Thank you Father, I'm hoping it will settle the lads down a bit and give me some quiet time."

Down the alley we hauled the round-screened RCA inside a paper cart with a sentry on either side holding and steadying the gem in place. We rubbed the top of it with our hands like a champion with his trophy as we pulled it over the cobblestone alley, falling deeper in love with every turn of the wheels. We had never treated any chore with such respect or care. We wanted to find an outlet right there in the alley and have a soiree with *The Three Stooges*. The trip took forever. We steadied our prize with each step and winced at each bounce off the cobblestones. We moved with the purpose and precision of a surgeon with a scalpel or a miner with TNT. And finally we pulled into the back yard and lifted the magical box up the stairs and into the house. It was only moments before we had the current flowing and *The Three Stooges* cracking each other. The afternoon was total bliss and euphoric, until we heard the car door slam: DADDY WAS HOME!

We were jolted from our high. Panic set in and bodies went flying, bumping into each other and mumbling about what to do. Our euphoria had masked the dread of the inevitable moment... that we all knew was coming...when Daddy got home.

"He's at the stairs," someone shouted.

"Christ, what are we gonna do?" Megan had raced upstairs and came hurdling down with an old sheet in her hand and threw it over the evil box. We scattered, picked up a book and feigned reading as Daddy strolled through the door. There was quiet. He knew something was up. These weren't his sons reading on a summer afternoon.

Megan took the lead, "Hi Daddy, how was work?"

He only grunted as he looked into the room from the hallway.

He turned his head and noticed the pall draped demon, "What's under the sheet?"

"Chair has a rip," Megan said. He nodded in disbelief but seemed too tired to challenge Megan's assertion. He left and headed straight for the dinner table where Bridie had prepared one of his favorite dishes, slowly simmered corned beef and cabbage. We needed every advantage before we broke the news and Daddy with a belly full of corned beef would help.

We all exhaled and fell back knowing that we had dodged a bullet, but for only the moment. The spikes of the antenna lifting the sheet like a puppeteer ghost in a store window backdrop only reminded us that the devil would soon have to be paid.

"Dinner," came Bridie's call. And instead of rushing into the kitchen with our usual hunger laden charge, we tiptoed like ballerinas embracing the grace and silence that was about to end. We all sat down in silence, awaiting the big moment when Megan would drop the bomb. We had strategized that bringing the "tellie" in before we had Daddy's consent would force his hand. Megan, his favorite, was again, the designated legate. If she couldn't convince him, no one could. There was much silence and trepidation around the dinner table, and when Daddy finished his boiled potatoes and let out a timid burp of satisfaction, Megan broke in. With a full belly he was as ripe as he would ever be.

"Daddy" she started, as we all looked on attentively, "The priests got a new TV at the rectory."

"Oh, so that's where my donations are going." he barked.

"Their old set was still working and in all their graciousness they offered to give it to us," she continued. "We're the only ones in the parish without one you know,"... extending the sympathy card.

"Good one, Megan," I thought.

His piercing look didn't soften.

We were all cowering with our eyes peeking up at Tom Brennan, waiting for the bomb to go off. Megan continued.

"I know that it's a point of contention but there are very good educational programs on TV that are required in some of our classes and everyone promises to watch it only after their homework is done." Keep going, Megan, you're selling him. "Could we please keep it, if only for a little while, pleeeease?" There was silence.

"Under one condition," he bellowed, "That it's never on when I'm in the house."

"Agreed!" We all chimed in. Nice job, Megan. We would have agreed to anything. And thus the gauntlet was dropped and the now famous TV wars began.

Tom Brennan never sold himself on the worthiness of TV, or even tried. He hated it and would always hate it. He was just outnumbered and he knew it, and all those sad supplicant eyes looking up from our boiled potatoes may have gotten to him.

As time went on Daddy regretted his agreement and when he finally decided that he had made a bad deal, started to pull tubes from the back of the TV. When we found his hiding place for the tubes, he started to cut the plug off the chord and hide that too. That didn't stop us either because we learned how to splice on a new plug.

In an emergency we'd cut the plug off a lamp and irritate Bridie as well, when she found the bared wires. You see, all that creativity that Daddy had taught us was paying off. He taught us too well. Daddy cut the plug and we spliced, again and again…until the chord was too short to reach the outlet. No problem. We stole an extension chord from his tool box. No one was giving up.

On Thursday nights we'd wheel the TV into our front walk-in closet before Daddy got home, just to watch *"The Untouchables."*

Some nights there were seven of us in there all straining to be quiet at the good part. Giggling was not allowed.

"Oh, Elliot is so handsome," one of the girls would lament.

Daddy had to have known we were in the closet with the TV because the house was never this quiet, but he never busted in, most probably enjoying our ingenuity (or our absence). If he ever caught you lying down and watching it though, you'd get his boot in your arse, right before he cut the plug or pulled a tube. And on and on it went.

The TV broke down often and that's when we found Mr. Pearson, the TV repairman and the nicest man in the history of the world. We should have known the priests weren't letting go of any bargains because the old relic needed Pearson regularly. Bridie would stuff Pearson with tea and soda bread, his favorite, just to let him know that we appreciated his kindness. We'd raid every piggy bank in the house, rounding up payment, but Mr. Pearson would never take it. Bent behind the TV set, he sensed our plight, as we hovered near him. Could he save the old relic again this time? He always had one more Band Aid in his tool chest and one more ounce of magic just to keep the box alive for another week or two.

"Thank you, Mr. Pearson," after he had worked his magic.

He never failed until one time when Mr. Pearson was on vacation and couldn't come to Cloonmore and in a state of total panic, we scoured the yellow pages for a substitute, even though we knew there couldn't be one for Mr. Pearson. When the new repairman showed up we knew that we'd have to pay when the old German turned down Bridie's soda bread. By the looks of his sweater this guy had moths for roommates and probably needed payment more than we did. After his inspection, he peeked his head from around the TV and reported, "Bad vertical transformer, $29.95 to fix." We'd gotten worse news, but not often. We declined his expertise because our kitty couldn't make the bill. We started praying to the saints for rain, wherever Mr. Pearson was.

So until Mr. Pearson got back, someone had to man the vertical control button while we watched. We rotated on that job too. And so the Great TV War went on, fixing, splicing, replacing and gorging ourselves on TV shows when Daddy wasn't home. It didn't matter what was on, only that it was *on*.

Over time, we began to realize that Daddy was right and that "doing" was far better than watching and our viewing subsided. Even *The Stooges* started to bore us. When we weren't watching, it kept us motivated and creative and when we were watching, passive and dormant. Daddy was always reading, sewing, cooking, playing his accordion on the front porch – anything but watching TV. The only time he was ever in front of one was to turn it off or cut the plug or pull a tube.

And so went our assimilation into the conveniences of modern suburbia and our attempts to fit in. I'm now proud to be able to say that I spent a large part of my childhood without a "tellie". Thanks Daddy.

After all the shock and awe of seeing the modern conveniences, our lust for partaking waned. We started to take pride in the fact that we didn't have any of the stuff and didn't need it. We knew how to make do.

As we grew and dreamed more and more about what was beyond Cloonmore, came the era of independence. Each personality was different from the one before it and each of us found a different avenue for our dreams. Tom found weights and tracks, Padraig a drum set and an old Ventures recording, Mike a girl and a dark gangway, Boroimhe a side door to run from the nuns, me an atlas to ponder, and Phelim two different colored gym shoes. And the older girls… men; who wanted to be an old maid?

It was Tom though that shattered the mold and sent the boys on their paths to discovery. He's never read a manual or followed a rule and if there is an accepted way to do something, Tom's not interested; he'll find his own way. He's kind, giving and selfless. If the score is forty-two to zero, Tom thinks the good team should fumble on purpose, just so the losers can have a little joy. He built our first basketball hoop on the garage roof, borrowed the plates off the Lake Street El for our first weightlifting set, raised chickens in the attic, sent away for fishing, art and karate lessons in the back of comic books, was the first to have a paper route, built a steam room in the basement out of a baby pool and some plastic and built our first indoor basketball court when he cut the seat out of a chair, taped a net to the rim and hung it off of a 20 penny nail that he had driven into the woodwork. He was a garbage man, a caretaker, a gardener, a paper boy, a baker, a choir boy, a grocer and a caddie, all before he was eighteen. Best of all though, he drove the nuns nuts. They couldn't get him to do anything. When they cracked him with their rulers or the pointer he just smiled.

Tom was our hero when we were young. No one worked harder or was more adventurous. I think that the abject Catholic ideology and school curriculum drove him mad because his true nature was to just dig a hole, or raise some chickens, or fantasize about the world he'd seen pictured in the back of magazines. He was never going to do what they wanted him to. Finally, when he was nineteen, he had had enough and bugged out for Oregon, where he wanted to be an opera singer and long distance runner.

In later years Tom opened up to me and told me how he felt. "I couldn't stand being told what to do. I had to find out for myself. I knew what I didn't want, and had a sense of what I

wanted, but could never find the confidence to make it happen …
I ran and sang and tried to smooch and lifted weights, but when it
came to the next step or the next idea, I never felt confident that I
could make it happen and wondered where it would lead me."

It breaks my heart to think of where Tom would be today if
there had been a little recognition of his independence and talents,
combined with his verve. The old way was to just jam traditional
education and Catholicism down your throat, ignoring your innate
talents and desires. "Shut up and listen!" "Don't ask questions!"
"You want to do what?" "How could you have such thoughts?"
"You'll never amount to much thinking like that." You only had
two choices; shut up and bury your thoughts or run…and Tom
ran. He tried hard to pursue his dreams but "It's tough when you
are all alone and unsure and sometimes confused," he said.
Despite all of that, he still is the only person I know that has
always done exactly what he wanted to do when he wanted to do
it. Anyway, if you look at a family photo you'll see Tom's
independence splashed across his face with exactly what the
photographer didn't want.

For the most part we all followed the Catholic sex rules, (or
the no sex rules) mostly because of the threat of Hell and not
wanting to disgrace the family. And disgrace it would have been,
so we all maintained the rules of abstinence until it was okay not
to… I think. Despite all of the authoritarian presence of the
church and its inane rules and the fears they brought with them,
we all had Bridie and her common sense approach. "Respect
yourself and others, help the less fortunate, act with a true heart
and most importantly, make someone feel good about themselves
today."

Back in the sixties the hippie influence never got much past
Cloonmore's front door. There was just no time. Between school
and work and practicing your music, everyone was just too

occupied to care much about Mick Jagger. The girls were commuting to and from their Catholic colleges and looking forward to the day they could leave Cloonmore and get their own bedroom and closet. It was back in the day when a single twenty-two-year-old girl was an old maid. The hunt was on for eligible bachelors and they arrived often because the sisters were cute. With the latest prospects, just inside the front door, Bridie and Daddy gave them the old once over, and so did we. The lads would sit perched at the top of the stairs and relish in the squirming that the suitors would go through.

"Have you finished college?"

"Do you have a career?

And the most important one, "Are you Catholic?" No prods were allowed.

Most of the girls knew the basic filters and wouldn't even bring a marginal candidate along. But Kaitlin was different. Molded in the same shape as Bridie except for a mane of strawberry blonde hair, when Kaitlin got an idea no one was changing it. Kaitlin's beau was Mickey who had taken only a couple college courses and liked cameras and dark rooms…with Kaitlin. His path was not the prescribed resume as far as Pops was concerned. One day in the foyer where all altercations seemed to end up, Kaitlin announced her bethrothal to Mickey and the proverbial shite hit the fan.

"Mickey and I are getting married."

"No you're not!"

"Yes we are!"

"He doesn't have college!"

"He doesn't need it."

"Is he even Catholic?"

"It doesn't matter!"

"You haven't finished college!"

"Someday!"

"How are you going to live?"

"We'll figure it out."

"He doesn't love you."

"Yes he does."

"You're too young."

"No I'm not."

And finally Mickey stepped in and said, "I don't care what you say, Kaitlin and I are getting married!" and it was over.

There was no money, but lots of care, and Daddy loved putting on a show so the plans were laid to spruce up Cloonmore for the wedding. The emergency call went out and all the old sod Irishmen showed up with their paint brushes and hammers and plaster trowels and before you knew it Cloonmore was glistening like the gem that it was. They patched and painted the walls, whitewashed the basement, fixed the balustrade and polished the woodwork. And all it took was a bit of poteen.

The wedding was a huge success. All had great fun and within a year Bridie had her first grandchild and all was forgiven. Fifty years later Mickey with several degrees and a few letters after his name and Kaitlin are still together. Even Bridie could be wrong sometimes.

The grand Cloonmore as it looks today.

The Jimmy Dean look started where?
Sean (left) and Phelim on Mozart Lane circa
1956, displaying brotherhood and sporting
the jeans and white shirt style that would
soon engulf America. Sean hid his money
in his cuff.

Phelim (left) and Sean posing in
Cloonmore's back yard. All right…the
lawn mower had rusted blades and
I forgot to mention our swimming pool.
But it was really for one of Tom's
ducks, Oona. I'm holding the catcher's
glove that Sr. Anna Lee
kicked to the wall.

"The Lads". The six Brennan boys posing in full game time regalia in the backyard at Mozart Lane. Back row, left to right; Padraig, Tom, Michael. Front row left to right; Boroimhe, Phelim, Sean. Uniformity was never our game, whether expression or dress.

The Cloonmore Alley Cats; From left;
Boroimhe, Lizzie, Marv (in front), Paddy the
graduate, Frankie, Sean, Turk, McCaffrey.

The Brennan Lasses. The first ladies in the
Irish Navy, circa 1946.

Sean and Jo posing before the 1969 prom.

Sean, Aunt Molly and Bridie in 1977 on
our return trip to Cloonmore. Back left is the
original house (now the barn) that all of the
Coleman's were born in.

Part II

Intro to:
The Boy

Without a "tellie", Bridie's six sons were very busy and very creative. Tommy, the oldest, had set the tone because he was a complete nonconformist and true pioneer. He never followed a rule or mandate and viewed the world as his oyster of discovery. He just plain ole drove the nuns nuts because he was unafraid and nothing they could do would ever phase him. Only Bridie recognized his way and let him be.

The bottom five all looked up to Tommy and his adventure, maybe for the good, maybe for the bad. But it was always fun.

One year Tommy won a new football in a newspaper contest. All the other paper boys and the six of us, mouths agog, were at the "Age" waiting for the manager to pull the winning ticket. When he lifted the ticket from the hat and read the winner, he looked up at all six of us and our gaping mouths, back down to the ticket and then back to us and yelled, "Brennan." This guy had a heart.

The football was a piece of junk and floated when you threw it. Coincidentally as we played with the football on the front lawn, the village was repaving the street. As our frustration grew with the floating football and the steamroller rotated back and forth, flattening the asphalt, Tommy grabbed the next pass, raced to the curb like he was scoring a touchdown, posed like Heisman himself and dropped the ball under the steamroller. A loud POP followed and as the steamroller passed on, there in the street, pasted to the asphalt was the winning football, flatter'n a pancake.

"Anyone for hoops?" he said.

Yes, Tommy's to blame.

For most of our childhood mischief was prevalent. It was mostly innocent and always the result of boredom or the chance at excitement from a good chase. If you knew they didn't want you to do something, you were motivated. As time went on and reputations grew, it became easier to point the finger at Bridie's lads because the accusers were usually right. Mostly it was a neighbor or a nun and sometimes a copper but Bridie was always wary, waiting for the next shoe to drop. The poor woman never knew who or where it was going to come from…but she knew it was coming. It was…coming.

The Paper Boy

The nearby church bells of St. Edmund clanged five gongs just as Bridie hollered, "Routes." It was our daily wake-up call and abrupt jolt from childhood slumber. Wearing only our underwear, we'd groan and throw back Uncle Tom's Navy issued wool blanket, and get slapped by January's energizing chill, a chill that crept its way through the numerous cracks in our Victorian manse.

"Feet on the floor," she'd chant and like the fine lads that we were, we complied. Our toes would hit the frigid oak floor and curl in response. There was no carpeting save an occasional discarded damp towel. The only thing between our feet and the oak were the dust balls that Bridie had missed on Monday; dust balls that skimmed across those ice cold planks, propelled by the drafts. Old Cloonmore may have been a Victorian manse, but it was filled with cracks and vents that let the cold in and most of the bad stuff out. Daddy the fuel-oil man, kept the neighbor's homes warm and cozy and his own economically chilled.

Down the hall we'd hop, clad only in our blown elastic, bandless jockeys with our arses kissing the frigid morning air, and our hands clasped between our thighs for warmth. It was our version of the Irish jig: we hopped and sidestepped the cold slats and splinters. We headed straight for the stock box at the end of the long hallway and first major decision of the day.

The stock box, itself pilfered from the back of the local food store that once held a gross of eggs, contained every sock that any of us owned; none of them matched and most had holes. On our knees, we searched for two socks that might faintly be a match. Black and blue, brown and dark brown or black were close enough. Any paired with white called for lowering your cuffs. If one had a hole but blended in hue, it would do. We'd tug down the top of the hole or try to slide the bottom up so the hole wouldn't show and we'd consider it a success. We'd grab some of the orphaned extra-large, heavy socks, and use them for mittens. It was an exercise in negotiation and selflessness and came in handy growing up with ten other siblings.

After adorning our '*spogs*'as Bridie called our feet; we dressed with anything that provided warmth. Our lone closet was crammed with pants, shirts and jackets of all sizes, but few were assigned to any one lad. There was little ownership with anything, mostly community property. Besides the few things that we gratefully and proudly owned, there was the community wardrobe, where, what someone else didn't wear was yours.

"Layers," Bridie would advise, because our coats were a bit needy and more of something was better. Eventually we donned all the wraps that were available and headed to the kitchen, belching out frigid air with each breath in hope that Bridie had cooked up something warm for us. And she always did.

Bridie made sure her six sons ventured into the frigid January mornings with a full belly. Every morning on the stove was a pot of bubbling lava-like oatmeal, a kettle of hot tea brewed from loose tea leaves and slabs of warm Irish soda bread, studded with raisins, smothered with butter. We didn't have to do a thing; just eat and sip. And we always sipped our tea.

Bridie's kitchen was her realm, short on style but long on touch. Here is where she cared for her own and all of the neighborhood refugees... and there were plenty. Here is where surgery, confession, counseling and care were daily staples. Here is where Bridie took her vacations and had her spa days at the sink, washing and rinsing her brown Irish mane, careful not to spill the small dark bottle at her hand: Bridie's single vanity-her lush brown hair was always going to be brown. Her kitchen was where she brought smiles to the forlorn, food to the hungry and calm to the worried, in a word, the sanctuary for the neighborhood.

As we devoured the oatmeal and bread and sipped our strong Barry's tea, Bridie would peer into the recesses of our earless cups, and find the damp, stranded tea leaves at the bottom: Every morning, my mother "read" the leaves and spoke as a seer to declare another day of good fortune and fortuitous events. Each clump of leaves always formed a picture and always told a story. Bridie's imagination was as wild as her hair and just as beautiful.

There has never been anything more natural to an Irishman than a story. Bridie would stare down at the damp leaves and intone:

"See the arm there and the leg over there."

"And there's the sun…" when there was a wayward leaf looking down on the others that might have been interpreted as dire. She helped you through every reading and searched hard till she could see good fortune somewhere: a more hopeful leaf. There was no need for any bad omens. Her oracles never included money or material things, because there had never been very much of any of that stuff nor much hope of getting any of it. Bridie knew what worked and that you couldn't buy it. Her oracles were wrapped round acts of kindness and thoughts of happiness and good fortune. She could even foresee the boy's sports triumphs:

"Oh, there's the shot going in the basket and the ball flying over the fence." And every morning you could somehow find all those happy predictions inside the fateful clump of tea nestled at the bottom of the cup.

Sometimes it took a second look if the leaves were a bit muddled but eventually the oracles always made sense, and after awhile we didn't need the second gander. Bridie's sorcery was always full of good fortune, and also full of story-like events that demanded all of your wit and wisdom in order to fend off any adversary or solve any dilemma that you would face that day.

"The wheel looks a bit bent, so be careful on your bike today."

Wondering at what point in the day that we would need the wisdom from the oracle, we donned the last of our layers, waved good bye with the sock-for-a-mitten hand and went off to enlighten the world. As we descended those creaking backstairs and ventured into the outdoors and felt the *real* cold for the first time, we'd look back over our shoulders and see Bridie holding back one side of the lace curtain with one of her powerful farm girl hands waving with the other. She had done all that she could do to make the morning work and now the rest was up to us.

We started taking on the newspapers at age ten. Phelim, the eleventh of eleven children and I, the tenth, often shared our newspaper delivery route: Rain, snow or shine. We would deliver the stack of *Chicago Tribunes*, and a smaller bunch of *Chicago Sun-Times*. In the morning, there were too many papers to carry in a bike basket. We used an old wooden cart we stored in the garage.

We'd back our newspaper cart out from the listing garage, wobbly from years of abuse from basketball games, bad drivers and Chicago snow storms. When it snowed, we'd wire an egg box to a sled and play Santa. Most days, one of us would push the cart and the other would lie supine with feet dangling off of the edge, inside the coffin sized cart. We took turns pushing as we did with everything. This particular day was my day to push. With ten sibs it was pretty hard to get selfish and still survive. Candy bars were cut into fourths, bottles of 'pop' were passed in a circle and consumed in sips and bubble gum…everyone got a stick.

The newspaper cart cast a rhythmic tune, as the wooden wheels bounced off the cobblestone alley, blending with the peaceful quiet of the morning. All alone with the beat of the cart and the silence of the morn' before few had risen, the world was all ours. For a bunch that shared their baseball gloves, rode three on a bike and slept three in a bed, we truly owned something that was all ours, the glory of the morn'.

Just a short jaunt from our house was St. Edmund, our parish, school and church. Adjacent to the parking lot was a marble statue of Jesus standing on a pedestal, garbed in a flowing robe and holding out one hand as if he was waving to the passers-by. Often as we passed the back of the Church a parish priest was tucked inside a gangway, sneaking his morning smoke at Jesus' back and swatting at the smoky plumes in futility as we approached...we knew.

Priests had to hide everything you know – smokes, booze, girl-friends, boy-friends... and in general: anything that was fun or human. Human trappings weren't needed. They had to look and act divine. We knew they were only human though, because we got to see them dress and undress in the sacristy just as regular as you or me with two legs and two arms, wrinkled undershirts and some normal talk that wasn't a hymn or a prayer draped in Latin.

The Church put priests on a pedestal because they were the closest thing to God on earth. Not a nun or a missionary or a volunteer at the Salvation Army could match them. The Church cloaked priests in long flowing robes, some red, some black. When the Priest walked by, you stepped back and bowed your head and looked down, slightly out of respect and slightly because you didn't want eye contact or anything that could lead them to know any of the guilt that resided within you. There were no high fives.

"Can you help inside the sanctuary this afternoon, Sean?" he yelled cupping the Marlboro.

"Not today Father," I answered. "Afternoon route and the news can't wait."

"Stay clear of that one," I admonished Phelim from the corner of my mouth. "There are rumors about what he wears under that cassock, if anything."

Phelim was too young to understand my quip, there being a couple years difference between us and hours of alley sex education by my classmate Murphy. That's where we learned about sex – in the alley. Murphy and the occasional *Playboy* magazine found in the trash provided the curriculum. Murphy came from the city just like us but his mother let him out a lot more than Bridie let us, and he had an older brother who majored in anatomy over at the pool hall.

"Have a good day Father," I schmoozed and the march of our paper route continued.

Rumbling along, the Agency, our newspaper depot, was our next stop. And that's where our workday began.

The "Age" as we dubbed it, was a dimly lit, garage-like, wooden depot where we picked up our morning newspapers. The lighting was dim; bare bulbs hanging from the rafters. Seating was provided by hay bales that softened the clamor and heated the dirt floors. There were wooden tables that housed machines that folded and wrapped the papers in string and were the envy of every other "Age" that had to fold by hand and use rubber bands. But you always kept a box of rubber bands in case the string broke or the machines went down, which was often.

When you pulled into the Age, you'd grab the bundle marked with your route number and hustle to a folding machine. If none were free, you muscled your way in and took turns.

After folding all of your papers, you'd stand them on end inside your cart, wedging the last few so they stood above the rest and then head out into the dawn, tugging the loaded cart into the dark morning. Our motto was "Get the news out and…now." We were businessmen with a duty.

The crew at the Age was a pastiche of moonlighting old guys down to the next generation of newsboys, the Brennans. Ollie the Kraut ran the joint. He counted the newspapers, repaired the carts and filled in for the slackers. He swore like a sailor and smoked like a chimney, introducing us to both bad habits. He could throw bundled newspapers like a champ; hit third floors with the Sunday *Trib* and front porches from the middle of the street. He was the Babe Ruth of newsboys. Best of all though, he took us to White Sox games.

Armed with a brown bag filled with Bridie's famous cheese sandwiches, Ollie would pack us inside his old blue Ford and deposit us in Comiskey Park's left field bleachers. There, Minnie Minnoso patrolled the outfield and Louis Aparicio combed the infield. This is where heaven began and ended for us and where we planned our fantasy big league careers. There was no other place we would rather be. Ten cents was your allowance to buy a pop to wash down the cheese sandwich, which by the time you had sunk your salivating teeth into, had melted just a bit.

There were always enough sandwiches to go around, some even for the strays, because Bridie's worst nightmare was a kid that would get left out. It never happened under her watch. When the game began, your next thought was catching a foul ball, which never happened but that didn't matter because it was the White Sox and Bridie's slightly melted cheese sandwiches.

Chris Dates was an immigrant Greek with too many kids and too small a paycheck. He had paws the size of an ape and would often shake hands with five of us, all at once. When it rained, he'd drive around the block numerous times just to hit a puddle he liked. He organized our gang and distributed the water pistols and rubber knives when we had meetings. He loved women and taught us to be gentlemen when we bird dogged. "Short quick ogles, don't stare and never get caught." Dates wasn't winning any

Hollywood roles with his looks, but he loved admiring God's female creatures and every time he saw something that he liked, which was often, he would mutter from the curved corner of his mouth, "nice material." Dates had the work ethic of a mule and the manners of a dandy.

The Kreeger brothers were another story. Cross eyed and cantankerous, they led the Age in complaints. You got a complaint when you missed a delivery. The "K" boys usually came to work straight from the bars, groggy, bruised and scratched. Curt wore a service uniform, something to do with maintenance and the "r" in his name tag looked like an "n." It wasn't wise to give the Brennan boys an opening, because we'd take it, and we did. We were quick too, so Curt never could quite catch us after we greeted him in the morning. The booze and bad knees would slow him down and we'd apologize from across the rail tracks in the tall grass, stopping to taunt, knowing that he had the will but neither the eyesight nor the energy to catch us.

"Sorry Cu_t, you really oughtta get that name tag fixed so we can be friends again." We all looked and sounded alike, so he'd forget pretty quick who had greeted him with the barb. Each morning started with the slur, the chase and his surrender.

Reilly-Roo was the last of the old timers. His plight reminded us to stay in school and do our homework. You knew when he was pulling in because most of his car was dragging on the street. There were no shocks, no muffler and the windows were stuck open. The clang of Reilly's car was a wake-up alarm for the neighborhood and the frozen windows, a refuge for the rain. He had last weeks, now mossy editions still piled high in his back seat and his trunk was filled with the junk he'd pick as he did his route. Early to rise, gave you first dibs on the good junk left out for the garbage men and was for Reilly, the real reason he had a route.

Finding a good junk pile was rarely good fortune but that didn't matter to Reilly because every pile was a treasure. Every wagon we found had three wheels; bikes had two flats and you could have all the *National Geographic*'s that you wanted. It was mostly junk, even to us, but gold to Reilly.

The cart clunked as it crossed the threshold that separated us from the Age and the task at hand, bringing yesterday's news to the world. Route 5 was mine, inherited from my big brother Tom, who had graduated from routes to working in the neighborhood as a caretaker and fixer-upper. Tom's the one that got us into this racket, looking for ways to pay our tuition. Yep, that's right, we paid for our grade school; three bucks a month, twenty-seven dollars a year, straight to the Cardinal. We could have gone to the public school for free but that would have exposed us to pagans and heathens and surely a one-way ticket to Hell. There was a good public school near us, but it was unthinkable to attend. We were not to socialize with the other side, or any side that wasn't Catholic.

Our routes began in the pitch darkness of night but carried us into the dawn of the new day. There were perks: We inhaled the early morning aromas: Strickland's Bakery, George the Greek's sizzling bacon and pancakes, Dee's brewing coffee and the incense from Fr. Walsh's early-bird mass. The early bird mass was a shortened version that came in handy on Sundays, when you had to attend or risk eternal damnation. You could fulfill your duty in one short ½ hour because Walsh, hungover from the night before would forget parts of the mass and didn't have to give a sermon, and everybody was in favor of that, even God. In a jif' you could fulfill your weekly duty, stave off damnation and have time to spare to get to the first game in the alley. But that was only on Sunday.

During the week, there were other perks: most mornings I was treated to a fine secret peek into Pinkie's basement window in the alley behind Dee's. There Pinkie'd be breakfasting at her kitchen dinette: a pretty almost young blonde, garbed only in pink panties and a frilly bra and sometimes on a hot morning, only the panties. The first time I saw Pinkie was by accident. I took a glance, couldn't believe my eyes and then another. We had something in common...no bathrobes. I couldn't get over the sight of her: I was ten-years-old.

The second gander cost me ten "Our Fathers" when I eventually confessed a couple of weeks later...after much thought. An accidental first peak was excusable if you turned away fast, but that second gawk cost me the prayers and quite possibly some time in Purgatory if God didn't buy my sorrow and contrition.

Purgatory was where you went when you died, if you were only a little bad and still redeemable. It was kind of like a holding cell until God knew what to do with you. Reasoning was, sometimes things like looking at Pinkie, although very serious, wouldn't be bad enough to get you sent to Hell. Every morning though, it got easier to look through Pinkie's window and every morning I looked forward to it and liked what I saw more and more.

Pinkie was introducing me to something more than the durty pictures that Murphy showed me in the alley. Pinkie was making Murphy passé which I never thought was possible. My daily voyeurism started to bring depth and detail to everything Murphy talked about and gave it some meaning. It was the start of what this sex stuff was all about and created much trepidation. I wondered if I was even ready for any of it because whether you were looking or fantasizing or God forbid touching, it was all forbidden, especially for a young lad like myself.

The first time I confessed to the Pinkie sightings, after much torment, it was very traumatic and I gave a great deal of thought to how it would be in Hell, because that's where the priest said I was going. He tried to get my name out of me but I was smart enough to know that my anonymity in the confession booth was the only thing keeping me from complete disgrace. Even though the priests couldn't speak of any confessional matters, I suspected that there was always chatter at the dinner table.

The priest's response was severe enough that I never mentioned Pinkie again. I rationalized that I wasn't hurting anybody but myself and that my damnation was so far off that I still had time to repair myself before I was sent to Hell. Besides I had an out.

The Church had this thing called indulgences that Luther used to buy to help finance the Popes' wars. The indulgences got you some good graces that you could save up and use to buy your way out of a tough situation or erase the stains on your soul. They gave you hope if you ended up in Purgatory and not Hell, where your fate was completely sealed. Once inside Hell, there was no getting out. If you saved up enough of the indulgences, you could buy your way out of the 'Purg'. It worked like frequent flyer miles – save them up for when you would run into a high fare and then use them to fly free. You would never use the indulgences for small stuff like stealing candy bars from Meltz, the Jewish candy man – that was like using the flyer miles for a cheap flight to Florida. You used them for major transgressions like Pinkie or missing mass on Sundays. Indulgences were a great trump card and let you have a few dances with the devil...but not too often. Repeat offenders lose their sway.

Almost every morning thereafter, Pinkie would be posed, seemingly ignorant of my adolescent glances. And every morning, I was confronted with the dilemma of looking, degenerating a bit and needing to be saved or passing on the Pinkie peek, ignoring the chance at debauchery and keeping my soul white. The temptation and opportunity was too much for a young lad like myself and I succumbed to the devil's work and took a slight soft glance the first few days and then longer harder ones as the days went by.

Each day it got easier as I started to look forward to Pinkie's generous display of herself. The threat of Hell went away mostly because I stopped telling the priest about it. It wasn't so much what I saw but the chance to see it that kept me gawking through Pinkie's kitchen window. How could I pass this up? And besides, I wasn't hurting anyone so why the Hell shouldn't I look? And maybe Pinkie knew that I was looking and wanted me to, and I couldn't disappoint her.

My peeks at Pinkie began to lay a crack in my foundation of absolute allegiance to Catholicism and each day the split widened just a bit until finally, I didn't feel any guilt at all when I looked through the window. It was the first time in my life that I ignored the dos and don'ts of Catholicism and went ahead and did something bad. It wouldn't be the last. I had seen the window of true enlightenment – the chance to feel free.

Seeing Pinkie was too major to hog to myself, so often times some of the boys would meet me in the alley and enjoy the show together.

"Am I supposed to like those things?" Phelim asked on his first visit.

"You are, unless you walk on the wrong side of the street, young man," I told him. Some mornings we'd park ourselves behind the bushes when we wanted to fully absorb the show and giggle and strain to be quiet as we watched, still too young to get much from it but bragging rights.

It was major and it was ours, because the morning was ours. Pinkie outclassed the magazines in the alley and gave us a glimpse of the future. It was her gift to the next generation and one that was well appreciated. Now we knew what was under the nuns' habits. Murphy had won his bet.

The next free performance on my route was of another sort: "Hairy the Ape", a man who lived near the end of our route, retrieved his newspaper in his birthday suit. We'd stomp up the wooden stairs of his dingy building, pound out a beat that was sure to wake him. I'd fling the paper just short of his door so he'd have to leave his doorway in order to retrieve it. It became an art; flipping that paper to just the right spot. The boys would take a position down the hallway just around the corner with our heads sticking out, one above the other.

And then he'd appear, ole Mister Hairy Butt. This guy was so hairy you hardly knew that he had a dingy. The "Pup" as Bridie would call anyone who was indecent, would march for the paper like he was taking a walk in the park and then he'd bend over to pick up his paper and a collective *"phewwwww"* would come from the paper boy gallery, as he stooped over. Hairy was another one that didn't have a robe.

Our morning routes were full of unexpurgated scenes like that. There was the time I encountered a young lad going AWOL from Bishop Quarters, the military school on Lake St.

"Good morning Colonel," I saluted, trying to connect.

"You need to learn your ranks," he advised, in a curt tone.

"It's Captain and I'm done with them," he said as he strolled by garbed in his military uniform. He continued on in military fashion and seemed to know where he was going, so I didn't intervene.

Next was the heel clicking whistler who belted out complete musical scores as he walked down the avenue. He never looked east or west, just straight ahead. It was only me and the jealous birds that were there to enjoy it. It was symphonic warbling, and gave me my start whistling. And to this day I think of him when I whip up a little *Summertime*.

One morning a transient with a wimpy gait stopped me and confessed to having a foot fetish and asked if I'd be kind enough to help him with it?

"What?" I said. Murphy never mentioned a fetish. "All you have to do is take your shoes off." Unsure of what I'd be getting myself into, "Oh no, too cold for that."

His face saddened and he politely strolled off after apologizing. I was more upset with the desperate pervert giving me a new word to look up than fending off his advances. At least he had manners.

Every morning it was something different, weirdos or inclement weather or just the simple, cold loneliness of the dark, frigid mornings.

We'd finish our routes in an hour and feel like big shots as we wheeled our carts home, when all the other kids were still tucked in their beds. Hands covered in paper ink and the tips of our toes cold with the morning chill, we felt like men of the manor bringing home the bacon.

Most days were the same -- Pinkie, Hairy, the whistler, the Kreeger brothers in pursuit, the dark alleys and back stairways of the indifferent apartment buildings, the sleepy houses, the warbling birds, the clunk of the cart on the cobblestone street, the fear of the darkness, the honor of our trek. Each day making us more and more of the lads that Bridie wanted us to be.

One day, however, would prove different, and leave a blot on my soul. A voyeur was one thing, but a thief? That day, I encountered the usual daily stuff but as I pushed my cart home, I passed by the back of St. Edmund School and was tempted.

Today for some reason, the milkman was early or I was late, I don't know which, I saw something unusual; a rack of fresh new chocolate milk cartons delivered for the day's morning break.

Every morning, halfway through classes, the nuns would call for a short rest and proceed to hand out "chocos" accompanied by a cookie to the rich kids whose families had paid for the perk.

The underprivileged proletarians would sit there, stomachs grumbling because the morning's oatmeal was starting to wear off and we would have to watch the doctor's son and the lawyer's daughter nosh on the treats.

Often, I thought of donning a cape and assaulting one of the choco sippers, ripping the treat from their hands and gulping down the choco with one hand as I held the privileged brat down with the other. As I was being escorted out of the room the other unfortunates would be cheering wildly as I let out a big burp and threw my fist into the air. It was one scheme that I left unfulfilled but brewing. Bridie was appalled at the practice of giving the favored ones, the chocos. "If you don't have one for everyone, keep it in the closet."

Chocolate milk was an unattainable and distant comfort for us. I stopped and paused, just to make sure that I was seeing what I was seeing, as the chocos began tugging at my soul. I knew they were for the break brats and I thought that it might be time to even the score a bit.

"They'll never miss one," I began to rationalize, and "who will ever know?" It was just me, the morning darkness and that beckoning choco. I slipped over and grabbed one, holding it against my leg just in case there might be someone watching. The overhang blocked me from the Lord above and the early hour darkness from anyone else, or so I thought. I'll just take one and down it at the end of the alley.

And that's just what I did, slipping the booty into my cart and proceeding down the alley, propelled by lust over how that choco would taste. I stopped behind Conroy's garage and gulped all eight ounces, savoring every drop of that luscious, velvety choco.

"Ahhhh," I sighed as I finished it, burped, threw one fist in the air tossed the evidence into the dumpster, looked around one last time for witnesses, exhaled in triumph and went home to get ready for school.

"How'd it go?" Bridie chirped as I came in.

"Just grand Ma," I said, "Nothing different today, still quicker than the Kreegers."

"Are you sure?" she said, her eyes narrowed, staring into mine.

"I took another look at the tea leaves after you left and thought maybe I saw something that wasn't so good." A couple of the leaves had dried out and fallen and it changed the picture a bit, looked like someone had taken a bite out of the halo that was etched above your head." The guilt started to set in. *Who saw?*

Could Bridie *know?* It was dark and there was nobody around. Doubt crept in. I had just added a lie to my theft, "Nothing different today, Ma."

I knew it could only get worse…all for the sake of a choco. Why'd you do it, you idiot, I asked myself. Succumb to temptation, again and again. Aw Hell, just forget it, you'll be fine. No one was awake and it was still dark out. Bridie couldn't know.

Off to school I went hoping today would be a quick one. I passed the scene of the crime, slyly glancing over where the milk had been. By now, they had brought the rack inside and I prayed they weren't counting the cartons, discovering the one empty compartment. The Hell with it, what's done is done, there was no going back. I told myself , "Everything's all right; one choco won't be missed." I wasn't convinced. I was shaking in my jocks. Peeking through Pinkie's window and now stealing. Oh! You fool.

I met up with the boys outside the main doors waiting for school to open. Everything was normal except my inner guilt. It was chewing at me enough for my buddy Turk to say, "What's wrong Sean, you don't seem yourself."

"Oh, nothing Turk, just a little tired from my route," I said. And sick to my stomach from that choco I stole, I thought. Come on boy, just get through today and never do it again, I told myself.

When the gold in-laid school doors opened, I looked up to see who was playing sentry. It was the beady-eyed Sister Anna Lee who thought that I was behind every caper and would gladly condemn me to Hell if she had the power. Anna Lee resented my penurious roots and consistent good performance in class and tried to bestow as much penance on me as possible as often as she could. She couldn't stomach the poor kid outdoing the doctor's son, which happened more than she would have liked. She did not accept indulgences.

I got behind my other buddy, Lurch, who towered over me and I tried to slip through the door unnoticed, but her arm came down behind Lurch's back and stopped me cold. She said nothing but her gaze ripped right through my soul. I could have imagined her piercing glare as unintentional because she looked like this most of the time…but not likely. This nun knew everything and had eyes in the back of her head, especially when I was in the room.

I stumbled on the threshold and gasped at the same time. She saw the guilt on my face and the shame in my heart. The taste of the choco soured.

I slipped into my home room where Anna Lee was the warden, holding out some hope that they didn't know and plopped into my desk, spent from the worry. I got out a book and tried to fill my head with thoughts of Lincoln or Jefferson or Aparicio or anything but my heist. Nothing was easing my torment and Anna Lee's glare kept stabbing my heart. Don't look up or sideways or anywhere, I thought. In a daze, I studied the carvings on the desk in front of me. "Someone is looking," the etching said.

The crackle of the P.A. jerked me from my fright and the morning announcements commenced. Every morning Sr. Michael, the Principal, would broadcast the day's events, awards and inquisitions.

"Subscriptions for *The New World* are due Friday" she barked. *New World?* That was the propaganda rag that the diocese put out. We had to sell subscriptions to spread the word just in case there was someone out there who was unfortunate enough not to be a Catholic. There was a page for the Cardinal to rant about our decaying society and another page for all of the events that would keep you cloistered in the Catholic community, and of course one for a small contribution.

"They'll be a special mass on Friday morning commemorating St. Luigi," she continued. Who? They had more saints than you could keep track of and each one had a special association. There was a patron saint of sinners and firemen and policemen and if you lost something and if you needed to sell your house or good fortune and a saint for anything else you could think of. There were so many saints, every circumstance was covered. When something good happened you'd hear them exclaim. "Our prayers to St. So and So were answered." Yeah, that's because there is a saint for everything. It was brilliant marketing and kept you wanting to be a part of something so fortuitous, especially with our luck.

I quit praying because I knew that someone else always would and even if no one prayed these saint guys would come through a lot. Every time we got bailed out, it was the saints who had come to the rescue. The faithful always knew there was a little help in the skies above. And fast, I tried to think of the bailout saint for thieves, liars and dumbos. Nothing came.

"Would Sean Brennan please come down to the Principal's Office?"

"Hail Mary full of grace," I was back to praying.

"Another award for Brennan," Soledad chanted from the back row. That was Reno Ray, who got his nickname for being the pitched pennies champ in the alley. Reno was one of my best buddies and my biggest fan but he'd be embarrassed to know me today...or maybe proud, the way he operated. Reno loved looking for a short cut. He had a route too, but it was for the weekly circular rag. When the bundle of papers was delivered to his house, Reno would put them in his basket on his bike, act like he was going to deliver them and then find the nearest dumpster.

His grandmother, who loved getting the coupons from the rag, turned him in when she had to pay full price at the drug store. Reno got fired and shrugged his shoulders when his mother told him he was a disgrace to the family.

No, this would be no award, only disgrace. My heart dropped a few floors and that bailout saint was still not coming to me. Hell, there was no saint for my crimes and the indulgences didn't matter with the nuns.

"The Lord is with thee," Oh no, he's not.

I got the nod from Anna Lee that it was okay to head down to the principal's office, and I slowly rose from my chair. Her piercing stare turned to a smirk as she knew that my execution was near.

Everyone stared at me as I moseyed out. Their looks were full of compassion and pity too, because most of them knew it wasn't good being singled out for a trip to the principal's office at the start of the day. Only Reno held out hope and he was looking for company in Hell.

Down the empty, marble floored hall I went, alone and terrified, with only the click of my heels to interrupt the damning silence. I felt like I was walking to the gas chamber, each step got me closer to doom, each step left less of my life to live and all for a choco. Hell, Cagney got a bank roll for his crimes.

As I neared the office, thoughts of veering left out the door and heading west entered my mind. That won't work, my bike had a flat and Bridie would surely miss me. What's that saint's name? Nothing! "Blessed art thou amongst sinners." You got that right, ole pilfer boy.

I turned into the office and ran right into the reason for my capture and straight into the key ring on the massive, totalitarian Albanian maintenance man's belt. The impact caused a clang of the keys that spelled my death knell and left an imprint on my forehead much like the ones at the Salem witch trials. Alfred was the grim reaper, the executioner, the extra set of eyes for the nun's wanton search for victims. Alfred helped the nuns keep their detention list full and the halls echoing with pleas for mercy.

Alfred looked down at me in delight, rubbing his massive hands together. I looked up at the behemoth brute...I was finished and I knew it. He'd bagged another transgressor an Irishman to boot, and fed him to the inquisition.

It dawned on me at that very moment that Alfred's house was across the alley from the school. From his kitchen window he must have seen me, even under my imagined cover of darkness, pilfer the choco. How could I have been so stupid not to think that this henchman for the nuns wasn't spying, wasn't watching me fall into the abyss of temptation, wasn't perched on some stoop stalking my simple path waiting for me to become fodder for his rapacious hunts? And now the only question was the punishment. How much disgrace will they bury me under? How many corporal hours will I serve? What stake will I be burned at?

What oak tree will they hang me from as an example for any others tempted to sin?

"Our Father who art in heaven," one place I'll never see.

Still no bailout saint; my panic was setting in.

I walked into the office, strained, scared and mortified. Across from me behind a massive oak desk sat Sr. Michael, the Principal; the desk was just another altar I had to stand in front of, laden with guilt.

The nuns often gave up their given names and assumed new ones, male monikers to honor a brother or father. The practice left the nuns with absolutely nothing of their own, which the Church liked. They didn't have clothes or money or cars or bikes or anything but the rosary beads that swung from their waist. They called it the vow of poverty and it kept them needy and dependent and without even their own identity, just the one the Church gave them. Someone had convinced them that the less you had the better you were and the closer to God you would be. They were prisoners and now I would be one too.

In the corner, perched, curled up like a worm that had been left out in the sun, in a worn oak chair was a crying Junior Tearney. It must have been his choco that I stole. The lawyer's son was crying over one little carton of choco, an everyday quaff for him, a once in a lifetime indulgence for me. And that's what I thought. Life! That's what I was going to get.

"Hallowed be thy name." One name...any name...help! Still nothing, I was begging to the very guy that was going to condemn me.

"Mr. Brennan," she began by offering me a chair with her long narrow hands, "Do you have something you'd like to share with us?" That's how they always started their inquisitions, impersonal, they never used your first name. Squash your identity and rip your self-esteem from your gut. They hoped you were so humiliated that you might spill your guts to the crime at hand and maybe something in the past that they improbably missed, one committed while Alfred was on vacation. That way they'd get you for some old capers and save some detective work. They'd clean the blotter...and your soul...at the same time. It was their mission, nab the transgressors and keep the world free of sin...except theirs.

I knew their game and weighed my options; an eyewitness in Alfred and a sniveling Tearney to support the shortage, way too much evidence to overcome.

"You know, Sister, it's a bit stuffy in here," sticking my finger down my shirt collar and prying it back, trying to buy some time.

"You know you're not in much of a position to be making requests, but I agree." And she rose and lifted the window and rolled away the stone that was blocking my resurrection.

A wave of fresh air with a scent of emerald came sweeping in and swirled around my head and nestled in my bosom. My mood brightened. Bridie's second look at the tea leaves and that broken halo had been harbinger of my fate and circumstance. The bad reading put her on alert, like a doctor in a triage center, the energies of my angst, a call for her magic and now the open window an avenue for her cure. And down the alley and west, right into the office it came, timely and omniscient. I felt it, tasted it, caressed it. It came to me suddenly. How about the mercy defense? And that's what I decided on. They were going to get my best sob story and a stab at mitigation.

I came clean. "Yes, Sister Michael I took the choco and drank it." They liked when you used their full name and she was only getting one confession this time. Past crimes would stay in my archive and on their unsolved blotter.

"But it was a dangerous situation, Sister. After rising at five for my route and bearing the morning freeze, I felt faint and thought my blood sugars were low and I needed a boost. I'll pay for the choco when I get my Saturday bonus and I'll clean the erasers after school," I pleaded.

"So you felt faint," she asked.

"Oh, yes Sister, it comes on me unexpectedly."

Tearney was still crying.

"And how long have you had this ailment, Sean." Her use of my first name indicated some leniency. "Mr. Brennan" would have meant the death panels. "Oh it's been a number of years, it runs in the family. Usually a bite of candy or a glass of juice will do the job. They say I'll grow out of it eventually."

"Well, I certainly hope so, Sean. I'd hate to see you stealing milk cartons when you're in college."

"It should be cured by then Sister, if I get into college," I said. A little self-deprecation helped.

"Well Mr. Brennan I can't very well let you walk on this one, especially with the way Tearney is taking it."

"Sister, I'll do the erasers and drop my paper route bonus in the poor box." They loved that poor box stuff.

"And a trip to the confessional, Brennan," she followed, back to the last name only.

"This afternoon, Sister."

"Let's keep this one to ourselves," she asked.

And it was over. Well almost…there was still Anna Lee to deal with.

She gave me the, 'Get the Hell out of here nod,' and I complied, leaping out of the chair and easing myself out the door. As I turned out of the doorway, I bumped into Alfred again who had been spying just outside. I just missed the metallic branding by his keys; I looked up and gave him a smirk as if to say, 'Not this time.'

His disappointment was obvious. He wanted blood and carcasses and got only a slap on the wrist.

I took a few cocky steps backward, bobbing my head and keeping my smirk fixed on the apelike goon. I turned and picked up my pace and left him with his disappointment.

Cleaning the erasers got me out of school and the fifty cent bonus would feed someone needier than I, if it really went to China, liked they promised. And the confessional? I could sound as mortified as a prostitute at the altar and promise all kinds of future good behavior. Most times I made up my sins, but this time it would be a real sin and my repentance would be true because I really had taken something that wasn't mine…even if it was Tearney's. A few Hail Mary's wouldn't hurt.

I could still hear Tearney's sobs as I fled. My backward gait turned to a skip and finally a trot as I slowly turned and disappeared from Alfred's glare around the corner and into complete freedom. Well…not quite yet, I suddenly remembered Anna Lee.

I felt worse for Tearney than myself, seeing someone cry like that over one little choco, but I knew he'd get his choco back tomorrow and that the crying would probably stop and the next day I could watch him tease the unfortunates again as he sipped his choco treat in front of everyone, knowing that I had righted the scales of justice, at least for a day. I was starting to feel better.

When I got back to my classroom I paused at the doorway and reignited my bravado with a deep breath and came strutting into the room, head held high. My air drew puzzled looks. Anna Lee looked confused and disappointed. She, like Alfred, wanted blood and carcasses. Hadn't this boy just been at the gallows? She sensed that I had gotten off too light and her glare foretold some future torture.

I settled back into my seat, turned and looked over my shoulder and gave Reno the thumbs up. Maybe we won't end up in Hell if you let me do the talking.

All eyes were on me. "All right, back to work," Anna Lee yelled and all heads returned to the math problem at hand.

Sister Michael had promised to keep the heist quiet, which left only Tearney to blab about it and nobody would believe him. I knew Sr. Michael didn't believe my story but I think she gave me some points for ingenuity and some lenience for Bridie's contributions at the church. And the bailout saint? Well let's just say that wave of serendipity in the principal's office had a hint of Eire. Ste. Bridie? I'll take it.

I left school that day in an aura of triumph and on my way to my afternoon route I ran into Turk.

"Hey, I just jimmied the lock on the gym window," he said, "Hoops this afternoon?"

"Alfred gone," I asked.

"Yep," he said.

"See you at five."

The Altar Boy

Without any discussion, in fifth grade, you became an altar boy. There were few ways in which an eleven-year-old could attain status at St. Edmund School in Oak Park, and altar boy was at the top of the list. You could also choose to be a crossing guard and wear the shiny, orange belt around your waist and the strap that ran from shoulder to hip, and help the little ones cross the streets. You could be in the band and learn to clang an instrument or join the choir and sing to the angels, or get really daft and help the nuns on Saturdays, but nothing held the high esteem of donning a red cassock that ran from shoulder to toe and a white, lacy surplice that cloaked the cassock, and then go parading before the altar with the priest, to kneel in front of the tabernacle and otherwise direct a Catholic's most treasured rite: the Mass.

The priest would arrive at our school every eight weeks and hand out report cards. When he entered, the room would fall deathly silent except for a few of the girls irrepressible giggling, "Oh, he's so handsome." The presence that the priest commanded was enthralling. Sometimes you thought you were looking at God. And who could ignore an audience with him? The priest would stand at the front of the room and call out each kid's name, peruse the report card to examine your progress, and then offer a critique as he handed you your grades.

"Excellent work," to the smart kids.

"You're better than this," to the so-so kids.

"Needs a little work," to the not so-so kids.

And to the Bradley's, the slackers, the kids who were never going to get it and didn't care, "Make sure you show this to your mother." But their mothers didn't care either.

And when the cards had all been passed out, and with them a dose of glee to some, humiliation to others, the priest would belt out, "Are there any volunteers to become an altar boy?" This was an invitation from the priest, the closest thing to God on this Earth, to stand with him on the altar in front of the congregation and look proud and solemn. Every boy's hand in the room went sky-high in response, except Bradley's. Bradley was looking out the window; he couldn't care less. The girls sat, bored and neglected, knowing that only the lads could serve God: *There were no altar girls.* Some thought being an altar boy was the first step to the priesthood, and every Irish family yearned to have one...a priest, that is. A generation ago, my father, Tom Brennan, was the priest designate for his family and enthusiastically entered the seminary. My cousin Paddleboat was the chosen one in his.

When you joined the seminary, the Church sequestered you from mainstream society as a way to assert complete control and keep you from all the worldly temptations. The biggest temptation was girls, and you know what that meant. Sex was forbidden, and if Jesus didn't have any, neither should you. They didn't even want you to want it. That was a sin, too, and lowered you to the level of the Protestants and anyone else who appreciated a good-looking woman.

Daddy admitted years later that life without girls was a bit too much to ponder. But that wasn't the big reason Daddy left. Six years into the seminary his father died suddenly and Tom Brennan was forced to become his family's bread winner. By leaving, he incurred the wrath of his mother and the bishop, too.

"You can't turn your back on God, Tom," his mother said.

"And watch you and my little brother Pat starve."

The ascendancy didn't like losing recruits either. Daddy was ostracized by the whole Catholic establishment who were incensed that someone had the gall to reject "God's Calling." That's what they called it to make you believe that you didn't have any choice. And for many there was no choice. You were going to be a priest no matter what *you* wanted.

And then Bridie showed up…in the choir of all places where Tom had a spot in the tenor section where he could keep a close eye on the new sopranos. And one day she was there and Tom was watching…at Our Lady of Sorrows on the west side. Still fresh from Cloonmore in Eire, with her rich brogue and direct blue gaze, she cast a spell on the unsuspecting ex-seminarian and ruined the script for good. Tom would never go back to the seminary, not that he wanted to now. Daddy' instincts took over, and he succumbed to the allure of the tall, Irish farm-girl immigrant with the fine mane of thick, brown hair and "a way about her." It was Bridie who wrote the decisive chapter in the plan that God and Grandma had laid out for Daddy. And could you blame the poor lad for abandoning theirs and adopting the one that included Bridie.

Daddy lost everything when he bolted – guaranteed salvation, a scripted future and being the closest thing to God that a human could be – but he got Bridie. *Nice trade,Pops.* He was damned and ostracized and left isolated as if on an island for a few years, a disgrace to the family. But that didn't stop him. Daddy wasn't one to be intimidated. And exoneration finally came years later; you see, Bridie and Tom Brennan saw enough of each other to add eleven new faces to the parish enrollments.

The Church loved numbers of worshippers and their monetary contributions, too – perhaps even more than they loved enlisting new priests. The pastor was always prospecting for new seminarians or altar boys asking often, "Do you have the calling?" You always said, "Yes," because you couldn't say, "No," to him. He was smart enough to never ask Murphy or Turk or Bradley because he couldn't count on their answers, and their pedigrees were lacking.

But I saw the perks: You gained some status when you became an altar boy and the extra cash from weddings and funerals helped too. Our portfolios had only the lint in our pockets for company.

I could forecast the two pinnacles of altar boyhood: attending the annual Altar Boy Picnic – a sports outing that let you have a full day out of the cage – and the greatest glory of all: the possibility of playing a key role at the Christmas Eve mass. All this promised some money, time off from school, and more than a little glory. My hand flew up, along with most of the other boys. So I became an altar boy, inching my way closer to God and heaven.

"Tomorrow after school for the first practice," the priest announced. By the next day, half the volunteers had thought better of waking up early for Sunday morning services and neglected to show up for the altar boy rehearsals. I showed up – the perks were too irresistible. Within months, I became an old veteran at serving, ringing the bells, swinging the incense, lighting the candles, carrying the cross. In a weak moment Sister Michael, the principal, made me head of the fifth grade altar boys. It was a huge honor to preside over God's little servants, and it got you out of school too. Sister Michael's motives were unclear, but I think that she had a soft spot in her heart for the less fortunate candidates who were an unlikely choice for a position usually assigned to the doctors' and dentists' sons.

Sister Michael knew that she was taking a risk putting me at the head, but her plan was to shame me into conformity. "Don't let me down," she said, adding more pressure and angst.

Our Altar Boy careers began engulfed in an angelic aura. It gave us lofty status assisting the priests in bringing mass and the

Eucharist to the congregation. The night before I served, Bridie would make sure I was well scrubbed and the next morning, my hair combed before she sent me off to serve God. Crisply garbed in starched cassocks and lace over garments, my cherubic face would gleam under the altar lights and flickering candles. We wore red for happy masses and black for sad ones. Our duties were crucial and varied. We prepared the cruets, full of the wine and water that became the blood of Jesus and then watched in angst, with a sour smirk, as the priests sipped it at the consecration which is when all the magic was taking place. We rang the chimes at the critical parts of the mass; timing and a practiced touch were required. At funerals, the short guys would carry the candles, and the tall guys would carry the crucifix. We'd swing the silver thurible, a container that housed the incense, and send a good plume of smoke over the coffins and relics. At communion, that's when the priest laid a thin wafer on your tongue, the Body of Christ, we'd hold the patens, a small silver plate, under the recipient's chin just in case the host went wayward. The worst part of our job was looking down everyone's throat and at their spotted and discolored tongues wondering what the Hell they ate yesterday.

To the boys in our neighborhood who hadn't slept in, we'd give a wink and press the edge of the paten to their throats, basking in our power as Jesus was laid on their tongues. No moment was so sacred that we couldn't inject some kind of mischief. But we were always required to look solemn and serene. There was no smiling. That was how mass was: solemn and dour. The more somber you looked the holier you were, and most hammed it up pretty well. Murphy would be in heaven if God couldn't recognize a faker.

Your solemnity started the moment you walked into church. In moments, you'd go from screeching and laughter on the lawn in front of church to more solemn and more somber with each step as you climbed toward the church's front gates. Once inside the front door, the curtain was totally drawn, and complete silence was required. The only snickers you'd hear were when Murphy snapped the hat-clip on the back of the pew and sent a crack echoing through the church. The nun would come from behind as the crack slowly faded into the nave and she'd look down each pew searching for the culprit. The only evidence was the giggling that followed, but everyone was doing that so most times the crime went unpunished. It was the height of frustration for a nun…witnessing a trespass and being powerless.

The chimes would sound, *ding dong ding,* and from the sacristy, the hidden room behind the altar where the secrets were kept, the priest would emerge garbed in flowing robes, looking like Jesus would have if he'd had money, and flanked by an altar boy on each arm.

The silence and solemnity would deepen as the priest slowly walked to the front of the altar, raised both arms to the sky and God, and let out a chant in Latin. And for the next hour the altar boys had to pretend that we were paying attention, which we weren't. The kids in the pews only looked straight ahead for fear the nun behind them would sense their indifference and come up behind and clip them one. The whole exercise was painful, and we didn't much understand what it was all about, only that painful stuff made you better. Pain was at the core of their everything.

The sermons were always about how sinful you were and how you needed to be more like Jesus. Often, as I was perched on the altar playing altar boy, looking out at the drawn faces, I'd wonder why this couldn't be like the Black churches, hoppin' and boppin'. No one was having fun in our church, and no one was supposed to. This was church, dammit, your weekly commitment that kept you out of Hell.

When mass was over and when you weren't serving, just after the final blessing that gave you one last injection of goodness, you'd start to file out of your pews. You'd be so eager to leave, you'd knock into the person in front of you so you could get outside and feel life again. When I'd take my first step outside, I'd breathe deeply and go charging down the steps, taking two at a time and the last three in one lunging jump, knowing that the next dreaded holy hour was a good seven long days away.

All this was somewhat balanced by some major payoffs for being an altar boy. One perk was serving early mass at the local hospital where they gave you a full buffet breakfast. The buffet ranked high because you got to eat as much bacon, doughnuts, scrambled eggs and pancakes as you could possibly stuff inside yourself in one morning. The buffet had all the things we never had at home, and boy, were we hungry. The hospital always lost on this one.

It was a whole new experience, a real trip at the hospital. The chapel was empty because most of the people who were supposed to be there were upstairs dying. The priest was Father Duffacy, who seemed like he was a hundred years old. At six feet two and 120 pounds his profile was hard to spot. They kept a bed open for him just in case…you never knew when. He walked by inches, not steps, and when he genuflected the cartilage in his knees would pop and fill the chapel with gunshot sounds. I ducked the first time I heard one. He couldn't talk anymore, only mumble, but halfway through the mass, he'd raise his voice and you'd hear, "Haila the Mary Fullo the Grace," and everyone present would be cleansed of their sins and the mass official. It wasn't long before we lost the hospital duty…something about, "We can't afford these guys anymore."

But the Altar Boy Picnic was the really special perk: we got a whole day off from school, got to wear plain clothes and play baseball, and got to leave the uncommitted boys behind with all the unde*serving* girls, who couldn't go because they weren't good enough to serve the Lord. We got to ride in a big yellow school bus and spend the day at Pottawattamie Park where we could run, play, slide, swing and swim until we couldn't stand anymore. It was the highlight of our year and the payoff that made all those masses worth it. The Altar Boy Picnic was our yearly vacation packed into one glorious day. The bus ride was a trek of just a few miles but, in our minds, a journey to heaven. It was the day when you got to show up to school in a sweatshirt and jeans, punching the padding out of your baseball glove, if it even had any, and dreaming of pure joy without one nun to say no to you or tell you what to do or remind you of your shortcomings. It was nunvana…*er, nirvana.*

Anticipation built as the day of the picnic approached. I had no reason to sense the disaster ahead. The day of the picnic was chilly, but there was no rain, at least, not yet. My newspaper route was done, and my excitement grew as I pulled on my worn blue jeans and White Sox sweatshirt and laced up my gym shoes. Bridie bid me *adieu* at the back screen door, barking out "be carefuls" and stuffing a strip of sheet, in lieu of a cotton hanky, in my pocket for the inevitable "shnotters" that you'd get on a chilly day. At the last minute, she asked, "And your jockies?" Her primal fear was that you'd be in an accident and as you were being undressed in the emergency room the doctor wouldn't find any or discover a *smather* that needed attention. The old screen door, with its holes and rips, slammed as I took the last three stairs in one leap. I looked back and could see Bridie waving.

"Be a gentleman," she warned.

Her admonishment fell on deaf ears…gentleman and the Altar Boy Picnic were worlds far apart. Today would be gluttonous, overindulgent, excessive and extravagant…hedonism at its height.

As I continued my mad dash for the alley and my road to ecstasy, I looked over my shoulders and yelled back to Bridie, "Ma, I forgot. How'd the tea leaves look?" I was looking for a little assurance that the morning would go well and what better place to find it than in Bridie's sorcery with the tea leaves.

"A bit muddled today. There was a wayward clump that could either be sunshine or a big cloud. Be careful," she warned one more time.

'Muddled...' I thought. That wasn't like her to be evasive the day of a trip or not find some silver cloud in the residue. I hesitated at the back of the garage and thought about a second reading to clarify things and then heard Maloney yell from the alley, "We can't miss the bus, let's go."

Aw, Hell, maybe she had read someone else's cup, and even if she didn't, a dark cloud couldn't stop this wonderful trip. I kept up my trot and ran to pick up my buddy Lurch, whose real name was Paddy and had gotten his nickname because he was tall and lanky, screwed things up a lot and had a nasally voice. Lurch lived two doors down, and I caught up with him at the garbage cans, but I was really starting to feel unsure about the prospects of the day. Bridie was always positive about her readings, especially on the day of an outing. 'Muddled...'

Aw, to Hell with it, muddled couldn't be that bad. All that mattered now was getting on that bus before anyone in charge could change their minds. I started looking forward to the first great moment of the day when, as we left the classroom and headed for the bus, we could look back at the other kids stuck in their desks, and the next pleasure would be stepping across the threshold at the front door and into the free world, the one without the nuns, and letting out a loud whoop.

This was the day that I could scream till I was hoarse and play till I was black and blue and near death. It would even be okay to die…but right after the picnic. Nothing could stand between me and this deserved reward. Lurch and I hurried down the alley, knocking over a couple garbage cans along the way. Halfway to school, as we were planning the day, in between breaths and under a crystal clear but chilly morning, one little old gray cloud appeared out of nowhere. I told Lurch about the muddled tea leaves.

"What could possibly go wrong?" he said in his nasally voice.

"We won't let one little gray cloud stop us, will we, Lurch?"

"Not on your life, Bridie couldn't be wrong," he guaranteed. Lurch's assurance made me feel a little better…just a little.

We got to school in time and linked up with our fellow soldiers of Christ, warming our arms up amid the diesel fumes of the school bus. The hum of the engines was like symphonic arias, filling the pauses between our ecstatic cries of excitement. Between each toss, we'd look over to the school doors to see if they were opening. In just a few short minutes, we'd all be sailing out to Elysium though past experience had taught us that nothing was a lock until we were clear of any nun's reach.

Today, a right turn at Oak Park Avenue and sliding across North Avenue would be our lock-in point and when the whoops would get really loud. We'd be free, and there'd be no going back. Even then we'd still check the rear windows for a screaming nun chasing the bus. As we warmed up our arms on the lawn just outside the school doors, I got a bit saddened looking at my classmates in school garb who weren't going, but then I reminded myself that today was my treat for seeing my duty to Jesus and performing it in a timely and dedicated manner. No more sympathy for others left behind: this was *my* day.

The heavy, mosaic front door of the school began to open, and my heart started beating faster as I knew our departure grew close. I took my eye off the next toss and dropped it. No problem.

I grabbed the ball from the dew-laden grass, and we let out a collective huge cry in response to the opening door, anticipating our escape, throwing our arms in the air and letting out a big whoop. The whoop died as fast as it had been given birth as I saw Sister Anna Lee stick her head out of the partially opened door and scan the crowd with her beady eyes. Remnants of the whoop faded to nothing. There was silence. Her executing look could do that to the highest level of excitement. Why wasn't she opening the door and letting us in? Did Bradley forget his homework again?

No, this was more serious than that. Her glare scanned the crowd until it landed straight upon my head, and I sidestepped to see if it was me she was after. The glare followed.

"Oh boy," I thought. I remembered the one lone gray cloud in the teacup and Bridie's admonishment. I couldn't imagine what Sister Anna Lee was after and then I saw her index finger beckon me in with an ominous "Mr. Brennan." My name, with that "Mr." in front, was the gravest, most chilling and isolating thing that I ever heard… gravest and most chilling because there was always catastrophe at their end, especially without my first name. Dread filled my countenance, Sister Anna Lee was no fan of mine, and every chance she got to prick my puff she took. Anna Lee had a small, sallow face, her eyes forever narrowed in suspicion. I shuffled my way inside like Duffacy at the hospital, trying to delay the inevitable as long as possible, stopped and stood before the great inquisitor, wondering how and why the axe would fall this time. The heavy door shut with a thud behind me like someone slamming a coffin lid on a despised relative.

The hallway was empty except for Sister Anna Lee and me, like Jesus and one of his souls on Judgment Day. She stood erect, hands clasped below her belt with a frigid and piercing look. Well, actually there was a trace of delight too, right at the corners of her mouth.

"Yes, Sister?" I popped my glove with my right fist, trying to hide my fears, pretending her face was in the pocket. There was no way I was going to use her whole name.

"You, sir," she started, "Missed mass in February and once in December, and in good conscience and because it wouldn't be fair to the other servers who haven't missed, I must deny your attendance at the picnic today." She puffed her chest out, smirked and raised her heels in symphony and lowered them slowly, as if to make the pain last. If she had stabbed me in the heart, she would have been kinder.

"But, Sister, those were snow days, and my route took extra time." My right hand left the glove, and both hands fell to my sides, lifeless. The glove slid off my hand and fell to the cold, marble tiles below. The thud was all that filled the deadly silence. Tears welled in my eyes. I knew the dye had been cast and nothing would change this inquisitor's sentence.

"You should have gotten up earlier," she said, assuming we knew the weather forecast.

"But, Sister, I didn't know it was going to snow," I begged. "We don't have a "tellie"."

"A commitment is a commitment, and I don't tolerate excuses," she argued, turning the knife in me one more rotation. "And when you do serve, your attention is wanting."

'Can't argue that one,' I thought.

My tears flowed, and my breath came in gasps because I knew it was over. There would be no Altar Boy Picnic for me today. I mustered every ounce of courage to make one more plea and ask for some mercy, but my lips were quivering and unresponsive, my breath short, and nothing came out. Numb from her edict, I dropped my head and inched down the hallway, like Duffacy, and stopped at the threshold of my classroom and took one last look back at Anna Lee and my solitary glove lying on the tile floor.

Anna Lee kicked the glove to the side. My pain doubled, but I was too weakened to put up any fight. I found my desk in the empty room and collapsed into the chair and cried and gasped. Nothing entered my mind but the sheer cruelty of Anna Lee's actions. I tried to think of some way to…but her dominance and my catatonic state wouldn't let me. It was over. I would be left with the undeserving today. With one cruel and incisive edict, all of my allegiance and service to God had been in vain.

The bell rang, and the other kids filed into the room laughing, pushing and shoving like usual, until they saw me slumped in my desk in a state of total shock. Their quick pace turned to a Duffacy crawl, their laughter turned to silence and their gazes to stares. Everyone was stunned by my uncontrollable tears. Forgetting their manners, they all just stared at Anna Lee's latest and favorite victim, slouched in his desk.

"In your desks," Anna Lee commanded, reasserting her control. And all the kids jumped and filed into their seats. It seemed like eternity, but finally the bus driver came to the door to collect the responsible altar boys.

"Gentlemen," he cried out, and in unison the good boys all rose and began to exit. Out of pure desperate hope, I started to lift myself out of my desk, caught Anna Lee's glare and slumped back. For sure it was over now. When the last *Champion of Christ* cleared the door, I filled the air with one last wail. Lurch heard the desperate cry and came back, stopped in the doorway and cast a glance that said, "I'm sorry," knowing that he'd miss his catcher today. Anna Lee sat on the edge of her desk with her arms folded, delighting in my pain. I would be left alone with Murphy, Bradley and fifteen girls, all wishing they could take me in their arms and dab my tears.

Word spread fast of Anna Lee's latest execution and got back to Bridie at Cloonmore. I was still crying and breathless when she walked through the classroom door, her head cocked and lip curled.

There was complete silence except for my singular sobs. She recognized no one until her gaze circled the room and stopped at my gravesite. The teachers had switched classes by then, and I've often wondered where Sister Anna Lee would have been deposited had she been there.

Mrs. Wright looked at Bridie and with a shrug of her shoulders recognized the sheer cruelty and lunacy of the moment. Bridie, with a jerk of her head, summoned me and I, still numb and sobbing uncontrollably, shuffled toward her and walked straight into her open arms and a big hug. The hug didn't last long, but it didn't have to. Her farm-girl grip infused me with instant comfort. Out the door we went and down the street we walked with her arm around my shoulder. Each step allowed me deeper breaths and by the time we got to the corner store, I was beginning to think I might live through the pain and shock. There, Bridie ordered me up a fresh chocolate donut and chilled chocolate milk. Life started to be good again as I downed the donut in between my last few tears.

"Come on, Sean, we'll have our own picnic today," were the first words she spoke. We hopped on the elevated train, Bridie gave me the preferred window seat and we headed downtown. The sound of the metal wheels on the tracks and the fleeting roof tops disappearing into the past massaged our thoughts and elevated our mood.

As I stared out the window, still in a daze, she grabbed my hand in hers and said, "There are two things I'd like you to take from this, Sean...actually, three. Number one, you can recover from anything given the resolve, and a hop in your step tomorrow will kill her glee. Number two, no sin is greater than gaining happiness from another's misfortune. And number three… you don't need such drama to get a choco out of me."

A new sweatshirt with my favorite "Aparicio" printed on the back, a hamburger deluxe from the Silver Diner and the latest cowboy movie at the State Theatre filled the afternoon and completed our picnic, all without a single ant. When we came out of the movie, the sky opened and cracked and rain started to come down, and I hoped that the boys had gotten their baseball game in at the picnic and were now sliding in the mud. Doctor Bridie had saved the day again with her favorite remedy; a little distraction and a new thought.

When we got back, as we walked from the train and headed down Oak Park Avenue toward Cloonmore, she reached down and grabbed my hand, squeezed it as I looked up and she gave me her softest Irish wink.

"Don't ever let a meanie ruin your day," she said.

I responded with a skip and then another. I had that same hop in my step the next day when I went to school. Fixed and focused, I sauntered into the room with my head held high, greeted Sister Anna Lee with, "Good morning, Sister" – I still wouldn't use her whole name – and sat at my desk garbed in my new White Sox sweatshirt. I lifted the top of my desk to pull out my English book and found my catcher's mitt with a note in the pocket, "We missed you, eight passed balls."

I snickered and looked over at Lurch and then straight into Sister Anna Lee's eyes with a resolve that appeared to upset even her. I knew then that no one can get you down unless you let them and that, most of all, an ounce of Bridie's potion and power was too much for a handful of anyone's evil, even a *Bride of Christ's*.

Incensed

Bridie had ridden to the rescue again using her usual love and magical wisdom. She had soothed my trauma and instilled in me a new resolve to perform like never before at school and on the altar. In an ironic way Anna Lee's vengeance had made me a better person…but not too much better as I still found a way to sneak in the gym, knock over a few garbage cans and launch a few spitballs.

Anna Lee's reputation had taken a hit because her actions were just too cruel for anybody to justify. Sr. Michael, the principal, was one of the good nuns and knew the line between abject discipline and having a heart. I can only think that Michael felt like she owed me one and laid in wait till an opportunity presented itself.

It was December, and midnight mass on Christmas Eve was just around the corner. Four altar boys were needed, one from each class, fifth, sixth, seventh and eighth. The call came from the cloth-covered speaker tucked in the front corner of the room during morning announcements.

"Would Sean Brennan please come down to the office?" Sister Michael beckoned over the mystery box. The usual taunts, whispers and speculations rang out.

"He's snatched another choco," from Reno.

"Forgot his homework again," from Haggerty.

"Caught kissing girls again," from a jealous rival.

It was always great to see everyone's confused expressions. Was it jail time or juice time? I looked to Anna Lee to get my release nod, and Anna Lee, sensing that Michael was throwing me a bone, reluctantly gave me a slight 'get the Hell outta here' dip of her head and off to the principal's office I trotted. I was pretty sure this wouldn't be punishment, because I had been a good boy lately…well, mostly. I slipped into the principal's office and all signs seemed fine. There were no sobbing victims in the solace chair, or red penciled assignments on her desk and the bane of my existence, the hulking Albanian janitor, Alfred, who'd caught me stealing the chocolate milk, was nowhere to be seen…I haughtily approached the wooden desk, so reminiscent of an altar, the desk partially hid the tall and lanky Sister Michael.

"Well, Sean, you haven't appeared on my blotter lately, and I'm always one to give someone a second chance. How does Midnight Mass sound to you?"

I was breathless and tongue-tied. I had just been offered the plum duty of the year and quite possibly my entire altar boy career.

"Midnight Mass?" I stammered.

"In one week," she said. "You best start getting prepared. That is, of course, you agree to serve."

I wiggled my cheeks and swished my tongue, trying to build some moisture in my mouth "Yes, Sister, I'm your man."

"Good," she said. "You're rounding into a fine lad."

I am?

When I got home, bursting through the door in a fit of excitement, I yelled out. "Ma, I'm serving Midnight Mass!" The kitchen was ominously empty as the door slammed and sent a call out for the missing Bridie.

It was just moments before the Bridie, clutching her ubiquitous dish towel, came running, panting, around the kitchen corner; she was never far from the kitchen.

"Oh, Bejasus! Oh, Bejasus! Oh, Bejasus!" She reached down and wrapped her arms around my waist and lifted me in the air and swung me around.

"How'd you pull this one off?" Bridie asked, always a bit incredulous at one of our successes.

"Sister Michael called me into the office and everyone thought that it was for another punishment and then she asked me to serve Midnight Mass."

"Has she gone daft?" Bridie joked.

"Ma, she had that, 'I owe you one' look' on her face and then said that I was turning into a fine lad."

"She did?"

"I couldn't believe it either."

For the next week, I practiced every night with the Father and other altar boys on my specific duties. The whole experience had my brain in a whirl, and when they told me that I was to swing the incense on the visiting relics, my knees knocked.

Relics?

Christmas Eve arrived, and Bridie and Daddy couldn't have been prouder. Bridie ran up and down the block to find a camera to enshrine the moment in posterity. Mary Maloney came through, and with the whole family and a few neighbors standing on the porch and crowding the stairs, Bridie pushed the flash button on Mary's box camera and captured the moment. The look on my face will go un-interpreted, much as the Mona Lisa's, and open to speculation: wisp of smile or smirk?

"My God, he looks like Jesus himself," Mary uttered to Bridie.

The night descended. The moon and our excitement rose like the expectations of a Roman coronation. And I got nervous… with theological stage fright. In the sacristy, the room behind the altar, where the celebrants prepared, I paced, rehearsing my duties. Occasionally I'd peek out at the expanding crowd through the round window on the sacristy door. The church was in full regalia, with bunting and cloaked statues, flowers and candlelight and puffy cushioned chairs for the hierarchy. I finally spotted Bridie and Daddy in the fourth row, which was good seating for them because they were always late and usually landed in the back. And as each moment passed, I got a little more nervous.

"Hey, Staunton," I asked the eighth-grade altar boy with the thick glasses, "Where's the relics?"

"On the side, you dope."

"Gee, thanks."

The clock struck twelve, and the church bells pealed like gongs from heaven. They were announcing the birth of Jesus, the fulfillment of the Lord's promise to his people. Everyone in church slid to the edge of their seats in expectation and then rose as the full entourage emerged from the sacristy door.

In front were three of the altar boys, including me, walking abreast, one of us holding a candle on each side of Staunton who was in the middle carrying the crucifix. We were followed by the main priest and, behind him the fourth altar boy holding his trail and finally the other dignitary priests all garbed in long flowing robes and mitered hats fit for kings. It was a sight to behold.

Along our procession, I sneaked a look at the beaming Bridie and proud Pops. The mass unfolded with bells and readings and blessings and hymns. And then the church went silent, and nothing happened, and everyone began to twist and turn, and finally Staunton whispered, "The incense, the relics."

"What relics?" I whispered.

"The ones on the side," he commanded

"Now?" I asked Staunton as panic set in.

"Now!" Staunton commanded again.

I rose and retrieved the incense at a pace even Duffacy would be proud of, rehearsing my duties...what duties. I didn't know what to do. I swung the thurible buying some time and to make sure the chain was free. And then I remembered something Bridie had once said in the kitchen.

"How old is that old Father Duffacy?" I asked.

"Aw, Bejesus, he's a relic."

"Okay," I thought, "Now I understand. Here goes."

Full of new found confidence and wearing my most solemn expression, I paraded proudly over to the dignitaries, each priest older than the next, and gave them all a good incensing. All three waved their hands to disperse the smoke and let out a couple of coughs. I returned to my spot as proud as any Pope after an Easter blessing.

"The relics!" hissed Staunton.

"Got 'em," I whispered.

The Mass continued and ended on a high note with the whole congregation singing "Hallelujah." I felt exhilarated. We paraded off the altar the same way we'd come in, slowly and with a deep sense of protocol. And when we were finally inside the sacristy and the door closed behind us, I let out a deep breath, and Staunton let loose with a, "You dope! The relics are the Saints' bones in the small, glass case. You don't incense live people, only dead ones!"

I was crushed. And I looked it. "Weren't the relics over there somewhere?"

One of the older dignitaries stepped over and put his arm on my shoulder and said, "Yes, they were over there, and I've always loved the smell of incense. You did a fine job, son."

The dignitary made me feel a little better but all I could think about was just getting the Hell out of there. I ripped off my altar boy cassock and threw it in the closet without hanging it up, grabbed my coat and burst through the door and raced down the stairs from the sacristy, again taking the last three with a leap looking for some kind of comfort somewhere. The frigid air on my face made me feel alive again like a wild wind, free from the fetters of prescribed duty. I breathed a deep breath, turned and found Bridie and Daddy. Bridie threw her arms around me and said, "If there was ever an angel on Earth, I'm holding him, how about some bacon and eggs?"

"It's all I want for Christmas!"

The three of us walked home in silence, embracing each other in the frigid night. At home, the party started round the kitchen table, where every party started at Cloonmore. The whole clan was there by now laughing and chiding my latest mishap. Bridie broke out the cast iron skillet and facetiously threatened each of the chiders with it. But before long, the kitchen was filled with laughter, the smell of frying bacon, basting eggs and steeping tea. Bridie made the eggs the Irish way – sunny side up, basting them by softly spooning the bacon grease over the yolk.

"You know, Sean, I was wondering how the dignitaries felt about getting doused with incense?" It was Daddy, spearing my yolk.

And as Bridie spooned a perfectly basted egg on my plate, "Sure, don't the old boys have one foot in the grave and the other on a banana peel...It's never a bad idea to get a head start."

I turned and looked out the window.

"It's snowing!"

It was all perfect then...My maiden Midnight Mass, crisp bacon, golden eggs, warm, buttered Irish soda bread, a spot of tea...and now the white blanketed night.

Merry Christmas.

The Other Boy

It had only been a matter of time before I would give in to temptation and find my way into the old mansion down the street from Cloonmore. I had spotted it on the day we moved into Oak Park and since then the mansion, which was cloaked in mystery, had consumed us. No one ever saw anyone go in or out of it. Speculation ran rampant as to what went on inside but nobody knew. That is, until one morning I saw the "HOUSE SALE" poster on the front lawn. After finishing my morning route, I decided that some detective work was in order and I biked over to the mansion. It was in its usual state: large, gray, lifeless, foreboding and completely quiet. I stashed my bike behind a shrub in the back yard and climbed the backstairs, bold but cautious. I had a story ready in case anyone asked, "I'm selling subscriptions to The New World." It was the weekly rag that the Archdiocese put out. I knocked lightly on the back door, not really wanting anyone to answer, and when I got my wish I slowly turned the handle, pushed the door open and set foot inside my next adventure. And what an adventure it would prove to be. I waited for a moment making sure the house was empty, all the while circling the room with my gaze and wondering just what went on in this mystery house.

"Hello, Hello, anyone home?"

There was no one around and not a sound. Discretion would not be the better part of valor today and I continued my snoop. I snuck from room to room and floor to floor without encountering anything out of the ordinary. Each piece of furniture had a price tag on it and I quickly determined that most of it was out of my league. The stuff wouldn't have matched anything at

Cloonmore anyway. Everything seemed normal until I approached the attic door and a sign that said, "No admittance."

Well, the quickest way to get me to go somewhere or to do something was always to forbid it.

'Welcome', is what I read.

"Oh, thank you! Nice of you to invite me in," and through the door and up the stairs I went.

The motif was plush and red. Shag carpeting, red hued lighting and a massive bed in the middle of the room. I wondered if they were selling the big mirror over the bed or the rack in the corner. Did they hang their wet clothes on that thing? 'This was no ordinary bedroom,' I thought and took a running leap onto the bed, jumped up and down a few times and landed on my back looking straight into the mirror – a time for self-reflection. I had never felt such a twinge of excitement; safe, alone, protected…in my own castle.

I jumped off the bed and did a couple of flips and landed on my arse, right in front of a dresser.

'What's in the drawers?' I thought.

Inside were some old shoe boxes, 'Funny place to keep their slippers…' I popped the top off one. It was full of photos.

'Let's meet the family,' I thought. 'That's odd - the Dad doesn't have any clothes on…and neither does Mom… and what are the neighbor women doing? Oh my God, what the Hell is this!?'

I couldn't believe what was before my virgin, altar boy, Catholic, prepubescent eyes. The boxes were full of pictures of naked men and women doing complicated things to each other that had never entered my mind and I'm sure not even Murphy's. Every sexual act and position known to man appeared, and all to my astonishment. I was stunned, not only because I had never seen anything like them, but because now that I had looked, I knew that a mortal sin had been committed or maybe a thousand of them because there was no going back or known forgiveness for something this disgusting and rank. This was way more serious than spying on Pinkie in her brassiere.

My soul immediately blackened. I could feel the tar seep down and drape my conscience. Not even lye could help now. There was no amount of "Hail Mary's" or "Our Fathers" or Rosaries or any other penance that could extricate me from the depths of the chasm that I had just fallen into. My precipitous descent meant complete damnation. I could see Hell and its flaming fires. There was no putting the paste back in the tube.

I dropped the photos and took a deep breath and thought, if I just met eternal damnation, I might as well get something out of it here on earth. I know with the way everyone gawks at the dirty magazines in the alley, my popularity will soar with this kind of booty and if I get them to look, I'll have company in Hell. And maybe…just maybe, they'll get me in with the big boys at the park. It could be a lay-up as bawdy as those guys were. My damnation suddenly provided my big chance and I was ready to jump on it. I had always wondered what it would be like to be part of the cool guys at the park, where the grass *seemed* always greener.

I slipped a few of the pictures into my pocket, just a few so they wouldn't miss any, straightened the covers on the bed and tiptoed my way back down the attic stairs, softly opened the door to find a still empty house and slid out the back door. Once outside, I knew that no one could catch me and I raced to my bike and took off. The alley was empty, so off I rode to the park where being a cool guy was just a few pedals away, hoping the whole way that I wouldn't get hit by a car, die and have my filth laden pockets emptied in the emergency room. My legacy would be one of mortification and disownment.

"I had only five sons," Bridie would say.

I dodged the traffic and made it to the park. There were only two of the cool guys there, Langdon and Murphy. It would be easier to win two of them over rather than the whole crew. Besides, Murphy was the ring leader and one of the few who might know about the stuff in the photos and could appreciate the debauchery.

"Hey boys, what's happening?" I called. No response, still on the outside. "Just thought you might be interested in these pictures I found," I said, knowing that Murphy wouldn't turn down a chance to exhibit his profane reaches.

Murphy, the pup, answered first. "Pup" was Bridie's term for sinners who did sexy stuff in public.

"Oh yea, whatta ya got?" he perked up.

"Take a look at these," and I handed the pictures over. Langdon choked and Murphy gasped. He tried to fake that the photos were ordinary but they were too much for even him.

"Holy sh...t," Murphy said, his breath leaving him like a billows in search of a hot ash. He went through the images one by one and then a second time and a third, at first appearing astonished but then catching himself and acting like he had seen stuff like this before and had probably tried some of it. "Wow, look at the size of that one... Wow she's got big...This guy's doing it wrong...I've seen better one's than that."

"Sure Jim."

"They're yours," I said and I couldn't have felt better about being rid of them and putting them in their proper place... with Murphy, Langdon and their soul mate, the devil.

"You guys hanging, tomorrow?" I asked. They both shrugged. Why was I chasing these dopes? And suddenly their allure died. A light went on inside of me making it clear that I was better off being on the outside. Kissing up to these bust-outs was dumber than carrying the pictures across Washington Boulevard and risking death and Bridie's damnation for looking at "durty" pictures. That would be worse than eternity in Hell with the devil.

I got back on my bike and sped home trying to figure out how to cleanse my soul and very happy to be rid of the durty pictures. I pedaled hard and harder until my lungs were burning, using my effort as an act of self-immolation. The breeze flowed through my hair and I was hoping through my soul. I was in deep rhythm, the clang of my broken bike spoke chiming with the beat of my pounding heart.

I started to feel free again and hopeful that I could somehow whiten my blackened soul. I pedaled harder and harder. It was working. My dread lightened, my soul became ashen and then the front tire popped, the bike slowed and my catharsis paused. I had found a way to partially extricate myself from this abyss of muck. It had to be personal and isolated. The subject matter was way too egregious to bring up in the confessional and I wasn't going to share it with anyone else. This expurgation would have to be between me and God. Cleansing my soul, if possible at all, would take a while, I was sure. I stopped and turned my pants pockets inside out, recognizing that anything that the photos had touched needed purging and started to walk with my impaired bike. In moments I was back at Cloonmore and safe in its sanctity and refuge, or so I thought.

I pushed the bike into the bridal veils that protected the front of Cloonmore, ran up the steps and plunked myself on the porch swing. With each gentle pass of the swing, I could feel my pernicious burden lighten. It put me in a pleasant state. All was starting to get better as I closed my eyes and rocked, promising myself to tame my future adventures, forget what I had seen in the pictures and leave Murphy and the boys with the photos, the filth and anything else that came with it.

As I was saying my first "Hail Mary'" as part of my one-on-one with God, a navy blue police car pulled up in front of the house. "Must have the wrong address," I thought, "Murphy lives a couple of blocks over." An imposing figure dressed in dark blue to match the squad car emerged from the front door and headed up the walk. Her steps were long and determined and each one clicked as her heels met the pavement. The click grew louder with each step and suddenly I realized it was Mrs. Miller, the truant officer. I had never seen her before but knew her pedigree from Murphy's accounts of his past slants with the old battle-axe.

"Jesus!"

My pleasant state now turned to dread. Here I was cleansing my soul of my own volition, turning over a new leaf, and now none of that mattered as Miller's next step landed on our stairway with a thud. The wood groaned from the pressure above. There were no more clicks, only the next step and the next groan and so on and so on until she was on the porch perched atop Pop's golden shamrock that he had painted as a welcome mat. Above her was the Cloonmore shingle swinging back and forth, and with each swing a slight squeak, the music of friction.

"Needs a little oil," she said to no one in particular. There she stood, an emissary of execution, big, bold and looking for prey.

I stopped swinging and could only hope that Bridie had left for some far off land and wouldn't answer the door. Is this how judgment day would feel? God can't look like that. I raised my right hand slightly and wiggled my fingers in a salutation of welcome and stopped in mid-gesture, knowing that soft soap was useless against this hardened inquisitor. My mouth went dry, my breath short, my heart racing.

"Your mother home?" she demanded.

"Not sure," I was able to croak.

Ignoring my answer and in a froth for justice, she pushed the doorbell button that had never worked and got no response. The only "ding dong" was in my heart. Mrs. Miller tried the bell again and then with all the patience of a dog in heat, attacked the door with three demanding raps. Bridie came running in response to the clamor, drying her hands in a dishtowel and opened the door.

"Yes," Bridie said. "Is someone hurt?"

"Mrs. Brennan?"

"Yes."

"I'm Mrs. Miller, the truant officer, and I'd like to talk with you," ignoring Bridie's query.

Bridie came out onto the porch, saw me on the porch swing and told me to leave.

"No, no, he stays." Miller ordered.

I can't describe the dread I felt. 'What's she doing here? I haven't ditched school.'

And then…I thought, '*The durty pictures!*' If there had been a cliff nearby, I would have leaped…a train, I would have jumped in front of… a standing saber I would have fallen upon the blade.

I cowered.

"Mrs. Brennan," she started, "We have two young lads in the station who claim your son is 'the other boy.'" That rat Langdon, that rat Murphy!

"The other boy for what?" Bridie asked.

"These pictures were circulating at the pool and we traced them back to your son's friends." Not my friends any more, those traitors.

Miller handed Bridie the photos and waited for her response. As Bridie thumbed through them you could see her heart shatter into smaller pieces with each photo. She went pale and silent. "Why I never…" was all she could muster. And she had never.

I was devastated, not for the avalanche that was soon to bury me, but for the humiliation I had just brought to Bridie. A tear ran down her cheek. After a deep breath and a moment of thought, Bridie spoke, "May I handle this internally and spare the jail cell the disgust of housing my son?"

"We wish you would," Miller said. "You seem capable of handling the situation."

"Don't you worry," Bridie declared.

Miller wished Bridie good day and took one more contemptuous look at me, before starting for the stairs to leave. I said nothing as I stared down at the floor and in a fit of irony, hoped that Miller wouldn't go, because I knew what was coming and soon.

'Have you had lunch, Mrs. Miller?' I silently asked.

But she did leave, stomping down the creaking steps of Cloonmore and getting back in her car. Miller's car squealed as it sped away, leaving me with the silence, dread, and the only inquisitor who had more bite and sting than any of the others.

Without a word, Bridie walked over to me, swatted me with the towel like I was a pesky fly, grabbed me by the ear, lifted me from the swing and marched me down the stairs and up the street toward St. Edmund and the Monsignor. No ordinary priest would suffice for this cleansing, it had to be the Monsignor. She gave me two more good swats with the towel and ignored it as the towel went flying with the second lashing. It caught a breeze and fluttered onto the neighbor's lawn like a pall being draped over a coffin. I could feel her rage with each footstep and each tug on my ear. I had to do something to ease her fury…to soften, if only a bit, what I was in for.

"I only looked once, Ma," I begged as we waited for the light, taking a stab at mitigation.

"Once! Once! Once!" she said as she twisted my ear another half turn. "I should gouge out your eyes and rinse your memory in lye," she said. "You'll never be the same!"

"No more, please," I thought, wincing from the might of her two fingers.

Still gripping my ear, Bridie and I, in my stooped state, climbed the stairs of the rectory and she gave the massive oak door three hurried raps. The raps rang of catastrophe because the priest's secretary answered the door as the last rap echoed into the afternoon.

"Could you get the Monsignor? We have an emergency," Bridie said to the lady.

I looked up, and the secretary looked down at me realizing the severity of the moment, and left us at the door in wait.

"Monsignor, Monsignor!" she wailed.

When Monsignor Carroll emerged, Bridie, still with a piece of my ear in her grip, didn't even take time to say Hello.

"Monsignor Carroll, I don't know what you have for blackened souls, but whatever it is, I'd like you to double the potion, double the servings, dunk every body part and rinse every vein. You don't need any more explanation than it was a sin of filth, and I don't know if I'll ever let him back in the house."

"Could you leave him with me for a bit, Bridie?" the Monsignor asked, recognizing the need for intervention.

"Keep the bugger as long as you'd like," she shot back. Bridie finally let go of my ear and planted the side of her foot in my arse. I lurched forward in response, rubbing my ear and then my arse, never feeling happier to be free from Bridie's clutch. She turned and descended the stairs never looking back, threw her arms into the air and called upward to the highest power, "Good luck, Monsignor, and God himself... you've got a job ahead of you... he's all yours!"

There was a moment of silence and I couldn't have been happier that she'd gone.

Eternal damnation with the devil was looking better than life with Bridie. I never thought that I would ever yearn for an afternoon with a priest. The Monsignor led me into the castle like rectory and plunked me into a chair that could have housed three of me. With my feet dangling above the floor, the Monsignor asked, "Can you tell me what happened, Sean?"

I told him the whole story about the abandoned house, wanting to be with the cool guys, finally emphasizing that I only looked once and didn't really know much about the content, only describing it as "durty" pictures. I didn't know what the Hell they called the stuff the people were doing in the pictures.

The Monsignor's face softened and a smile came across it and eased my heart rate and slowed my breath. For the moment, I was happy to be removed from all women and their grasp. He asked if I'd had any physical reaction to the pictures, like a surge or a rise or anything like that.

"Oh no, Father, I was too ashamed when I saw them." What the Hell was he talking about? Didn't he know that I was Irish and five years from puberty? He asked if I could forget what I had seen.

"What pictures?" I quipped.

He smiled.

"Well we can't let you off without some penance, lad," he said. "And I think your real penance is going to come when you get home. I want you to attend confession and Mass every morning for a week. I think that will cleanse your soul and get you back in the good graces."

"Who's?" "It's not Him I'm worried about."

But I gladly agreed knowing that *I* would have to come up with something to get Bridie's pardon. He rubbed me on the head and wished me good luck.

"Now go give me a few 'Our Fathers' in the church," he concluded.

"Thank you, Monsignor."

'Why weren't the nuns like this guy?' I thought. 'Is compassion masculine?'

After leaving the church and feeling a bit better from the penance, all I had to do now was deal with Bridie's wrath. *All I had to do?* I moseyed my way down the alley with my hands deep inside my pockets, taking my time and planning my approach when I would see Bridie. The Monsignor had made me feel better and had assuaged my guilt a little bit, but the real test was still in front of me: the moment when I had to look Bridie in the eye again.

I decided that total supplication was the only way to go. I knew where Bridie's soft spots were. I didn't need a saint for this one. I inched my way up the back stairs at Cloonmore, rhythmically stepping to the creaks that came from the dried-out wood, pushed open the patched screen door and let it slam behind me, announcing my arrival. I stopped and pondered my next move.

Bridie was at the stove boiling some stew, stirring as if she was in a therapeutic trance. The bang of the door had no effect. She didn't move or respond. She just kept stirring. I stepped across the threshold ready to confront the only person, out of all of them, that mattered to me and I began, "The Monsignor has worked out a penance plan for me and he thinks my soul will be white again in about a week. I promise I'll do double the 'Hail Mary's' and be cleansed a bit sooner. I'm very sorry, Ma, for what I've done and how I made you feel, and I'll never look at a durty picture again."

She said nothing and continued stirring.

"Would you please forgive me, Ma, because your forgiveness is more important than anyone else's, even God's!"

There was a crack in her countenance as the strain in her shoulders eased a bit. She took a deep breath and spooned some of the stew onto a plate, backed away from the stove, turned and came to me with the steam rising from the stew and embracing her face. She placed it on the table and looked straight into my eyes. Her own eyes were a bit red from the tears.

"Sit down there, Sean, and don't let your dinner get cold."

My left ear ached for several days after being the object of Bridie's wrath. No greater sin could have been committed by her *by,* other than thinking durty notions. And anything sexy was durty. Although Bridie's standards were generally higher than the Church's, and she lived up to them far more often than did the Church, they both looked on durty thoughts as a very serious violation. Lying, stealing, and cheating were sins that paled in comparison. Durty notions and sexy endeavors were for sure the work of the devil, and in order to remove the soot from your soul, needed to be treated in a direct, firm fashion. If you died with those ebony stains, usually in the form of a big black mortal sin, you were for sure spending eternity and a few lifetimes with the devil... in Hell.

"Mortals" were the worst kind of sin and required immediate and intense treatment. That's why after looking at the filthy pictures, it was so important to get to the Monsignor as fast as possible and get my soul cleansed. If you died with a "mortal" on your rap sheet, it was all over; there was no extrication from the underworld.

"A good scrubbin'," is what Bridie said I needed.

By order of the Monsignor, I was to go to Confession every day for a week. One session would never suffice because of the disgusting nature of the pictures and the added onus of carrying them around in my pocket and letting the filth seep through my clothes and into my soul. Each Confession would cleanse my soul a little bit more and each day would get me closer to God's good graces.

The confessional was the place where a good Catholic went every Friday to get his soul washed so he could welcome Jesus, in the form of communion, on Sunday. Confession was the Catholic rite that started in second grade and sent seven-year-olds into a dark chamber to confess sins they didn't even know they had committed. The process filled the children with fear, guilt and confusion. It was another of the Church's tools for mind control and allegiance, all under the guise of contrition. It made you fret about everything that you did, if it was good or bad and how good and how bad. You started to look over your shoulder all the time to see if Jesus or one of his commandos in the form of angels was looking. And then when you did do something wrong, you had to walk around suffering deep guilt and fear that your soul was stained. You had to hope that you wouldn't get hit by a bus before the next Friday and go straight to Hell, because that's what would happen if you didn't get to Confession and get a soul scrubbin'. It was a lot for a seven-year-old to carry around and really ended your early years of free thinking and innocence. The Church and the confessional were the only place that you could get the scrubbin', so membership stayed strong.

The confessional booth was a built-in oak kiosk just west and east of the nave on each side of the church. There were three compartments, the middle one for the priest, who would do the scrubbin' and the two side compartments for the sinners. Above each door was a little bulb that was green when the compartment was empty and red when somebody was in there getting cleansed.

And on the outside a long line of contrite sinners waiting for their turn to enter and go through the process of washing the soul.

When it was finally your turn and you opened the heavy oaken doors, there was always a long and loud creak that heightened your state of dread. Alfred could have easily oiled the hinges, but I think the squeak was left to heighten your fear. Once inside, the door would slam from the tension of both the spring and the moment, shutting you out from the whole world. A heavy silence and musty scent of the leather walls, body odors from the nervous perspiration of previous supplicants, and an occasional puddle from a really nervous kid and then one last squeak from the kneeler as you descended. All of it engulfing you. The door shut and slowly you sank into a dark and quiet tomb of dread. You were locked in. It was just you and the priest for the next few minutes. After kneeling you'd place your face in front of a small panel that remained shut as the priest cured the sinner in the other compartment. It was a way of automating the process and absolving mass numbers for the following Sunday, one sinner on one side getting cleansed and another on the other, awaiting his absolution. You knelt motionless, head bowed, hands clasped together in a perfect steeple, anticipating how severely you would be treated and apprehensive about which priest was on the other side of the screen. There were nice priests and mean ones with bad breath. When it was your turn, the priest would slide back the panel leaving only a small lattice grill between you and him. The open window allowed just a bit of light into your chamber, casting some shadows and making you feel like Amantillado had felt just before the last brick was laid, sealing his fate.

The priest sat sideways facing the front door in his compartment, with either his hands folded in his lap or his arm resting on the sill in front of you. He was garbed in a long black cassock with a sash that he had kissed and which gave him the power of absolution. That's what they called the scrubbin': "absolution." Bridie liked scrubbin' better cause you knew what was going to happen to you; as far as I knew, "absolution" was something you got at the end of a math problem.

As soon as the priest slid open the window and exposed his large shadowy figure, the penitent opened with, "Bless me, Father, for I have sinned, it's been (one week) since my last confession." And then I'd begin to lie about how many times I swore or talked back to my parents or how many candy bars I had stolen. I made it all up, every word. And I'd put some big numbers with each category. Oh, I did that twenty times and this thirty times and on and on and on. And then the big bomb after I had looked at the durty pictures, "Father, I looked at some durty pictures."

I heard a big gasp from the other side and saw him twitch in his chair.

"What kind of durty pictures?"

The details were important in order to place the sin in the right category of severity and give him something to bring back to the rectory for dinner conversation.

"Uhhh, Father," I stumbled and fell silent.

"What kind of durty pictures!" he demanded.

I came clean. "We found durty pictures in an old shoe box in the alley and looked at a picture of a girl without clothes on…and a man with a…" No need to go into the details of the breaking and entering here, I'd seen enough of Mrs. Miller. And besides, my ear still had a mark from Bridie.

"Where'd you find 'em? Do you remember the house?"

Another gasp.

I don't remember Father, it was a dark morning…and…"

It didn't matter what house because it had to be a Prod's. They were the only ones with durty stuff. No self-righteous Catholic would house pictures like I found. The Church hadn't figured out yet that the fastest way to get someone to do something was to forbid it. And so we paperboys would trek the alleys and search discarded piles of literature looking for a durty picture or two… mostly we'd fail, disturbing the centipedes and slugs who had found a home in the bundled, damp, newspapers and magazines.

The Father eased his inquiry.

"All right forget the house. How long did you look at them?"

"It was only a side glance that I took, Father, and I immediately turned away," I confessed, trying to mitigate my sin.

The priest admonished, "Well, a little look is just as bad as a long one." There was no scale of severity with this priest, either you did it or you didn't. "Did you have a physical reaction when you saw the picture?"

"I did get a rise out of it, Father, but it was mostly my shoulders lifting as I took a deep breath, cause I never have seen one of those before."

"What did you see?"

"It was the, the, the….you know the… the," until he couldn't take it anymore.

"All right!…do women have them?"

"Well, I'm not sure but the one in the picture did." No way was I going to say what I saw. He gave up.

"Don't be doing this stuff anymore!" he commanded.

"Oh, no Father it was an isolated incident, it won't happen again." More lies.

"Did you get rid of the pictures?"

"Oh, yes, Father." I didn't rat out the guys who turned me over to Mrs. Miller.

"Give me twenty 'Our Fathers' and twenty 'Hail Mary's and leave the durty pictures where they belong…in the garbage."

Twenty was a lot but it seemed the punishment fit the crime. I wasn't going to complain. "Thank you, Father." I pushed up and away from the kneeler, stood and left the confessional, wondering if he'd recognized my voice and knew who I was. The door slammed behind me and I looked right into the eyes of the next supplicant walking in for his few minutes of cleansing and feeling a bit of empathy for the poor bastard. The hard part was over for me but just beginning for the next guy in line. Next was finding an open pew, because some of the earlier atoners were still serving their penance. Sometimes that was how we'd know someone did something real bad, because their penance took a long time. It was one of the ways we gave some of our critics something to think about.

'How could he be that bad if his penances are so short?'

Next, I had to kneel down again, bow my head and bless myself, and slowly lift my eyes to find the sentinel statues tucked into the alcoves. Left to right I'd turn until I found my favorite saint and start to get sad. You had to get sad before you did your penance because supplication was mandatory. The statues helped you get there because they all looked so sad. Mary, Joseph, Peter, it didn't matter what statue you looked at because somber was always the mood. Even the paintings were sad. Some were of angels all naked lying on clouds and playing the harp. Others were of condemned souls burning in Hell and hoping for a glass of water. Still others were of more condemned souls with snakes wrapped around their necks...and you knew they weren't getting away. Once I got the sad and penitent look on my face, I'd rip through penance often losing count and short-changing Jesus. "Done. Get me the Hell outta here, there's a game in the alley!" Most of the time I did feel better after the cleansing and penance, and with my newly whitened soul I tore down the stone steps taking the last three in a leap, proud that I was good to go for at least a week. Ahhh, the feeling of guiltless freedom…it never lasted very long.

Every day after the durty picture incident, I would drop into the church after my paper route, enter the confessional and kneel on the kneeler. After the priest slid open the window I'd begin with, "Bless me, Father, for I have sinned, it's been one day since my last confession; I looked at some durty pictures."

By the fourth day, the Father said, "All right that's enough, you're wearing out the scrubber, you're good to go, your soul is back in order; I don't want to see you tomorrow." Scrubbin' the durty pictures away had taken only four days.

The Church Confession was the easy part because it became so rote. The wrath of Bridie was harder because I had to live with her and feel how terrible she felt at knowing that one of her *bys* had seen such durty stuff. I still couldn't look Bridie in the eye. Each time I crossed her path, I looked as humiliated as I possibly could. And I was good at it; curling my shoulders downward, slumping my head and not looking up and generally speaking in muffled undertones. Each morning I'd fold my hands in prayer at the kitchen table just before one of Bridie's bowls of oatmeal and finish the prayer with a deliberate sign of the cross as I stared up to the sky.

To Bridie having a clean soul was as important as having clean underwear when you went to the emergency room. If you left this earth with either your soul or your underwear soiled you were doomed…and so was the family name. You could have an accident but not if Bridie could help it.

After the fourth day of my catharsis, Bridie turned from the bubbling pot of oatmeal and said, "All right, that's enough, you're foolin' no one. I want the old Sean back…without the durt."

"But Ma, it's been helping me clean my soul and forget the bad photos."

"Well, sometimes the cure is worse than the crime and I don't think I can take much more of the sainthood stuff. I'll take you with the stains and all."

The durty picture scandal was finally over. Bridie had decided that enough was enough. She had run me through the Monsignor, the confessional, penance and her own brand of reclamation. There was no sense kicking a dead horse.

The Alley Boy

The alley was where everything happened, football, baseball and basketball. It didn't matter what season only if you had the right ball. And when the games were over the mischief and tomfoolery would start. The summer was especially active as the afternoon waned and the evening arrived. That's when we let the girls play, only because you might get a smooch. Out in the open there was 'kick the can' and 'dodgeball' and 'hopscotch'; and in the recesses of a darkened garage or shady hedgerow, hide and go seek. "Wanna hide with me?"

During the day, the girls didn't matter, it was game time. In the summer it was mostly softball with a sixteen inch orb. Our field looked like a squeezed diamond because the alley was so narrow. Third base was only steps away from first base. You had to hit it up the middle. Home plate was always an old newspaper, first base the pole that protected the neighbor's garage, second base another newspaper and third the corner of old man Shoppe's garage. To the left of second we had a home run porch between the corner of Mr. Dean's garage and a telephone pole. The ball had to fit perfectly inside the opening or we considered it foul. There would be no cheapies in this league.

Deano was a tight ass and took pride in his perfectly organized life and impeccably manicured estate. He and his estate had been a long time target. Only an opportunity was needed, and it came one day when Deano, ensconced in some kind of stupor, left his garage open. Deano was one of those guys that owned every toy. His garage was a showcase, perfectly arranged and abundantly stocked. He never did anything wrong or different...until today.

As Deano drove away with the garage door agape like a yawning window of opportunity we knew our big chance wouldn't last long.

His arrivals and departures always put a hold on our games and we were never too happy about that either, especially because of the time he would take to precisely back his car into the garage. If he didn't get it right the first time he did it again and again, impervious to our mission, always holding up the next pitch.

We ran to the garage and looked in, our mouths agape like a kid in a candy store with no shop-keeper: This guy had everything and it was easy to find, neatly organized on steel racks right there in front of us.

"Can't pass this one up," I said. We had waited for years to put a dent in Deano's armor. We tiptoed in and surveyed the pickings; paint, fertilizer, tools, you name it.

"Paint for the bases?" somebody belted out.

"No, how about the fertilizer for Bridie's garden?"

"She's good enough without that stuff."

Everyone stopped, looked and in unison screamed, "Paint for the bases!"

We had committed a fair amount of larceny before and had the heist procedures down.

"Lookouts," I yelled.

"Jimmy you're on the roof; Barney down at the corner and whistle if he's coming."

Next: someone to slip into the garage and abscond with the paint and finally an artist to finish the job.

"Your turn," someone yelled and all eyes were on me. I hesitated knowing that I would be the culprit if anything went wrong and decided to go for it. I tiptoed into the garage, hamming it up a bit to entertain the boys, and looked left onto a shelving unit and saw the neatly stacked cans of paint like soldiers in a line.

Each was considerately marked...blue, black, white ...yes green? I picked the green for emphasis and started to tiptoe back out when someone yelled, "You need a brush!"

We were wasting precious seconds and I turned and saw a paint brush hanging on a hook on the wall. We had the tools and within minutes, with Varilla our artist at the easel, had home plate and second base glistening in the afternoon sun.

We were all euphoric: it wasn't just the new bases. It was catching Deano with his pants down, seizing the chance, weighing the options, planning the caper and pulling it off and then waiting to see if we'd get caught... We didn't use much of his paint and put the can back after carefully wiping clean the rim and resealing the top. We used McAffery's t-shirt for that.

Done, nice job... except...suddenly... not a second too soon – we heard Barney cat call from down the block:

"He's coming!"

"Shit!" simultaneous expletives from six guys at once. The scramble started, bumping, squirming and spinning. Deano's car eased down the alley.

"The brush!" The wet brush was still in Varilla's hand. I grabbed the brush from Varilla, ran into the garage and stuck it behind the paint cans. We got back to the game pretending to be deeply involved. Deano paused when he saw the unexpected open garage door and started to scratch his head and then shrugged an 'Oh well,' with his shoulders. Deano took his usual time backing into the garage narrowly missing the drying second base.

"What's the count?" when Deano finally had the station wagon with the St. Olaf sticker in the garage. The door closed behind him and we started to breathe easy and then it slowly started to open again. "Damn!" maybe he hit the auto button by mistake.

Auto button! That was Deano; he had everything, had shared nothing until today and easily became a target for our Robin Hood instincts.

As the door raised so did our angst…with each inch. The game was on hold. We were all frozen still anticipating Deano's next move. And finally as the door and our angst reached its pinnacle…

"Goddamnit!" Deano roared from the recesses of his garage. The door clunked as it came to a stop. And there was Deano, standing like a damning inquisitor, as he held the paint brush with his thumb and index finger like you'd hold a dead mouse by his tail. And pointed to the dripping paint brush with his other hand like a detective who had found the murder weapon. A solitary drop of paint descended and landed on his shoe top. He didn't notice.

Getting a "Goddamnit!" out of ole Deano was quite an accomplishment and very serious, especially coming from the church going, straitlaced Christian, who had a St. Olaf sticker on his car window. We hadn't figured out who St. Olaf was, but assumed that he was another prod Saint, who really shouldn't have been one because he never performed a miracle, the way the Catholic saints did. Later, Maloney took the time to research St Olaf and discovered that he really had been a Catholic and was known as Fat Olaf who walked around with an axe in his hand. The image fit the steaming Deano only instead of an axe he held the wet paint brush high above his head. St. Olaf didn't matter because we had never heard of him which made him no better than a prod saint in our minds.

"You little bastards," Dean forgot his faith again. Out of the garage he stomped, red in the face, wide in the eyes and then changed his grip and held the brush up for all to see. He had the look and strut of the Olympic torch bearer.

"Goddamnit!" He swore again, inching closer toward his God's bad graces, whoever he was. We didn't say a word, waiting for the accusation that was coming. Our minds started to spin, thinking of a creative comeback, always when an indictment was about to be levied.

Sometimes fear would make you spill your guts before the accusation was offered, but that was the old days and we were way too seasoned to make that mistake. It was always a good negotiating policy to get the accusation first, so you didn't confess to another crime that you had gotten away with.

"Which one of you son-of-a-bitches did this?"

The third curse put Dean's place in heaven in jeopardy as he held the brush higher and shook it a couple of times. Three more drops descended but missed Dean and landed right where the shortstop played.

We all followed the wayward drops to the ground and bounced our attention back to Deano as they landed. Shrugging our shoulders in unison, we winced our faces into an "I don't know" look, and joined together in a chorus of denials.

"Not me."

"I didn't do it."

"Couldn't have been us."

Dean had some detective work to do. He paused and looked around, gathering his thoughts but keeping his snarl. He scanned the crowd to see if he could pick out one of the guys who wasn't a good liar. Christians were good at that... finding the squealers. The inquisition comes to mind.

Dean was cooked. We had way too much experience and moxie, to puke that fast. He paused for a moment in contemplation, scanning the cement field and not finding a single rat and finally gave up, exhaling. He lowered the brush and put his fist on his waist and began to turn away…and suddenly saw second base. I tried to posture my feet to hide the green box, but size 5 in a kids' wasn't doing it. Dean had been near defeat and was suddenly thrown a trump card, a life vest. He was alive again and his posture proclaimed it. He puffed out his chest and began to rock back and forth like a math teacher with a solution.

"I never saw that base before," he confidently asserted trying to back us into a corner. He started to look cocky knowing that he had us.

We all looked at each other to see who would be the spokesperson. It was always good to have just one and keep the story consistent. I was on second, in the middle of it all. More eyes were on me than anybody else. Perched atop the forensic evidence, it was my case. 'Confess or lie?' I thought.

He knew we were the culprits, so confessing was useless, and I wasn't going to make it easy for him.

"We had some left over paint from painting the house," I offered. Pops and the brown baggers had just put a fresh coat of Kelly green paint on Cloonmore and trimmed it out with golden yellow. It was the talk of the town…the mustard and relish house. Our story made sense and he extended an air of superiority when he harrumphed while uttering, "Yellow and green?" "While I never." And he hadn't ever…stepped out that is. And never would. He would never feel like we did… taking a chance, letting it fly, jumping in, walking on the edge, running to anywhere. And we did it every day…all day.

"And the brush?" he said.

"Mr. Dean," I said, offering up a bit of respect by using his title, "We had a left over brush that the painters gave us and besides you always keep your garage locked."

His confident snarl eased and turned to one of confusion as he scratched his head with the hand holding the brush. A couple of drops landed in his hair. He was obviously torn between the crime at hand and knowing that his life always followed some kind of order. 'Leave the garage door open' NAH. At first, his pride in his idyllic, undented world won out and he turned and started to walk back into the garage knowing that he never left the garage open and then he looked questioningly at the wet paint brush and stopped... and began to turn to start the investigation over again and stopped again. Deano was gassed and confused. He continued into the garage tossing the ruined brush in his trash can. Deano was torn. Had he left the door open? He mumbled, "I couldn't have left..." as the garage door came down behind him, creaking as it lowered. He slowly faded into the dark garage, disappearing until the last thing we could see were his paint spattered shoes. Deano was ruined ! He'd never be the same. 'I couldn't have forgotten...I always'...

On the concrete playing field, there was a moment of still and silence... always a pause when you were on the chopping block, after you dodged one... but only for a moment.

"What's the count?" someone barked, breaking the silence and jumpstarting the mood.

"Three and one," I answered, trying to get an advantage and hoping everyone else forgot. They had forgotten, but they knew it was me trying to get another edge.

"Oh no, it was two and two," someone from the other side yelled, knowing that it wasn't three and one if I said it. And the next argument started. "Three and one."

"No, two and two."

"New count" I yelled, finding a middle ground. Playing was far more important than bickering. The argument was over and the game back on as the next pitch floated up to the plate.

I forget who won the game because camaraderie was far more important than any victories. If you lost you'd mope for just a bit…but just a bit because the next game was right around the corner and the rest of the boys wouldn't let you be a sore loser. "Get over it." "The sun will rise tomorrow." "It's over, move on." Life in the alley taught us much. Things I hold dear today. Mostly that your interests were no bigger than the rest of the crew and that the esprit de corp was paramount.

Beating Deano did matter, though. Matching our wits with a tight ass prod whose perfect world was so far from ours… and now had one solid dent in it, was big. We had to win that one.

After the game, I retrieved the symbolic brush from Dean's garbage and tossed it onto the garage roof that housed all of our other trophies… crushed beer cans, old baseball covers, a couple of water logged baseball gloves, a ripped b-ball net, and an old bra. It found a preferred spot among the revered debris and there it would sit and remind us daily that ole Deano had been broken.

"Where's O'Brian been," someone asked of a missing teammate.

"I think he's on vacation," came from another corner.

I started thinking… 'O'Brian', that meant potato chips. It was another of those things that we never had and everybody else did.

Cookies, pop, potato chips, peanut butter; they were all dreams and fantasies. Only this day, my fantasies would be fulfilled. Every time we went into a neighbor's home we were reminded of all the stuff that they had that we didn't. It wasn't always only the food. It was furniture that matched and table cloths and silverware and glasses without Smucker's written on the side and working toasters. But when I mentioned "O'Brian," I thought devilishly, "Bet they left all their great junk food out for us; I pictured a big tin of Jay's salted chips, jars of creamy peanut butter, and erect, statuesque bottles of Coca-Cola.

After the game broke up and the alley emptied, it was lunch time. I approached my brother Phelim and asked him if he could go for some potato chips? We hadn't eaten yet so I had him at my mercy. I was already salivating.

"Sure," he said. He didn't know yet what I had in my mind.

"Follow me." I could almost taste the salt, feel the crunch.

The two of us moseyed down the alley and up the gangway next to O'Brian's two flat.

"What the Hell are you doing?" Phelim said when we stopped just below the side window.

"I think they keep this one window unlocked," I said, ignoring his question.

"You're nuts,' he said.

"It's a fresh tin," I said, conjuring the Jay's. I could swear I'd seen a supply last time I'd been legitimately in the O'Brian kitchen.

"Don't be chicken." I interlaced my fingers palms up and directed him to put his shoe in my makeshift hoist, then a hand on my shoulder and push up with his off foot and grab the window sill.

"On three," I commanded.

"One, two, three," and *oomph* and Phelim was hanging from the window sill with his feet kicking like a horse thief at the gallows.

I squatted down and got one of his feet on each shoulder and stood up, pushing him higher and right at the window sill.

"Push up on the window," I commanded and he did and it slid straight up. One last *oomph* from me and he was halfway through the open window with his feet kicking as he wriggled himself all the way in and fell on the bedroom floor.

"Come around and open the back door," I said.

I started to taste the chips.

A minute later, Phelim opened the back door and let me in and again stated what a bad idea this was.

"Too late to turn back now, let's enjoy the chips."

On the counter was a large round tin with JAY's written across the side, the Mcguffin, the crown jewel, the prize. No one was around except us and the chips and a silent empty apartment. We munched on the chips and decided that we needed something with which to wash them down and opened the fridge door with the working handle. Inside was a row of Coke bottles neatly ordered: the glistening green glass bottles with red script were something that we had only admired from afar and until now, had only been a dream.

The silence was only disturbed by our pounding hearts. We took a seat at the kitchen table and noshed on the chips and quaffed the Cokes, finally experiencing the crème de 1960's modern suburban dining. The empty Coke bottles went back in the empties case and the top went back on the potato chip tin, still half full. Can't be greedy.

We weren't so dumb as to finish the chips, even though we wanted to crunch to the last. We got to the back door after closing the bedroom window and looked back to make sure everything was in order. I took one more gander at the Jay's tin, got seduced again and decided one final handful would complete the afternoon. I felt like a bank robber at the getaway door looking back to make sure I hadn't left any clues and seeing one more bag of money. Well, maybe a little greed won't hurt, knowing full well from the westerns, that that's what got most culprits nabbed. I tiptoed over, opened the tin and grabbed another handful of chips. We eased out the back door and down the back stairs, through the yard and into the alley looking over our shoulders to make sure the coast was clear and then disaster: We bumped into Mr. Shoppe who was coming back from the drug store.

"I thought the O'Brian's were on vacation," he said, inquiring as to our presence. I slid the last handful of chips that I was chewing over to my cheek just so I could answer the old snoop. Phelim was frozen.

"We just found that out, Mr. Shoppe, no one was home," I said, trying to deflect his accusatory query. I swallowed the last of the chips. Shoppe wasn't buying it.

"Oh, really?" he said.

We slid down the alley without exchanging another word, trying to act as cool and carefree as ever but fearing that our afternoon of gluttony had been exposed. When we got back to Cloonmore and parked ourselves in the garage, Phelim looked over at me and said, "Hey Billy the Kid, you got some loose chips on your cheek."

I wiped my mouth and looked into my hand. The small potato crystals looked back at me as much to say, "You better start thinking of an out!"

Everything had gone great except for that old snoop, Shoppe. But maybe he was too old and senile to remember anything, but maybe not. The torment of not knowing what we left behind at O'Brian's set in.

"If we get caught, this one's on you, buddy," Phelim warned, asserting his defense for the inevitable confrontation with Bridie.

My mind started to freak. Always after a crime, you started to wonder what went wrong.

"Hey, did you put the top back on the chips?" I asked Phelim, setting it up so I had someone else to blame.

"Yeah, but Mr. Glutton Boy went back for more," he said, shattering my strategy.

I had gone back. But I put the top back on the chips, didn't I?

"And did you close the window?"

"And where did you put the empty Coke bottle?" Phelim pelted me with doubt.

The caper was unraveling as fast as my mind was spinning. Damn, it was too late to go back. We had to hope Mrs. O'Brian was forgetful and couldn't remember how she had left the place. Not.

It was a few days of total torment before the O'Brian's would return. Each day I spent wondering if we had left the place like we found it and if we'd get caught? It was a dumb notion because we never left anything like we found it. Our prints were on everything. And even if we had screwed up, how would Mrs. O' know that it was the Brennan boys that had broken in and feasted on her chips and pop... another dumb question. The block had fifty some kids on it so it would be hard to pin it on us. Hard...not hardly. Every interrogation started with the Brennan boys. It was easy...like a cop who responds to the bank alarm and comes upon a muck covered bandit sitting next to the askew sewer cover, counting crisp, bundled bills. "I wonder who..." And now it was a break in, and missing coke and chips. "Lets see..." It was only common sense to start with us, because they were usually right. We couldn't run from our legacy but we often tried. "It was just some pop and chips," I started to rationalize. And then the hammer came down.

Coming down the alley, pushing my paper cart the next morning, I caught sight of Mrs. O'Brian leaving the back door of Cloonmore with her chest pushed out and head held high. It was the pose of vindication. She peered over her shoulder at me and smirked. I parked the cart and stalled but knew that at some point, I would have to pay the piper. Slowly I walked into the house knowing that doom awaited. It felt like the trip down the alley after the visit to the Monsignor, the walk to the Principal's office after the choco and now more disgrace and embarrassment for Bridie.

When would I learn? Would I ever learn?

I sidled up the groaning paint chipped stairs, slid past the screen door, closing it softly. I needed no announcement that I was there. I parked myself at the table as far from Bridie as possible with my head hanging low and waited for my bowl of oatmeal. In a futile attempt at more deceit, I folded my hands and mumbled a prayer and finished with the sign of the cross as Bridie placed the steaming oatmeal in front of me. It was no use.

Bridie barked, "Do you know what I hate the most, *bys*?"

There was no response because we knew it wasn't good. And who could choose, amongst our misdeeds…what Bridie might hate the most?

"Do you?" she insisted.

"No Ma," we finally choked out a response.

"It's when that pesky neighbor woman O'Brian comes down to the back door and tells me how my *bys* broke into her house and ate her potato chips and drank her pop. And does it with her head held high and chest expanded, all the while rocking on her tippy toes. And I have to look her in the eye, knowing goddamn well that she's probably right and I don't have a leg to stand on -- *That's what I hate the most!.*"

"And do you know what I hate the second most?"

"No Ma."

"It's when I can't tell her to bugger off because my *bys* would never do a thing like that even though I know they would."

"You see, Mr. Shoppe warned me about what was coming. He saw you down the gangway climbing through the window on his way to the store – you forgot to post a lookout! And on the way back he ran into you exiting the crime scene with chips on your cheek." She took a great, heaving breath as if it might be her last.

And you forgot to put the top back on the tin and close the window.

"Not only are you a couple of crumbs but you're bad crooks to boot – you're either going to have to get honest or smarter and you know which one I'm in favor of."

I snickered after the crumb part, sensing the pun was unintended. Her fury peaked in response to my giggle and next felt her hand come down across the back of my head. I slid to the edge of the chair, anticipating another blow by covering my head with my hands.

"Now, I can't blame Phelim here because I know it couldn't have been his idea. But he ought to know by now that his older brother is a real dope and he can't see past his nose when he wants some of the finer things in life and can't pay for them." She turned her baleful stare upon me... me alone. "And now he's folding his hands and mumbling prayers, trying to buy his way past his just deserve. Someone is always watching. Remember that one lads."

"You see Sean, you think that it's worth it to sacrifice your integrity for a bag of chips or a choco or whatever else you've stolen?"

Phelim was off the hook...well mostly. Her fury peaked and she raised her powerful farm girl hand and brought it down on the back of my head again. I knew there'd be another one if I didn't change the momentum, so I fell to the floor and curled up, holding my head, wounded. "Jesus Ma, it was only some chips. How come we never have any?" I rebutted, taking the offensive.

Not smart. Her ire peaked again.

She raised her foot to land one in my arse, and thought better of it and stopped. Bridie, still full of rage, got a hold of herself, lowered her foot and started to weep...and then took a deep breath. There was stillness and only the soft whimper of her disappointment.

"All I wanted was some chips," I pleaded, as I got to my knees while guarding my head with my forearms, trying to deflect the next wallop.

"You think your integrity is worth some potato chips?" she asked.

"All right, I'll get you some chips," she relented. "Can you try a little honesty in return lad?" She looked straight down at me, still with blue venom in her eyes.

"It'll never happen again," I declared.

I lowered my arm and peeked out, wondering if there was another blow coming?

"Should I go to confession, Ma?"

"It worked after the durty pictures," I said, still peering over my forearm and taking a stab at her mercy.

"Not for very long. I'll absolve you right here. She made a sign of the cross over a glass of water and then dumped the entire glassful down on top of me and went back to the stove.

I felt cleansed, the way I did when I rushed down the Church stairs after confession. As the water ran down my face, one solitary drop paused at the tip of my nose and dangled.

"It's not the confession or the 'Hail Mary's' or the 'Our Fathers, it's what's in the heart," Bridie said, still facing the stove.

"I'm sorry Ma. I'll try to be better."

"Sorry!"…"Sorry!" "They're just words," she barked. "Show me lad."

She went back to stirring the oatmeal. I wiped the bead of water off of my nose and flicked it onto Phelim just to make sure that he was scrubbed too. The oatmeal was cold by now and so was my heart. I couldn't stand seeing Bridie like she was and I jumped to my feet and rushed out the screen door, letting it slam behind me like the confessional door in church. Bridie was rid of me…for the moment. My soul was clean though, because Bridie's scrubbins' were as good the priests and always meant more.

The red light turned green.

The Lover Boy

As eighth grade ticked by your biggest decision was what girl you were going to try and smooch. Thoughts of the girls were filling my head, but they were only thoughts. Actually qualifying to hold someone's hand or giving someone a smooch didn't seem very realistic. I still felt very much on the outside and not a part of the in-crowd. Maybe I could find someone in the same dilemma, but she'd have to be cute, no lame ducks for this lad.

Choosing what high school you would attend was no dilemma. It was easy because there was no choice. You would go to the local Catholic all boys' high school if you could get in. There wasn't any discussion about other options. Just around the corner from Cloonmore was a five star public high school that was free, and included girls, but no good Catholic would risk the communal disgrace of not going to a Catholic school. You'd be committing blasphemy and heresy and anything else that was taboo, just thinking about attending. Besides, the Publics were going there and they were inferior and you were not to socialize with them... to any degree.

There were enough Catholics to go around and fill your social circle; so numbers were no excuse. Even if you didn't make it into the local Catholic school there was another one a bus ride away that would take you in. That was usually the one in the bad neighborhood that had the thermometer test; 98.6 and a check got you in.

So that left just one decision: what girl would it be? Socializing with the girls was a major challenge for me in grade school. They didn't play sports, which is all I did, and there never was any occasion that could initiate some hetero socialization, serve to break the ice, and end all of the segregation. You couldn't talk in class and by the time I finished my route after school, everyone was gone. Writing notes was just for the girls and no one had my address.

It seemed that the hierarchy coyly kept the sexes separated. Being shy and only five feet one inch didn't help either. There were only a handful that I was taller than, but I knew that it only took one, and as eighth grade wore on I was beginning to get an idea of whom that one could be. I'm not saying just yet but my plans were taking root, just like my buddy Lurch's sunflowers that were beginning to peak through the flowerbed in his back yard. I had serious doubts that anyone would be interested in a prepubescent lad like myself and the only women that I ever talked to were my sisters and Bridie. So, up until now I had hid inside sports, routes and serving mass at the altar, but my breakout was near at hand.

Despite all of the impediments, my desire to discover the world of girls grew and when Murphy the sex minister called one night, so did my first chance to blossom. Murphy was the big shot in the class. The guy who was light years ahead of everyone when it came to sex and gambling and girls and just about anything besides Math and English.

Bridie answered, cupped the phone as she summoned me and warned me of Murphy's treachery. Bridie knew Murphy's family from the west side and all their entries on the police blotters.

"Oh, Ma, he's all right," I assured, knowing that she was right. I didn't care. I was willing to get hoodwinked just to step out, take a look inside this alien world of girls and discover the other side.

"Yea, Jim what's up?" I started.

I knew he must have wanted something because he would usually never even give me the time of day.

"Hey thanks again for that math help," he said. His tone was hollow. I knew it hadn't done much good. He didn't call me to thank me, he needed something else.

"Yea no problem Jim, I know how it can be when you can't get those times tables down," asserting a semblance of superiority. Murphy could pick a horse at the track or draw to an inside straight but he didn't know ordinal from cardinal or a noun from a verb.

"Hey, there's a bunch of us meeting at the park tomorrow and we're all going to try and match up and maybe hit it off behind the bushes, you interested?" Behind the bushes, what do you do behind the bushes?

Murphy was organizing an afternoon in the park where he would match up the girls and boys. My antennas went straight up; why would he want little ole' me for the soiree and what girl would I get? There had to be an extra girl seeking the same things that I was…but who? Murphy would want a favor if he was offering any of the fair mares and I didn't have anything that he wanted except doing his homework for him, and the year was almost over. There had to be an ugly duckling and I was the sacrificial lamb. I can hear him now, 'We'll get Brennan.'

After a slight pause trying to figure out his motives I asked, "Who's coming?"

"Oh, the usual crowd, I can't promise you anyone in particular but there ought to be some decent pickings," he said.

I knew that he only needed me for some clean-up, but I was willing to get burned just to see what this girl stuff was all about. Maybe the math help was paying off if he was trying to get even numbers, besides, I had some one in mind who had caught my eye and she might be there and you never know.

"If you don't shoot you can't score," Bridie would say.

"What time?"

"One."

"See you there." I hung up nervous but excited. Bridie was lurking near the phone.

"What does *he* want?" Bridie asked.

"They need a catcher for a game tomorrow," I lied.

"Just make sure it's only baseball," she warned.

"Every game needs a good backstop," I shot back.

I knew the first thing I needed to do was get to the stock box early, scour it and find something decent. Early Sunday morning I hopped out of bed quickly and ransacked the box and at the bottom found a dark blue and black, loosely related and without holes, so far so good. I raided the community closet looking for some decent pants and found a pair in the recesses that were grown out of and weren't too tattered. I zipped through my route, dozed through Fr. Kelly's Sunday short version mass, feasted on Bridie's "Sunday Only" bacon and eggs, and then spent a distracted morning in the alley shooting hoops and mostly laying bricks, distracted by my big adventure.

"I've never seen you this off," my big brother Tom poked at me.

"Big date today," I jokingly answered knowing that no one would buy my interest in girls.

"No one wants a squirt like you," he shot back. And I started to think that he might be right.

The afternoon slowly approached and I agonized every minute over whether to go or not. I shot again, another brick. The torment came from Murphy's treachery and the chance of getting matched with a faulty feline for the afternoon without an out. I stopped and pondered and took a pass off my noggin and out of bounds.

"Hey airhead!"

"Gotta take a break," I said.

I had to go. I had to see what was out there. I slipped off the court and I'm sure no one was sad to see me go after the way I had played. I snuck around to Cloonmore's front door and upstairs where I had stashed my threads in the back of the closet.

The house and bedroom were empty and I dressed in the back of the closet just to make sure no one saw me. I slipped down the hallway and jumped in front of the mirror and took one long look at what Miss X was going to get today. I tiptoed and expanded my chest and decided after a quick brush of my golden locks that I didn't look too bad. Someone was in for a treat today.

I had a story in mind, just in case Bridie spotted my exit. Bridie wasn't ready to sanction cavorting with the girls so I had to sneak this one. I slipped down the hallway and inched my way down the stairs each one squeaking louder than the one before. At the bottom, still on my tippy toes, I looked both ways, saw no one, could only hear the whirr of Daddy's sewing machine in the next room, and I darted for the door.

From behind the living room doors I heard, "Where are you going, Sean?" I had one foot over the threshold and into my next adventure. Bridie could be as vigilant as Alfred.

"Oh, just over to the park for a game, you know the one where Murphy needed a catcher."

"Dressed so nice?"

"It's Sunday, Ma."

I saw the catcher's mitt thrown in the corner and retrieved it and gave it a couple of punches as if to certify my story. She smiled, feeling like all of her good rearing was adding finish to her boy.

"Be careful, and don't ruin your good clothes, err... whose ever clothes."

I zipped down the stairs taking the last three with a leap, just like after Mass, grabbed the handle bars and sprinted alongside the bike and in one huge hop was on the seat peddling hard.

"Be careful," she warned. "The tea leaves had a surprise." And I waved my right hand high without turning and sped off to my afternoon adventure.

"Cling, cling," the broken spoke sang, disturbing the silence and getting a bit louder as I picked up speed. My heart pounded as my trek unwound and I began letting thoughts of my first smooch enter my mind. A vision of that one girl that I had admired from afar entered my thoughts and a slight delirium came over me. My first smooch with my special someone…Well, let's not get ahead of ourselves…but maybe.

The special someone, I'm sure, had no idea of my affections. I was still an outsider to the in-crowd where she resided, and for the most part I didn't feel like I belonged anywhere except in the alley or on the basketball court. Well maybe she felt the same way and thought that she was looking in from the outside too. Not likely, and high hopes can only lead to disappointment. I looked back over my shoulder to make sure that I was free and started to pedal hard with a surge of adventure. The coast was clear and I was on my way. The whole ride I kept threatening myself to turn back, worried that my tongue would tie. The whole experience would be new to me and what if…. I filled my head with thoughts of what could go wrong. I pedaled on convinced that I needed to step out.

I got to the park early and stashed my bike behind a bush so no one could see the wreck, ashamed it wouldn't match up with the other kids' newer versions, and into the wooded arbor I strolled. My plan was to scope it out from behind some bushes and then arrive fashionably late. I considered just escaping one more time but hung on enjoying the thrill that was tingling through me. 'You're in the on-deck circle, big boy!'

From behind the bush I scanned the landscape. The park was empty. Did I go to the wrong park? And suddenly, I saw someone approaching, garbed in a bright yellow sundress. It was her. Goddamn...I mean Goddamn. A surprise...Bridie had nailed it again. She sat on the park bench crossed her legs and looked around as if she was expecting someone. I'm over here...psst...over here, all in silence, too scared to utter even one sound. 'It's just me and her,' I thought, 'all alone.'

'Go for it, you dork.' I had to act fast, but I was frozen. We were the only ones in the park, she perched on a park bench glistening in the sunlight, lusting for her Romeo, and I crouched behind a bush with a mosquito circling my head and a lilac branch stabbing my arse. My mouth got dry and my limbs started to shake.

'Stay cool and be cool,' I thought, and then I took my first step into a blistering new world of love, lost my balance and fell into the bush.

"Oww!" I cried as the lilac branch stabbed me a good one. She looked and I laid low, silent, spying her glare from between the leaves. Despite the branch, I held my frozen pose. The branch dug deeper. She looked away, assuming a stray cat perhaps, then paused and looked again, straining her head to see into the bush, and then rose and strode toward me – I couldn't be caught this way. It was too humiliating – speared to a branch, a girl stalker. I groaned as I freed myself from the piercing branch and began to crawl toward my hidden bike.

"Who's there?" and she stepped closer. And then one more giant step and, "Is that you, Sean?" On all fours with my aching arse aimed at her eye, I looked over my shoulder and confessed.

"Sure is." The pain became secondary to my embarrassment. "Yea, it's me," I confessed having no other out while I rubbed my butt. She laughed.

"Okay," I thought, "Go for the humor approach."

"There's blood on your pants," the doctor's daughter observed, her tone alarmed. 'And shame in my heart,' I thought.

"Why don't you come up from there and join me on the bench," she invited. "It's much more comfortable there."

Are you kidding? Her tone was inviting. She was playing psychologist to boot, trying to minimize my embarrassment. I needed the help. It worked. I got to my feet brushed off the leaves and eased my way to the bench. She sat back down and patted the spot next to her.

Oh, boy! The welcome mat was out. Rubbing my arse to ease the stabbing pain, with a silly grin to add a bit of humor, I sat and jumped back up as if the pain was too much. She giggled. Good one. I eased back down on a spot a bit outside where she had patted and let out a breath as if the pain was gone. She giggled again. Nice. She inched over.

It was Haggerty, the class monarch, the doctor's daughter, the one that I had been dreaming about. There were others more popular, but none of them had Jayne's quiet confidence and aplomb. This was looking like my lucky day and a chance with the bases loaded. The surprise Bridie foresaw in the tea leaves! This was a gangbuster.

"What were you doing hiding behind the bushes?" she said.

I felt an ease come over me. I don't know if it came from making light of my situation in the bushes or Haggerty's overture of seeming interest in this tattered lad.

"Hi Jayne," I was finally able to gasp, looking down at the ground, not yet completely comfortable. She smiled like she was happy to see me. I only sensed her smile because I still couldn't look up.

"What were you doing in the bushes?" she asked again.

I wanted to say, 'I'm shy, I don't know what I'm doing, I'm afraid of girls, especially…you. I stammered, "Oh, I was looking for a…"

"A what?" she asked.

I never finished. She sensed my dilemma and retreated.

"Oh, it doesn't matter, it's nice to see you outside of class." Her tone eased all of my pain. I looked up.

"It is?" I said.

"Oh, yea, I never get to see you at these things and I always kind of hoped you'd come." You did!

"But that's in the past and now you've finally made it."

'What?!' I thought. 'Did I just hear that? Was there mutual interest?' I finally got the guts to look over at her and found cuteness and a demure smile that for the moment was all mine. She actually seemed to like being there with me. Nah, it's just pity…well maybe. My confidence started to grow a bit and I complemented her on her dress and happy glow. That one came from my brother Mike, "A complement will always get you to first base." And it did as Haggerty smiled and expressed sincere appreciation for my notice.

"Oh, thank you," she said and she inched closer. And before I could ratchet up my game, the one I didn't even know I had, clicking heels on the pavement shattered the moment and turned our heads. It was Murphy, barging up the walk in his Cuban heels and tough guy air.

"He, who hesitates…" my brother Mike would say.

I never got to tell her how I felt or that she was my dream come true or that Bridie's surprise oracle was the biggest one of my life or anything about how great this moment was.

"Sean, we hooked you up with Charlotte, she'll be here any minute," Murphy barked.

Charlotte! Ich! The air left my lungs, the high escaped from my head, the tingle from my bones. Bridie's bright omen was short lived. Charlotte! Although Charlotte was nice she was eight inches taller than me and way too much woman. Murphy reached down, grabbed Haggerty's hand and pulled her to him and shattered my heart and dreams at the same time. I looked up and into her eyes. There was a sadness that said she wanted to be back on the bench next to me. She couldn't possibly like someone who misses simple math like nine times nine.

Murphy turned and pulled her towards him and the two of them began strolling off hand in hand. "Charlotte will be along pretty soon, take good care of her," Murphy snickered out of the side of his mouth. Haggerty turned and took one last look over her shoulder toward me as Murphy marched her into the shrubbery. Her look dripped of petition as she disappeared behind the lilacs and I stood there, in shock, waiting for Charlotte and wishing I could just walk over to the lilacs, put my foot up Murphy's ass and take what was rightfully mine. I don't think Haggerty would have objected.

It felt like Haggerty was being forced to do something that she didn't want to particularly because now she had an alternative. The thoughts of chivalry and attacking Murphy, grabbing the distressed damsel, and fleeing entered my mind, but they left just as fast. He'd kick the Hell out of me. The door to Haggerty seemed to be open though, but it was no time to think about that now. Haggerty was no pushover and could probably handle Murphy for what seemed would be their last afternoon together.

I saw the yellow dress disappear behind the lilacs. Don't be too rough on her Murphy. And then I realized, steeped in my state of concern for Haggerty, that Charlotte was not too far away. I couldn't get stuck with Charlotte for the afternoon. I looked down the street and saw her coming, all five feet nine inches of her. She hadn't seen me yet. There was still time to scram.

Just then, I heard a "Psst" from behind the bush. "Sean," I heard next, and I turned but saw nothing.

"Sean, it's me, Phelim." Behind the bush was my little brother, the same guy who had his head stuck between the spindles when Murphy called the night before.

"Bejasus, Philly, whatta ya doing back there?" I whispered.

"Ollie came by with Sox tickets and we got one for you."

"How'd you know I was here?"

"I had my head stuck between the spindles last night."

Charlotte was coming closer but still far enough away that she couldn't see me. I froze for a second, wondering which way to turn.

"C'mon, we're parked down the street!" This was a no brainer as I took off down the path and stopped when I heard a loud slap and then... "You brute!"

Haggerty came out from behind the bushes and Charlotte came running into the park and threw her arms open for her best buddy, Jayne. Murphy came out from behind the bushes holding his reddened cheek and Charlotte grabbed him by the hair and kicked him right in the ass and then shoved him. Murphy did nothing but stand there holding his cheek with one hand and then his ass with the other, humiliated.

The girls turned and scurried toward the park exit.

Haggerty was safe and I was outta there.

"Wait for me!" I dashed for my bike, jumped on the seat and peddled like Hell and out the back entrance of the park. The pain in my arse was gone. I never looked back to see the look on Charlotte's face and the disappointment in her heart knowing that her diminutive first date had left her at the altar. Charlotte would have to wait for another day to get her first pluck at me, to hold my head to her breast and try to smother me with love. I breezed past a bum asleep on a bench and whisked the newspapers off of him.

"Hey."

"Sorry," and I bounced over the curb and down the street to a waiting Ollie and passage to freedom. Standing up Charlotte was no consideration when there was a Sox game at hand and now that Haggerty was safe... Ollie threw the bike in the trunk and off we went to the Sox game.

In the back seat with my head slung out the window feeling the breeze, I grabbed one of Bridie's lightly melted cheese sandwiches from the brown shopping bag, took a bite and let out a holler, "YEEHA!" I had just gone from nirvana to the depths of despair and back to the edge of euphoria and a date with the White Sox. Baseball had won out over girls, but just for today.

As we rode off in Ollie's old Ford, with my head stuck out the window enjoying the breeze, I felt bad that Charlotte would be fellowless and wasn't going to get smooched and that she would miss holding my head to her bosom, while she ran her fingers through my curls.

I allowed for one small thought of Haggerty and her reception and what might be ahead.

And I hoped there were a few mosquitoes descending on the brutish Murphy and his reddened cheeks.

Almost Quartered

Hoops was my game and I was determined to cherish every moment I had on the hardwood. It was everything that I wanted; a uniform, indoor basketball, nets and someone to pass to. I played hard, despite the inevitable outcomes and left it all on the court, all ninety-five pounds. During our eight game season, I cherished a single hope: that we could win just one.

Eighth grade was winding down and the end of my grade school days near. The basketball team had lost the first seven and we faced one last game against The Quarter. An answer to our prayers this season, we were thankful for having Bishop Quarter on the schedule, a school whose team was lower on the food chain than we were. The Quarter was a local military school that housed dispensable rich kids. They played basketball like they walked – stiff and erect, there wasn't much hope for a reverse layup from this lot.

As pathetic as the opposition was, The Quarter was our final chance to achieve a single winning game, to break the losing streak that threatened eight out of eight. I even resorted to what I resisted most... prayer. The nuns always advised us to ask God for something special when we prayed; you know, world peace, a cure for cancer, the pagans to be converted, goodwill for the starving Chinese or guidance for the misinformed Prods. It was essential to only use God's good graces for something very important. If the nuns knew that I was praying for a basketball victory over at the gym they would have torn up my prayer card. But they never specified important to *whom* and winning just one stinking basketball game was all I dreamed of. It was the end of the basketball season and we were down to our last chance, The

Quarter. I went down on my knees and prayed during the daily supplications.

"Who are you praying for today, Sean?"

"I think I'm going with the pagans today, Sister." I lied.

We needed a win.

You could use a standardized prayer like the "Our Father," or personalize the prayer and supplicate about what an unworthy sinner you were and how undeserving you were because you were such a paltry human and despite that still needed some divine guidance and just beg your ass off. "Oh, please Father, bless me for I know I have sinned, I know I don't deserve your grace but would it be too much to get one victory out of you this year?" All that mattered was that you were as sincere as the statues on the altar. And if God smelled a rat and sensed your insincerity and didn't come through, we always had a backup savior, the one over at Cloonmore and she was going to be at the game.

I expected my prayers to be answered and my target was an easy victory and some self-esteem. Feeding the Orientals and converting the Pagans could wait until the season was over. Just once a year we needed a little pick me up in the form of an easy sports victory to at least give us a little hope. I don't know who the Quarter boys found to provide them a morale boost but that was their problem.

This year we got lucky and had one chance to embrace what it felt like to saunter into a gym, cocky as roosters in a henhouse, and bask in the glow of the overhead lights, knowing that we were going to dribble around the military brats and bank a few in. At times I would feel bad about putting a lick on someone, but not these guys; they had nice uniforms and probably got dessert every night.

The day of the big game finally arrived and playing at night was special because everyone could make the game, Ma, Pa, Bro,

Sis, the neighbors. The game was away and that made it fun too because we all had to pile in cars and wrestle our way to the opponent's gym.

We felt like pros, exiting the cars with our shopping bags...er I mean... gym bags...all six of us. You see, the regular beatings had taken their toll and thinned the ranks. We had Lurch, Brennan, Turk, Maloney, O'Brian and the only pollock in the school, Kowalski.

When we walked into the diminutive and overflowing gym the home boys were already warming up. This was our time for intimidation, which we weren't very good at because we had never done it before. We strode down the sideline in formation from shortest to tallest; I was leading, the net grabber Lurch was trailing. We peeked over at the military brats, sizing up their game and harrumphed and sneered at their futile moves. A wayward ball rolled to my feet and I snatched it with my right hand and let a one hander fly and it swished. I had thrown down the gauntlet; you never took a shot at the opponent's hoop. I didn't expect this lot to know that tradition but then heard, "Hey, stay on your side. You've crossed the line!" I acted unaffected and indifferent but knew that I had egged on the enemy. Bridie always warned, "Don't wake a sleeping giant." Oops.

We kept walking like it wouldn't matter, hit the locker room, ransacked our shopping bags and came strutting out on the floor like we belonged. The gym broke out in uproarious laughter. Even the Quarter boys stopped shooting and fell into laughter, "Hey you guys, are you on the same team?" "Is your equipment manager blind?" "Doesn't mom know what school you go to?"

You see, three of us had yellow shirts and three of us had brown shirts. We stopped in our tracks and turned red. The intimidation was on the other foot.

"Gotta fix that," the ref yelled.

We ran back into the locker room humiliated.

"Goddamnit, shit, balls, Jesus Christ!!??"

"Whatta we do?"

"I know, turn your shirts inside out!" The three yellows suddenly became three browns just like the other lads and 12 became 21, 13 became 31 and 9 became 6.

Problem solved, but not the humiliation.

We huddled up. "Alright boys," I started. We still didn't have a coach.

"Let's turn this into a positive!" "Let's run out there like we did it on purpose, waving to the crowd and pumping our fists."

And that's what we did, bursting from the locker room and running in a big loop around the court and then into a perfect layup line with six browns, three in one line and three in the other.

"You guys should be in the circus!"

One last cat call.

The whistle blew. We huddled up and went over our strategy which was keep running and never pass to the other team.

The ref tossed the ball up at mid court, Lurch tipped it over to me and I stepped out of bounds. "Damn this gym is small."

We weren't used to the small gym and kept stepping out of bounds and before we knew it Bishop Quarter had a six point lead, which was huge because we only scored twenty-five points a game.

By halftime their lead was the same and our frustration was evident. These well-groomed but clumsy Quarter boys had a coach and a system that, despite our superior talent, made us look like we were standing still.

During our halftime, I addressed the team.

"We've got one chance all year to win a game and we're losing to these sissy-ass, well-fed, military brats who never shoveled any ice and never ran hot water over their frozen basketballs."

"GODDAMN IT!"

"We pick 'em up full court and press the wrinkles out of them.!'"

"Got it!"

"Got it!" they responded. I wasn't so sure.

We huddled up, put our hands in a pile and yelled, "Kick some ass!" and raced back out onto the court for the next and final half of the season.

Our basketball season started out with great expectations as Maloney's older brother volunteered to be coach. He was replacing old man Ruttigan, whose legacy was forgettable because he stood five foot four and had never played basketball. When you were in eighth grade, the players weren't supposed to be taller than the coach. His favorite piece of coaching was to dribble "low and slow." Low maybe, but the slow part kept us in the backcourt too long.

Devin Maloney, the new coach, passed the height test because he was taller than anyone on the team. Maloney's younger brother, Lurch, was our center because he was the only one who was taller than his mother. We called him Lurch because he was tall and thin and had trouble holding his head up. Lurch was pretty skinny and offered little resistance to the opposition but every now and then he could knock down some fifteen footers. He didn't want to be there, wishing instead to be planting sunflower plants in his backyard and baking cookies with his mother. The ridicule that he got for wanting out was too much, so he forsook the flowers and became a part of the futility. "Come on Lurch, you're the only one who can touch the net."

Devin, the older brother, was a decent player in the alley so we thought he might know something. And he did, exhibiting some common sense two weeks after the season started, by quitting. There was no letter of resignation or other kind of notice, Devin just stopped showing up. The challenge had been too much for him and the pay even worse. We understood. Wooden would have punted too.

So without much in the way of democratic processes, I declared my desire to be the head coach and met no dissent. The job didn't require much knowledge except knowing how to pick teams at practice and knowing when the games were, which was easy because we had one every Saturday. Getting my teammates to practice was no problem either because playing inside the gym in the middle of winter was a huge treat. We were finally in the gym legally which rendered the hulking Albanian, Alfred powerless.

Alfred didn't go away that easily, he often stood sentinel in the doorway, watching us, hoping that someone would spit or swear or be caught playing in their street shoes so he could rat us out.

That was another prohibition that they held over your head.

"Stay off the floor in your street shoes." You could understand if the floor was some exotic hardwood, but it was plain old linoleum that could withstand just about anything. It was just another rule that they could use to keep you from having a little fun. In case someone forgot their shoes and usually someone did, we kept an old pair of Lurch's gym shoes in the ball bag that was sure to fit anyone because he had the biggest feet. All we had to do was stuff some newspaper in the toes, if it was a short guy.

We'd meet every day after school and without any hesitation, start shooting. We were never too good at layup lines because eventually everyone would be in the same line and there'd be no one to rebound. We didn't know any other drills so we just shot.

Practice began with an all-out assault on just firing some shots. That's really all any of us wanted to do anyway. Just fire some shots where it was warm, the ball had air in it and bounced and the nets swung like a pendulum when you swished one.

With only three balls, one from the school, one from the doctor's son and one from the dentist's kid, practice would start. With only three balls, competition was fierce to get a rebound and get some shots in. Because I was so small, I usually deferred and waited on the perimeter for a long rebound, not wanting to battle with the tall guys.

Once we had warmed up, the real fun would start when I'd announce, "Game Time." This is where my coaching regimen began. There was the usual bitching about how unfair the teams were and I'd respond, "Quit your whining and play, we need the work." Normally you would shoot free throws to decide teams but most of us had trouble making one and we couldn't afford the time. We'd get the game going and play until we couldn't walk, sucking up every minute that we could legally be in the gym. This was indoor basketball with nets, we weren't going to treat that lightly.

Saturday would finally arrive after a long week of practice and beating the Hell out of each other. We played our regular season games at the local high school. The high school sponsored the league because they could recruit any good players without having to go very far. The recruiters liked when we played because they knew there wasn't much reason to be there and they could skip our game and have that extra cup of coffee in the coach's room.

We always showed up and took our regular beatings, because the thrill of having a uniform and being in a big high school gym were worth the price and never wore off.

Because of the regular trouncing that we received, morale was tough to maintain. Our rag tag look commanded little respect and with each game the roster shrunk. We didn't have home and "away" uniforms and we had to hope that our opponents had different colors and even if they didn't we were used to passing to the other team anyway.

Each game there would be one less player, someone else letting despair overcome any interest in continuing our futility. By the fourth game there were only six of us left and my pregame chat centered around watching our fouls, because they wouldn't let you play with four players and I wanted as much gym time as possible, even if we were getting our brains beat in, which was normal.

The opposition, already confident from pre-game reports about how weak we were, would smirk when they saw us emerge from the locker room in our mismatched jerseys, pale legs and lack of formation. Our booster section at games was rather thin. Once and awhile there'd be a mother present, concerned only that the abuse to her son would be minimal that day. The cheer leaders never showed up either, electing to spend Saturdays at the mall with the cool guys. Our season would be our own personal folly, full of uphill climbs and overcoming lopsided odds, which we never did. Upsets were not part of our vernacular. The memories would be shared by none… and all ours.

Barbs would descend from the stands "You guys should be in the girls division." But there wasn't a girls division. And who wanted to get beat by the girls anyway.

Hecklers attacked other areas as well, especially when they saw my lily white legs.

"You could use a little sun, Junior," and "That's quite a reflection your shooting up here" and "How 'bout some nylons for those sticks, cutie?"

I enjoyed the attention and would thank them with a blown kiss. The slants only gave me more motivation, not that it helped with the outcomes, but it motivated me to try and play as hard as I could each game.

Our pincushion status taught me determination and compassion, especially the game against the Christian school where we couldn't get the ball over half court. We kept trying and they kept stealing, another steal, another layup. Even the scoreboard got tired that day.

You'd think they'd get bored with beating the Hell out of you, but they never did, stealing and laying up, stealing and laying up. They never even tried to soften the slaughter, leaving the starters in to feast on our futility. At what point does dominance cease to thrill? It takes longer than you'd think.

Besides us, no one knew that our season ended, or started for that matter, which was okay with me. When it was basketball season, the rest of my world ceased to exist. There was no nothing except hoops. My only focus was the thrill of having that leather orb in my hand, trying to make anything happen.

Halfway into the fourth quarter the press had begun to work and we had taken a small two point lead. O'Brian fouled out on what I thought was a hometown call.

"Zebra!"

The ref heard me and whistled a technical foul. The Quarter boy hit all four free throws and put us down by two.

"The ref wears knickers," came from the stands.

It sounded like Bridie. Everyone laughed.

I called a time out.

"You're in my prayers, boys!" it sounded like Bridie again.

"All right boys, we're down to the final minute and I ain't losin'."

"Lurch, on our next possession turn your ankle on purpose, let out a yelp, grab your foot and when everyone stops, circle around your defender and I'll lob you one." "When we make the basket, everyone act like they're running back down the court and I'll double back and try to steal the inbounds pass. It's our only chance."

We inbounded the ball and I walked it up the court not trying to exhibit our panic…lose to the Quarter? At the top of the key I shuffle dribbled, did a tweener, Lurch yelled "OW!" and grabbed his foot, all the Quarter boys stopped and Lurch did a spin move around his defender and caught and layed in my perfect lob pass. We were tied.

"Wher'd ya learn that one?" guess who.

Our fans went wild and started to stomp on the bleachers. We at least had overtime.

The clock ticked down…ten, nine, eight. The Quarter boy, intent on getting one last shot, inbounded the ball without looking as we had turned and made it look like we were happy with the tie and welcomed overtime and started to run back down the court. Not me. I ducked behind their biggest player who was stunned at our lob play, saw the Quarter boy recklessly inbound the ball, stepped out and grabbed the wayward pass and headed for the game winning layup. Not so fast. The big goof that I was hiding behind suddenly came to life and charged my winning layup…three, two…

As I left my feet and started to push the ball with my right hand, his arm came down like an axe; I had only one out and switched the ball to my left hand and forced it up like a shot putter. He crunched me like a pesky fly and knocked me senseless onto the floor. One, zero and the buzzer and I opened an eye to see the ball hit the backboard drop onto the front of the rim, quiver and fall through the hoop. The fans erupted, I rolled over and pounded the floor with my fists and thought, 'Damn we're good…one and seven.'

I'll never know if it was my prayers to the Father or Bridie's goodwill to the team that got that ball to fall in instead of out, but I do know whose voice I had heard from the stands.

And before I knew it my final grade school season was nearing an end. We had one more game in the playoffs and had been invited not because of our record, but because they needed eight teams and some fodder for the Christians. It was like the lions and the peons in the coliseum… not much of a contest. We got clobbered in the final game and as I walked off the floor, battered and beaten, I had thoughts of continuing my hoop career in high school, knowing that it would take a lot of hard work over the summer if I was to compete with the likes of the Christians. My grade school career was over and so was my high school career, but I didn't know that yet.

The Caddy

"Who are you?" the caddy master barked as I approached the caddy shack. The master was garbed in a sleeveless tee, with tattoos running down each arm and a potbelly that evidenced some serious abuse. Above the "Love Mom" tattoo I spotted "Vinnie" in small letters. Vinnie's blackened and stained teeth matched his visceral protrusion. He was all gut and gruffness.

"I'm Turk's friend, Sean," I stuttered, intimidated by his manner.

"Yeah, he said you were coming. Whadda ya know about caddying? The last guy Turk sent was a bust."

"Clean balls are important," I answered.

"Do you know what a wedge is used for?" ignoring my quip.

"Get close to the pin," I said.

"Not bad for a rookie," he complimented.

Turk had given me a rudimentary class on what needed to be done if I got called. "Tote the bag, walk behind the golfer, keep the balls clean, don't talk unless spoken to, and look away if you sense them wanting to cheat. That should get you through the first day."

"Wait over there, I'll call you when I need you," the master ordered.

"Thanks Vinnie," I said, letting him know that I was observant and no push over.

"It's 'Mr.' to you," reasserting his station. "I'll let you know when you can use my first name."

"Yes sir, Mr. Vinnie."

I took a seat on a long wooden bench alongside the shack. All the other caddies were gathered around a penny-pitching Turk hooting and hollering his next toss. It looked like the championship as Turk lofted his next penny at the crack in the sidewalk about six feet away. Heads and eyes raised then lowered as the copper descended onto the asphalt, bounced, spun and then came to rest exactly across the tiny crevice. The crowd roared, except for the loser, who dropped his head in defeat. Turk raised both arms to the sky. It had nothing to do with Jesus and he let out a whoop, then accepted all the high fives and back slaps that he was due. He still hadn't recognized my presence.

"Hey Champ," Vinnie barked, "Loop on the first tee."

Turk pocketed his winnings and trotted off.

"Rematch," the loser begged.

"Duty calls, save your money." he cockily admonished the losing competitor.

And there I sat for the next two hours waiting for Mr. Vinnie to give me an opportunity to wash some old guy's balls. I'd taken this sort of 'job' in the hopes of earning more money for the private Catholic high school tuition and to spend more time with my best buddy, Turk. My birthday twin was heading off to a different Catholic school, one snootier than the one I was going to…if that's possible. So far, I'd spent the summer doing my morning and afternoon routes and saving every dime for my tuition. At forty dollars a month I would just make the three-hundred and fifty annual tab. It was the last summer of our best buddy relationship. The inseparables would be separated, and caddying together was my last stab at keeping us together even though I knew our friendship was hanging by a thread.

Turk and I had been through a lot together and much of my mischief was a result of his design. The fifth of an Albanian family of high achievers, Turk tired of their accomplishments and the expectations placed on him and sprouted a nascent bud of self-destruction. He would intentionally bring doom upon himself just to remind his parents that there wasn't a perfect mold or formula, and prove the black sheep theory. Naturally smart, his common sense lacked finesse. His parents both worked and during the summer when they left for work, the house was locked and Turk was cast to the streets. Over the years he had become one of Bridie's refugees, relishing in the cheese sandwiches and aesthetic pleasures of Cloonmore.

"I don't know why they have them if they're not going to raise them," Bridie would chortle in disgust over Turk's abandonment.

Cloonmore was a lot like my bike: there was nothing worth stealing so there wasn't much need for locks. The doors, windows and, most importantly, our hearts were all left open, naked to the world. Our only treasures were Bridie's homespun sandwiches, soup and comforting counsel, and it was offered to all, without cost. Her kitchen was the stage where she served up this wisdom, complete with the occasional fly that snuck through the holes in the screen door. Her quickness with a rolled up newspaper would fix them. Yes, Turk didn't get much love and comfort in his own home but he sure got a healthy serving of it at Cloonmore, wrapped in every cheese sandwich Bridie served him.

One summer day he lured me into breaking into his house with, "I got something to show you – wait'll you see this!" I always fell for that one. Making sure the coast was clear and Alfred wasn't nearby, we crawled through a first floor window and climbed the stairs into Turk's attic. Alone in the corner in front of us was a padlocked cedar chest. Turk pulled a screwdriver from behind a rafter and said, "Watch this." He removed the hinges from the back of the chest and raised the lid. Inside, the chest was filled with cash neatly bundled and stacked. I couldn't believe my eyes.

"Turk, you guys are rich," I gasped.

Turk slipped a twenty from the bottom of a bundle. "Just to be sure if they're watching the serial numbers," he said and screwed the hinges back on. We left through the back door and headed straight for the pool hall and bowling alley. That afternoon and many more after we dined and bowled our way to happiness.

It didn't take long for the novelty of the pilfered fun to wear off. The money got dirty, the fun it bought even dirtier and guilt set in. The hamburgers deluxe lost their taste and the bowling alley turned into one long gutter ball. Although I was often a willing part of these capers, I always thought that you were supposed to at least try to be honest. Turk woke every day wondering which way he wouldn't be honest, how to get around it, work some angle or outright snatch some cash. I began to dislike myself, the money and the pleasures. Earning my way and appreciating the things I had started to grow in value. I started to resist our treachery and decline his invites and so began the parting of our paths.

I should have seen it coming with all the dishonesty. And finally one day it happened, Turk's first mortal sin or at least the first one I ever saw. Had there been others?

One Sunday we walked to church together and as we approached ole' St. Eddie's, Turk made an abrupt left turn and headed across the avenue to Dee's coffee shop, where during the week he'd sit in a booth, drink cherry cokes, eat chocolate donuts and spend hours devouring the comic book rack, all with somebody else's money. Now I knew how he financed these afternoons and disliked everything he was starting to become. I had been a part of it, but those days were over. Today, however, was the first time I saw him or anyone else commit sacrilege. Sacrilege was bad and could send you to Hell without hope of atonement.

"Turk, where are you going?" I was concerned that he was missing Sunday Mass, a sure mortal.

"Over to Dee's," he curtly and nonchalantly replied.

"No Mass?"

"Eh," he said.

"You're committing a mortal," I warned.

"I have plenty of those already," he declared and "I ain't worried."

If you missed Mass on purpose you got one. Mortals could condemn you for eternity unless you came clean on your death bed. As the story goes, Capone came clean on his death bed and got atonement for all his mortals, but his was a special case, or so they would tell us when we asked how a murderer could get into heaven. "He confessed to our merciful Father." His funeral Mass was at the cathedral.

"It won't be the last," Turk promised.

"Won't be the last!" my mind echoed. I was witnessing the precipitous descent and certain damnation of one of Bridie's refugee's and my heart began to ache. Intent sealed your fate and Turk couldn't fake that.

Turk continued across the street giving me an 'aw your nuts' wave. He never looked back. I tried once more to save his soul, "But Tur…" My mouth was dry and my voice silent. I couldn't finish my plea. It was no use. I climbed the steps of the church in a complete stupor, slowly reaching for the handrail to steady my leaden legs. It seemed like it took me forever to finally sit down in the last pew and catch my breath. I buried my face in my hands and sobbed. I had just seen my best friend buy a one way ticket to Hell. I said a few prayers for his soul and gave it one last thought… 'If Capone got off maybe…'

Here I was, in complete devastation, worrying about Turk's soul, all the while he was downing a choco, sipping a coke, lusting over Betty and Veronica…laboring over redhead or brunette.

After mass and having fulfilled my weekly duty to God and doing all that I could do to save Turk, as I approached the church doors and fresh air, my spirits brightened. I took a long look from the top of the stairs and puffed up my chest knowing that for once I had repelled a sinful temptation and tried to save Turk's soul. I raced down the church steps in a state of euphoria and jumped to the sidewalk skipping the bottom three. There were no mortals on this soul, at least for the time being. Turk's fate was now his own.

After trying to save Turk's soul and weaning myself from the stolen money and pleasures, I realized that my first day of high school was right around the corner and I was short some tuition money. I had always wanted to try caddying and Turk in an effort to get back into my good graces, invited me out to *his* club. Playing big shot again, he said, "Yea I can get you in."

There were only days left to the summer of '65 and just around the corner was my first day of high school, so I said yes and gave it a shot. Turk had chosen caddying instead of routes to make a buck. Even though he had regular access to the family fortune in his attic, his mother made him get a job which eased her guilt, gave him a spot to hang and kept him off the streets. Now she could drop him off in the morning at the country club and not have to worry about him for the rest of the day. So one Monday morning I pedaled the five miles to the country club where Turk claimed to be a fixture. The whole experience was new to me. That first morning, I cruised up the winding path to the glorious Tudor styled club house with flower pots in full bloom adorning the entrance. A guy in a funny uniform and bow tie guarding the oak front doors welcomed me.

"You're supposed to use the back entrance," he barked, obviously disgruntled with my garb, broken spokes and paper basket with a couple of yesterday's newspapers still undelivered. "I don't want to see you up here tomorrow."

His attitude and the pristine atmosphere gave me a sense of foreboding that he wouldn't get the chance. I turned and took off down the path purposefully grazing one of the flower pots and catching a petunia in the loose spokes. The flower exploded and spewed its colorful shreds onto the spotless drive leaving a trail of welcome.

"Sorry," I shot back, in my most contrite tone, not really meaning it, peeking over my shoulder to get his reaction. He sneered as I rode over the grass just to make sure I had left a couple of tire tracks in his idyllic world.

At the caddy shack, no one said a word to me, viewing me as unneeded competition. But adjacent to the shack was a basketball hoop, nailed to a piece of plywood and bolted to an oak tree. I asked Mr. Vinnie if he had a basketball and next thing I knew he stooped down and rifled one at my head. I took a couple of shots as if I had never touched a ball before and dribbled a couple off my feet.

"Anyone for horse?" I asked. And two victims volunteered. From the way I looked and my first few dribbles, no one could have been very intimidated.

"Buck a game," I said. They both jumped at the opportunity. And in a few short minutes I had two bucks in my pocket.

"You set us up?" one of them accused.

"Nope, just needed to get warmed up," I shot back.

"Rematch," one of them ordered and in just a few minutes I had four bucks in my pocket. They resigned, not believing a runt like me could shoot like I did.

"We'll get you tomorrow, hotshot," not knowing that they had no chance of getting their money back today or ever because I increasingly sensed that today would be my last.

Before long, I was the only caddy left without a loop and just when I was going to hop on my bike and flee, I heard, "Brennan!" Mr. Vinnie sounded desperate. I jumped and ran to the window where Vinnie was sucking on a cigarette. He belched out a plume of smoke and ordered the first loop of my caddy career.

"Mrs. Dettle is at the first tee," he snickered.

I hesitated, not knowing where the first tee was.

"That way," he pointed. "And if you get by her you'll have a long career," he chortled. I took off down the path, hurrying to spend the afternoon with Mrs. Dettle wondering how bad this was going to be.

"Dot your eyes and cross your tees or I'll hear about it and I'm not in the mood," Mr. Vinnie warned.

Everything she wore was yellow, sun hat, slacks and blouse. Even her bag was yellow. I immediately sensed that Mr. Vinnie was trying to teach me a lesson by hooking me up with Miss Sunshine.

"Good afternoon Sunshi... I mean Mrs. Dettle," I soft-soaped.

"Easy on the butter," she warned.

"Yes, Ma'am."

"Do what I tell you and don't speak unless I speak to you."

"Yes Ma'am."

"Driver," she bellowed, and held out her gloved hand.

"Damn," I muttered to myself. Turk hadn't mentioned a driver.

"Did I hear you swear?" she asked.

"Oh, no Ma'am, swearing'll get you a sentence to Hell, and I ain't goin' there."

"Aren't," she corrected. "Am not going there." Further asserting her superiority.

I rifled through the bag looking for something called a driver. All I could find was a stick with a big "D" etched on the back.

'D'for Dettle or driver? This has to be it, I guessed, lifting it out of the bag and handing it over to the missus. I held my breath waiting for, "This isn't what I want," but she smirked at the missed opportunity to correct me, took the club and the wooden peg she had held between her front teeth and strolled over to the two logs on the grass. She stopped right in between them, bent over giving me a solid shot of what Mr. Dettle hadn't planned for back when he proposed, and stuck the peg in the ground. She reached out with her off hand, still bent over, and barked, "Ball!" I was mesmerized by the width of her moon, commiserating with old man Dettle's plight and how happy he must have been, being somewhere else for the afternoon.

"Ball!" she barked again. I panicked not knowing where the balls were and then noticed the pocket on her bag with the zipper a bit open. Hopefully... I put my hand in the pocket and got stuck by one of her tees.

"Goddamnit" I mumbled.

As she stood up, her moonshot flattened, sending my attention to the immediate task and my hand landed on a ball deep in the corner of the pocket. "Yesssss!" I wiped it with the towel hanging from her bag ("Clean balls,")Turk had admonished, and placed the glistening orb in her outstretched palm.

"You'll have to be quicker than that if you want any kind of a tip today, young man," she warned, setting me up for the big stiff later. Somehow I began to sense that there wasn't much chance of any tip. It was starting to look like this damsel would use anything to diminish my effort and keep my payday light. I began to wonder how I could wrest some glee from this foreboding predicament. I decided that I would compliment her into submission.

Her first drive was short and left and came to rest at the base of an oak tree. "Good shot," I offered. I sensed that I was in for a long afternoon but held out hope that ole Dettle could get a little better as the afternoon wore on.

"I can do better," she shot back.

"I'm sure you will," I predicted, "It's still early."

She flipped the club toward me and started the first of many wayward and zig-zagging marches toward her ball. I wiped the club clean, stuck it inside the bag, lifted the bag and threw it over my shoulder, stumbling from the weight of it and started *my* march down the fairway in pursuit of Mrs. Dettle's little white ball.

"What the Hell is inside this bag?" I thought. It weighed more than her ass, and I didn't want to carry that either. I tried my best, keeping my mouth shut and jumping to her orders. After she plunked one in the water hole I claimed, "Oh darn, bad luck again," and asked her if she wanted me to go in after it. Her palm reached out with her fingers beckoning a replacement.

"I don't think so," she smirked. I didn't know how to swim, so I was glad she said no. I knew where the balls were now and hastily found a replacement. The minutes ticked by and slowly turned into hours. Each moment I dreamt deeper and harder of when this Hell might end. 'There's eighteen holes,' I remember Turk had warned, as we passed the sign that had a big nine on it; nine holes down; nine more to go.

Soon thereafter we passed a little hut with a chimney belching smoke and filling the air with the smells of barbecued hamburgers and hot dogs. 'Halfway House' the little wooden plaque said. The aromas drifted down and ignited a salivating hunger within me; hamburger or hot dog… or maybe one of each? I couldn't decide but it didn't matter, I could've eaten the ass end out of a water buffalo. And all I thought about was sinking my teeth into whatever was served up. Dettle stopped, ordered a double cheeseburger and told me to wait at the next tee. "There's a water fountain over there," she said.

"But…"

I looked into her eyes and knew that she had absolutely no intention of getting me something. I felt like I did when I was in front of a nun's edict. Nothing would change.

I thought of Bridie and all of the times that she had invited the hungry world into her kitchen for a bite…of anything. It didn't matter what… a chance to give solace and comfort and love. She never missed one.

I rounded the hut with my protruding and gurgling stomach, took a drink, doubled back and peeked around the corner to catch her biting into the burger, leaving a *smather* of mustard on her cheek. She wiped it away with her sleeve.

'More yellow,' I thought.

My instincts, driven by my hunger and the callousness of the moment wanted me to sneak up behind her, rip the burger from her hands and eat it as I walked backwards, taunting her as I hummed, 'Mmmm , yummy, yummy, come and get me!' I resisted, still hoping that there might be a payday ahead. She teed off on the tenth after finishing the burger and letting out a loud burp. The tee shot was no better than the first nine and the only good thing about it was that it got me closer to the end.

"That one's a little better," I said. And I did mean 'little.'

The next nine holes were more of the same; lugging Dettle's monstrous bag, cleaning her mud-stained balls and muffling my thoughts with each crooked shot. On each hole, I lost track of the number of shots and wondered why anyone would keep at something they were so blatantly bad at. And then suddenly right before my eyes was the wooden placard with a green "one and eight" etched into it. "Yahoo! Jesus, Mary and Joseph! Whoopee, it was almost over!" I got one last final shot of her bending over and placing a tee in the ground and again thought of the mister. Her final drive was no better than the first seventeen but this was no time for despair, only hope, as the green on the horizon grew closer with each step.

"Best one of the day," I chirped, wondering how anyone could find the least bit of difference between this one and any other of her hundred and fifty shots. The end was near.

My legs were starting to buckle under the weight of the bag but I was determined. The finish line was in sight. After she tapped in for an eight on the par four, I retrieved her ball and wiped it off for the last time. My time with Mrs. Dettle was nearing an end. All to be determined now was the size of my payday. Could I have been wrong and underestimated this damsel's largesse? Was she just trying to toughen me up and then surprise me with golden philanthropy, or were my instincts right and the old, "You need to do better speech," in the offing? We got to the scorers' table and she told me to dig into the bottom pocket on the bag and hand me her purse. It was fat and solid, much like her. She unsnapped it and pulled a crumpled single dollar from a larger fold of crisp twenties and slid it across the table at me.

"It would have been two if you had been a little more attentive," she said.

"Well, it's just my first day," I pleaded, casting a sad look her way, looking for some sympathy and maybe a few more bucks.

"I can tell," she shot back.

"Yes, Maam," I replied in a very demure tone, keeping my disgust at bay. Her glee in strangling my fate was evident. Well, at least my time with her was over... but poor Mr. Dettle?

After five hours of toting this matron's golf bag around, getting bleached and burned by the sun and washing her balls until they shone, I had scored a single dollar. I pledged at that very moment that it would only be *my* balls that I would ever attend to again.

"Thank you Mrs. Dettle," I said, trying to cast a bit of guilt her way. The guilt bounced right off her arse and landed on the grass. I was done searching for a tip and whispered under my breath but just loud enough for her to hear, "You know if you lost a little weight...maybe..."

"What did you say!"

"Only that I just can't *wait* for my next day at the country club," wondering how people could be so heartless.

She harrumphed and strode across the path to the club house clicking her spikes on the pavement. I took one last gander at poor Mr. Dettle's fate and turned and walked away.

Starving and spent, I forgot to look for Turk back at the shack to thank him. I found my bike leaning against the caddy shack. The papers were gone. As I pedaled off in an exhausted and discouraged state, each turn of the wheels and clank of the broken spoke got me closer to freedom from caddying and a date with a juicy hamburger. This was one career that I could erase from my future. In the distance, as I exited the wrought iron gates of the club, I spotted a wooden marquis; "EATS," it said. And eats it was. I stopped at the diner with my crumpled five singles, four from my horse victory and one from ol' Dettle, all crying to bring me some happiness. I stashed my bike behind the bushes, naively thinking that someone would steal it and plunked my arse on the stool right in front of the busty waitress.

"You look a little sun-burnt, sunshine," she cracked. "I'll take good care of you my little lobster," she continued with the comedy.

"Menu," I commanded, too tired for a comeback. "Aw, Hell, forget the menu. Give me a double cheese burger, raw onion, choco malt, fries and if you hurry there might be something in it for you."

"Right away, my little lobster!" She flipped her hair back as if on cue and hurried off wiggling her backside to my famished delight.

I ate like an animal pausing only to look up and admire the waitress' melons. She wasn't shy about her built-in billboard and would breathe deep when I looked. The bill came to $3.75. I counted out the five singles like a maverick with plenty to spare and uttered, "Keep the change, delicious."

"With pleasure," she said in an alluring tone, again taking her cue as if she was on stage.

"Stop in again!" she commanded as she bent over and wiped the counter.

I got lost in the cleavage.

"I'll try my best."

"I'll be waiting, don't make it too long," she winked, standing, turning and giving me a profile and inhaling one last time.

"Aloe for the sunburn..."

Off I rode exhausted with a full belly, baked like a clam and broke, but with visions of the waitress replacing visions of Dettle. I got home, Bridie soothed my burns with a soft comforting lotion.

"Aloe?" I said.

"And a little love."

I slept like a baby, did my route the next day and never went back.

The Freshman Boy

My new high school was the standard bearer for status. Passing the entrance exam and being one of 350 accepted students out of 1,000 applicants was considered quite an accomplishment. I was one of the chosen. There were the usual legacy brats, sons of big donors and the well connected, but most earned their way in by innate intelligence and hard work. For the next four years, we would be regularly reminded of our status and fine breeding and I bought the whole package and exclaimed with pride: "I go to Dominican High School."

On the first day, at orientation, I was filled with excitement and a little fear. Excitement for venturing into a new world and fear for the kind of world it would be. I stood just over five feet; I still didn't weigh a hundred pounds. Prepossessing, I was not.

On orientation day I got into the first line that I found, thinking that I'd figure things out as I went. Bridie couldn't be there and liked for you to forge your own way and blaze your own trails.

When my turn came, a foreigner with a broken accent and severe halitosis started to measure my extremities. "Jersey's for basketball?" I asked.

"Blazers" his breath singed my eye brows.

"How will you be paying today?" asked a June Cleaver look-alike volunteer with static hair.

"How much?" I asked. I had four bucks of route money on me.

"Fifty dollars for one and seventy-five for two, so you have a back-up when one is in the cleaners," she said.

"Cleaners!" Lady we're still working on a washing machine with a window, toaster with a timer and fridge with a handle. I needed an out quick. I grabbed my crotch and panted, "Lady this can't wait." I pulled away from the tailor's grasp and ran to the bathroom.

I hadn't given my name and Bridie wasn't joining the Mothers' Club anytime soon; I was still anonymous. After ruminating through my piddle, I went to the phone and called Bridie.

"Ma, they want fifty bucks for a blazer with gold buttons! Any ideas?"

"We'll get your father on the sewing machine tonight."

"Get your arse home."

Fifty bucks was three months worth of route money including bonuses; all so I could look like Little Lord Fauntleroy. I had better ways to spend my scratch.

Bridie and I put the press on Daddy when he got home and he knocked out a blazer by midnight. Daddy was unique; He learned sewing from his mother and developed it into a lifelong passion. Every year, he made Easter suits for all thirteen of us. His workshop was an old Singer sewing machine perched on a corner of the dining room adjacent to Bridie's prized and revered China cabinet. It was fitting how both of their most treasured possessions had found a place in the same room eternally looking out for each other. Below the sewing machine Pop's kept an old Folger's can that he used for a spittoon. Every once and awhile Pops would chew a little tobacco or smoke a cigar, indulging in his only bad habit. We all loved the smell of his cigar and would beg him to light one up. One of his good habits was sewing; he tailored precise outfits for all thirteen of us that we donned on Easter Sunday and with a herd of photographers in tow, proudly displayed them as we paraded down Chicago's Magnificent Mile. And every Easter Monday morning, there'd we be -- splashed across the back page of the *Chicago Tribune* for the whole world to see.

On Sunday afternoons, it was in the sewing room that Daddy held us captive drilling us with spelling words and demanding essays. He was the literary judge with no "if's" or "but's," the jury without compassion and the executioner with no mercy. Word queries were met with, "Look it up," exit pleas with, "You're not done yet," and "I'm done," with, "You're done after I've read it over."

During especially tough moments, Bridie would sneak into the doorway behind his back and signal letters to us during the spelling tests that would follow the essays. She could gesture the whole alphabet.

Daddy taught you to dot your I's and cross your T's because if you didn't, you started over and no one wanted that.

The next morning, I slipped on my new blazer and felt something was amiss. It didn't feel right. I hopped over to the mirror and noticed right away that the buttons were brown. "Ma," I screamed, "The buttons aren't gold!"

"And that's the way they'll stay," Bridie chirped. "Buttons won't make the boy and the brown ones will lend you a bit of distinction," she said.

'I'm going to get laughed at,' I thought. I sat at the kitchen table wondering how I was going to handle this dilemma and consoled myself with the fact that at least my socks matched. All right, one of 'em had a hole but you can't have everything, right?

I scarfed down my oatmeal and soda bread and sipped my tea feeling ever like the Eastern prep boy. Bridie read the tea leaves at the bottom of my cup and declared "A day of good fortune."

"It looks like you're making a basket," she said. Every day, Bridie would read the tea leaves that hugged the bottom of the cup and always found a picture of good fortune. It wouldn't make any sense to see a bad one.

I posed for a quick snapshot in front of the pine that stood next to the sidewalk. Bridie had a small tear in her eye as she pushed the button on the camera that probably didn't have film in it, sealing the moment for posterity and then she gave me a loving shove that sent me down the walk and off to my first day of high school.

When I got to school I found my way down a long marble floored hallway with lockers on either side. Each locker was numbered and as I walked down the hall the numbers were getting smaller and suddenly there it was: locker five. A kid a head taller than me was loading up the upper half and I figured at my size, the lower half would do.

"You Brennan," he asked.

I put out my hand and said, "Sean."

"Mike Brand," he responded.

All around me there was the usual poking and picking at each other going on but I stayed uninvolved and used deep breaths to keep my calm.

The bell rang and we were herded into formation and into the gym and freshman orientation with the disciplinarian, Father O'Malley. I knew no one, so I took the first available seat in the bleachers and placed my brand new books next to me. My seat was right next to what looked like a legacy brat and four of his buddies. The gold buttons, designer tie and matching argyle socks gave him away. I figured I was safe with the monstrous O'Malley at hand. O'Malley stood well over six feet tall and looked like a middle linebacker. He was garbed in a shoulder to ankle, white, woolen monk like robe with a belt around his waist and a massive set of rosary beads hanging from the belt and swinging with each step he took.

"Gentlemen and I use the term loosely," O'Malley bellowed. "Today starts your high school career and strict adherence to our regulations."

"Cheap hotel pants, that's the kind without ball room, will not be tolerated." Everyone chuckled. I muffled my amusement, wondering if it was okay to laugh and then broke a slight smirk when everyone else chuckled.

O'Malley continued laying out the rules and regulations and penalties for breaking them. The general intent was to scare you to death and establish your complete allegiance to the code. Legacy boy next to me wasn't fazed and thought that he needed to exhibit his disdain for the protocol. He sucked all of the snot from his nose with one big snort, lifted the cover of my Latin book and then deposited the contents on the title page and shut the cover. Legacy boy sneered with contempt. His comrades giggled.

"Good one Sal," one of them whispered.

Incredulous, mortified and motionless, I took my hankie (Bridie would never let you leave the house without one) wiped my book clean and dropped the soggy snot-laden cloth through the bleacher and onto the floor below. In shock, I couldn't believe that someone in the interest of scoring points with his buddies would do such a despicable thing. I sat motionless and imprinted in my mind Sal's glee in my humiliation. I've often regretted that I didn't raise my left elbow into the air and bring it crashing down across his nose. But I didn't; I was in shock.

I never heard another word O'Malley said and sat there wondering if there would ever be an end to my dread. The bell rang. O'Malley wished us good luck. I was frozen and defeated. Everyone got up to leave as I sat in full humiliation. After everyone had risen and departed, I finally summoned enough strength to rise up and head to my next class, gym. Sal and his buddies had hopped down from the bleachers, high fiving each other and giggling about his heroics and what a sissy I was.

I walked toward the locker room in a stupefied slump wanting to turn right and head home into Bridie's arms. "Oh, no you don't buster, go get that gym uniform on and air it out," which is what I did.

As if I wasn't traumatized enough, when I descended into the locker room, I was immediately reminded that I had to bare myself and unveil my complete lack of any sign of puberty. As I stood in front of my locker I looked peripherally, without turning my head and knew I was in trouble. Everyone else there was...you know...hairy. And the hairs were sprouting around prodigious members. I delayed, running the risk of being late for class, and breaking one of O'Malley's rules. I was ready to risk anything just to keep my puerile condition a secret. My hope was that everyone would leave and I could get dressed without baring my soul, which is what I felt I was doing.

'I'll take the jug for being late for class,' I thought. I dawdled and fiddled and then felt a light tap on my shoulder. I looked up and saw this six foot strapping senior next to me who leaned down and said, "I went through this three years ago and there's only one thing to do."

"Just do it, it'll get easier every day." He rubbed the top of my head and departed.

It brought a calm and a determination over me. I stripped to the bone, stood there butt naked with my back to the room (I was not going to turn around) and hurried to get my jock and shorts on. Without owning much to hold my jock up, it hung loose, the satchel a long way from being filled out.

I laced up my Converse all-star gym shoes and sprinted up the stairs to the smells of sweat and sounds of basketballs bouncing off the hardwood. When I got to the top of the stairs, I looked out onto a sea of activity. Shots being fired, balls being bounced and basketball. Yes! My game, my stage, hoops; my dread was fading fast. I darted onto the court, grabbed a loose ball and proceeded to dribble through my legs, reverse spin and let one fly; nothing but net. The cure was seeping through my veins.

The whistle blew and my new bodyguard beckoned everyone into the center of the gym. "My name is George, I'm a senior and I'll be proctoring the class," he said. "Layups," was his next order and I ran to the line, dashed to the hoop and laid one in. Out of the corner of my eye I saw Sal at the other end of the gym. I watched his layups and studied his moves. I wasn't impressed. 'Maybe just maybe I can exact some revenge today', I thought.

After a few go a-rounds George blew his whistle and ordered everyone to the base line for some one on one. I was nice and loose now and had forgotten my trauma and was looking for some nice hard hoop action and a victim. I sidled over to George and whispered, "Do you think you can match me up with ole hairy legs over there?" I motioned to Sal.

"Not a problem," he whispered out the side of his mouth.

George signaled me to the front of the line just as Sal got to the front of his.

"Hey,' George bellowed, "You with the hairy legs."

Everyone but me laughed.

"You're next." Sal stepped to the front wondering what was up.

"You against the skinny kid," George declared. "Everyone else stop," George ordered. And the stage was set.

Sal didn't recognize me as the person he had just humiliated. His indifference didn't surprise me because victims don't matter to people like him. Bridie would always advise that vile behavior had no discretion.

I rolled the ball out to Sal and followed closely, declaring my intent with my stare. When he picked up the ball, I looked him straight in the eye and said, "Game to six, I'm spotting you five, make it-take it."

He nodded in agreement, believing all he had to do was make one basket and he would win.

His ego and my skinny-legged stance wouldn't let him turn down this challenge. In his mind, it was a lock.

"Make it-take it" meant that if you scored, you kept possession.

George blew his whistle and Sal cockily started his dribble to the right as if this one was already over. It was, only Sal had the wrong winner. I had watched his moves in layups and I anticipated the dribble. With my left hand, I made a backhand swipe and stole the ball, clearing it and driving around Sal with a stutter step and crossover dribble and drove to the hole for a layup and point number one.

"Five-one Sal," I said. Sal was a bit startled.

Possession was now mine until I missed. At the top of the circle I let him check the ball and get ready. It was more than he would have done for me. It was my ball now.

I had my next move planned and led with a shake dribble, crossover, step back and swished one from fifteen feet. I winked at George; he nodded.

"C'mon Sal," one of his comrades yelled. There was a little more silence.

"Five-two, Sal," I said.

The gym began to sense the intensity of the duel and everyone stopped their dribbles to watch the matchup. More silence. For now, it was just me and George's goodwill against Sal and a full entourage of his toads.

Sal checked the ball again, looking a little more worried.

I threw a shot fake, got the rookie off his feet, dribbled right around the stunned creep and laid point number three in. That was easy. Sal's collar tightened.

His toads implored longer and harder. "Sal you can't let this guy beat ya!"

I was just getting started. On my next possession, I started left, hesitated and dropped a 'tweener back right and scooted around a flat-footed and stunned Sal to score number four.

"Hey Sal, you gonna let sissy boy beat ya?" suddenly recognizing their earlier spit victim.

George cracked the back of the toad's head. "Cap it, toad boy."

Five-four and Sal looked exasperated. I sensed his desperation and anticipated something dirty but not the foot he stuck out to trip me. Down I went. The ball got loose and Sal scooped it up. I got to my feet as fast as I could but Sal was already setting to shoot. I lunged and just missed tipping his shot and watched as the ball hit the front of the rim then the backboard and rolled around the rim… and out.

"Thank you St. Whatever Your Name is… maybe St. George?" I felt awful indebted.

I got the rebound, cleared the ball and with Sal gasping for breath, fired one from the top of the key… swish and a tie game.

The game was in my hands and some show time in order. Sal was digging in. I dribbled right, reverse spun back left and watched Sal trip and fall down trying to cover the move. Enjoying Sal's humiliation, I stood in one place, dribbling, and waited for him to get up, giving him a chance to reset and extending his humiliation.

Sal's frustration was too much and he charged me with flailing arms, screaming as he came. Still dribbling, I sidestepped and ducked, missing his swings. He lost his balance and fell on his stomach. With no one between me and the basket, I dribbled right, tweenered back left, reverse spun back right, looked down at the fallen brat and laid the winning point in with my left hand.

The ball fell through the net and bounced three times listlessly. It was the only sound in the gym. Everyone was in shock. I gave George a high five as I strutted to the back of the line acting as nonplussed as I could. Sal was still motionless, face down on the gym floor. The skinny kid with the white legs, who chopped ice from the alleys in winter to learn those moves, had spoken. I looked over and one of Sal's toads was helping him up. Sal pushed him away.

The bell rang. It was over. I raced to the locker room, leaving Sal in my wake. Without a word, I stripped naked and walked straight into the shower room ignorant of anyone's glances. 'Might as well get all this done the same day,' I thought.

There were no bumps the rest of the day, only some talk that the skinny kid with white legs had pantsed Sal and made him look bad. I sauntered home immersed in feelings of accomplishment, knowing that I had gone from total despair to total vindication.

"It's not about getting knocked down, it's about getting back up," Bridie would say.

I slipped in the back of Cloonmore, slamming the holey screen door and declaring my presence.

"How'd it go today, Sean. Were the tea leaves on?" Bridie asked from the kitchen.

"For the first two hours I think we had the cup upside down Ma, but after that you called it like you had the script."

"And how'd the coat look?"

"Natty, Ma, only one without gold buttons."

Tryout Tragedy

Tryouts for the basketball team loomed as a big opportunity and challenge. I was nervous about my chances, being so small and skinny, but I was determined to throw caution to the wind and give it my all, come what may. Whipping Sal and asserting some semblance of game gave me a little confidence...but that was against Sal. The first day in the locker room had me worried, too, because I was buried amongst a lot of big hairy guys who were stronger and faster. Tryouts were right after school and that's when I did my afternoon route so the next hurdle facing me was getting someone to fill in. I recruited my brother Mike who reluctantly agreed. "You got three days, Bub," he said.

Tryout day neared. I had established some reputation with my battle against Sal but the coach hadn't seen any of that. After Sal's comeuppance, word spread that I had some game. I might not be able to beat you up but I could probably dribble around you and lay one in. Asserting myself on the hardwood kept the other dogs like Sal at bay. Thanks to my guardian angel, George, and the countless hours I played hoops in the alley I had retrieved my dignity and gained some respect. I was able to walk the halls with my head held high even though I still couldn't see over anybody.

Sal hadn't taken his beating by the skinny little kid too well. After getting embarrassed in front of his toads and being left lying on the gym floor like a discarded rag you would think that he'd be seeking revenge, but he never bothered me again. I think he knew my reaction would be a little different the next time he decided to be a rat, and I always had George in reserve. His henchmen were a different story, though, and saw an opportunity to get even with him because he treated them the same way he had treated me.

You see, Sal was rich and could only get friends because he bought them. It creates subliminal resentment and the quasi friends needed some payback too. They wouldn't let him forget it.

"At least you didn't get shut out, Sal."

"Does your little sister beat you too?"

"Why don't you try badminton?" were some of the taunts that got hurled his way.

"Every dog has his day," Bridie would say.

I turned the page and learned that the next time something like the 'big spit' happened, I would disregard personal safety and social positioning and attack like a rabid dog and hope that someone would break it up before I got killed.

Basketball tryouts could lead to something that I had dreamed of for years: making the team. I had spent hours chopping ice and clearing the alley, just to play hoops in sub-freezing temperatures. I had risked the wrath of the nuns by sneaking into the gym, just to experience a dribble on a warm hardwood. In grade school, I had gotten my brains beat in by the Christians just to feel what it was like to have a uniform on and have someone to pass to. And now it was my big chance to put all of that adversity to work and make the team. No one could break me now; I had already been broken and more than once by the nuns, Sal, the Christians. And now I was healed. And what's stronger than scar tissue?

My grade school career hadn't prepared me much for what the high school challenge would bring. We didn't have a coach, barely enough basketballs, barely enough players, barely enough games. The tryouts would be my opportunity on a much grander scale. The notice went out and the day of the tryouts came. I showed up, eager but scared. I stood with my lily white legs next to guys a foot taller than me, twice as wide and a lot hairier. I was the smallest guy in the gym without a single leg hair, very few muscles or even my one friend present. That's what hit me: George wasn't there. I was all alone. I had established some credibility with my whipping of Sal, but he was peanuts compared to the real competition I'd face at tryouts. My plan was to be smart and try my hardest. The tryouts would last three days and each day the numbers would be pared.

After the first day of flashing my ball handling and knocking down shots, I went to the bulletin board and found my name right below Brand's. "Yesssss!" I fist pumped. The next day Brand was gone but there I was right under Ahern, the funeral director's son; two down and one to go. There were twenty-five guys left for twenty spots. Day three came and I was sore and had blisters on my feet not ever having played at such an intense level. The scrimmage got tough and physical, not my game. I usually survived on guile and quickness and as the critical tryout progressed, I felt like I hadn't distinguished myself. Time was running out on my dream. Everyone seemed better than me.

On the last day with just minutes left in the scrimmage, I knew that I hadn't done enough to make the team. I got the ball on the wing, shot faked, got my guy off his feet, dribbled right and fired. This was no time for a pass. It swished through.

As the opposing point guard brought the ball up court I had noticed that he always went to the right on his entry passes. I anticipated his pass, knocked the ball down with my left hand, stole it and dribbled the length of the court. As I started my layup, I felt the point guard's rage and hairy legs coming down on my layup and threw a reverse spin move on him and laid the ball in. Unable to stop, he went crashing into the padded brick wall and slapped it hard sending a bang into the gym and drawing attention to the moment. Sensing his emotional state, I knew he would do something dumb and he did, flinging the inbounds pass without looking.

Bridie had taught, "You'll never do anything well when you're mad."

I faked that I was running back down court and suddenly reversed, snatched his errant and rageful pass and laid it in again. Take that, I thought. The buzzer sounded and day three was over. I had done all that I could and nervously awaited the next day's posting. On judgment day, school ended and I rushed down to the gym and scoured the list on the bulletin board for my name. Ahern was gone, but so was I. I turned and stumbled away broken hearted.

"Why the long face?" came from nowhere. It was the coach and I muttered, "…didn't make it."

"Check again," he advised and I raced back and went from top to bottom and there I was, right under Zanoni. He chuckled, "I don't know the alphabet very well and that'll teach you to check the whole list."

I must have been a second thought, ending up beneath Zanoni, but that didn't matter now. All that counted was…I had made it. Made the team! The coach put his palm out and I slapped him five.

"That move, swish and steal at the end sealed the deal," he said.

My excitement was unbridled and I skipped all the way home. When I got home my brother Mike with his ink stained hands greeted me with, "I'm not doing your route tomorrow."

The next day, I was torn between my responsibility to my route and the tuition that I would need to earn for school and going to basketball practice. I skipped hoops and did my route, and the next day and the next day… and I never went back. Earning my keep and my allegiance to those dastardly routes won out and stuck a pin in my life-long dream. I never went to my parents or anyone else to share my dilemma and no one ever came to me. It was the age of non-communication when troubles weren't discussed and conundrums weren't addressed and the end of my basketball career. My only solace was that I had made it but it would never be enough.

It will always be my biggest regret.

The Heretic Boy

After the basketball tragedy, and it was a tragedy, I decided to concentrate on doing the best I could at school. I kept the route going and saved my pay for tuition day, often wondering "what might have been" as I pegged another afternoon edition onto a porch. What would it be like heading down to the gym every day and slipping on my school colors on game day, dancing in the layup line with the cheerleaders looking at my skinny legs? I made up for the total disappointment of not being on the team by getting almost straight A's. I had to be good at something.

Each week on Saturday afternoons my fifty-cent bonuses were exhausted at the local diner on grilled cheese deluxes and chocolate shakes. I couldn't go back to Dee's where I feared running into Turk and his ill-gotten bankroll. My big chance with the basketball team was over and I had to satisfy myself and my fantasies with games in the alley. Why didn't the coach call when he saw me missing? I'll never know.

In school, I was taking all the standard classes, Algebra, English, History, Religion and Latin. And it was Latin that introduced me to my favorite teacher and next adventure.

"Zeus," Mr. Falla declared, as the lightning cracked on a rainy day outside our Latin 101 class. Mr. Falla was short in stature and wide in girth but highly respected by all. He added a hint of humor to our class which was much appreciated given the dour atmosphere of my other classes with the priests. My high school was serious and you'd better be, too. Falla taught us Latin, a requirement that made little sense to me then and even less now, since the language had been dead for centuries. Why weren't we learning about something else that would have application to our futures, like sex education, or typing, or personal finance or how to replace a broken spoke? Everyone would someday have a partner and a house and a kitchen and everyone had a bike.

But that wasn't the way at our school. As far as I could see we had to learn things that most commoners couldn't understand. It gave us a perception of heightened status, an elevated perch from which to look down upon the others. There was nothing common about Catholicism. Elevating our status was the exercise we practiced every day and, initially, I bought into it. At that time, I hoped to become a doctor and Latin would help writing those prescriptions that only the pharmacist could read.

Mr. Falla was a refreshing break from the authoritarian priests. In the priests' classes it was "think straight, sit straight, look straight ahead." There was never any room for digression from the subject matter, or any humor. Mr. Falla was different. After the bland Latin lessons he would leave room for open discussion, laughter and ideas. Despite my skepticism about the need for Latin, Falla introduced us to something that I learned to love – mythology and its glorious and entertaining stories. Reading mythology was much better than reading the Bible, whose stories were just as farfetched but were force-fed as true and the *Word of God*. Mythology enveloped the life lessons that were the intent of the whole religious exercise without the onus of trying to believe they had really happened. The myths with their gods and goddesses, nymphs and monsters, were fun reading, entrancing and stimulating. These rich tales fertilized the seed that bloomed into my skepticism of Catholicism and all its tenets.

My doubts about all of the Catholic theology had taken root in grade school and began with my inability to understand that there could be three persons in one being; "The Holy Trinity" they called it. We could get three in a bed and three on a bike but three people in one carcass? My queries were met with the ubiquitous trump card of, "You must have faith, Sean," and although I'd nod my head, I knew that I had very little and probably never would have enough. I was a rationalist. If something didn't make sense, I wasn't buying it. I had been challenged my entire childhood by having faith in more secular passions such as the White Sox and Bears and my prayers rarely worked. My teams always lost the big ones.

At the time I felt like the Catholics had designed a whole play book of fantastic events and ideologies which separated them from other ordinary religions. And that was the way they established superiority over the competition. There was the Immaculate Conception and the Resurrection and the Assumption, and Mary appearing at Fatima and Lourdes and Knock, and then all the miracles like the bread and the loaves multiplying and the Red Sea splitting and on and on and on. With ownership of all these glorious and supernatural events how could Catholicism not be the one true faith? How could anyone not feel that they were riding in the lead car, walking on the chosen path or flying toward heaven and eternal happiness? It was straight and simple: believe and you had it made. And for fourteen years I bought the playbook and ingested the tenets. That is, until the three-in-one and Mr. Falla's mythology aroused my suspicions and began to undermine my Catholic beliefs. Pagans and Heathens were our competition. And then one day I looked up what they were and discovered that they were people who just had a different take on things and adored nature gods. What is wrong with that?

Mythology taught the essential lessons of life and how to have wariness to its temptations, without the obsession of thinking that the fantastic stories had really happened. I knew that Hercules couldn't reverse the flow of a river but his efforts taught me creativity and determination. I knew that Pandora, the first woman, who was sent by Zeus couldn't introduce all evils by opening her box but it sure made me wary of women and their seductions. I knew that Prometheus had hoodwinked Zeus out of fire and given the incendiary tool to the common man but I didn't forget the reality that the cavemen invented it. It was great fun, all without the cost of ideological freedoms. Catholicism, on the other hand, insisted that you believe their fantastic stories and pay dearly if you didn't, with eternity in Hell or a crisping at the stake.

By the end of grade school, I had begun to fake my allegiance but my introduction to mythology upped the momentum. How could Jesus' mother bear him and still be a virgin? How could Mary herself have been the product of an immaculate conception? Why would innocent babies be born with original sin and need baptism to cleanse them? If they died without baptism, which happened, how could any reasonable God condemn them to eternity in Limbo? Is this something a loving and merciful God could do? And as for eternal life, who wanted to live forever anyway?

I finally got a chance to air my thoughts when Mr. Falla announced an essay paper on the effects of mythology in our everyday lives and how it related to Catholicism. I sharpened my pencil and began to write with a rapacious glee, finally embracing an outlet for my religious skepticism. This was it, the ultimate goal of education, getting someone to think and reason for themselves and display their original thoughts. I poured my heart out and all the doubts that I'd been harboring. I illustrated and drew comparisons between the acknowledged myth of the great Greek stories and the mandated belief in the Christian ones. I cast doubt on the Immaculate Conception and the Annunciation, a God who mouths mercy and invents Hell and Purgatory, the wholesale marketing of indulgences, the Resurrection, and just about anything else that sounded fantastic and improbable and was only concocted to elevate us to superiority. I let them have it and good, and handed in my essay with an esoteric joy. Then, the day came to get back our essays and everyone's name was called but mine.

'BeJasus,' I thought, 'they've mounted the work in the library or sent it to the Smithsonian for publishing!' A sense of pride came over me for my ingenuity and my growth as a student and brashness as an author. This would only be the start of many more such writings and the development of my reason and academic pursuit of the unknown.

"Mr. Brennan, could you see me after class?" Falla asked.

'No problem, I've got plenty of time for some accolades,' I thought. My route and the news would be late today and for good reason. When class was over I approached Mr. Falla with a sense of pride and accomplishment but noticed that he kept his head down and his eyes averted. This wasn't like him. He was usually exuberant about declaring an "Ace" for my work and I was sure that I had earned one.

"Was this all your work?"

"Yes sir, every word," I answered proudly.

Mr. Falla grimaced, placed his hands on the top of the desk and then slowly pushed himself backwards, pushed down with a grunt and slowly rose out of his chair. The chair made a slow scratching sound as it scraped against the tiles. Concern set in. 'Is there something wrong,' I thought. He stood up and looked at me with a sense of sympathy…for what…and started to walk toward the door. "Follow me," he ordered and down the hall we marched, me trailing in complete silence and now engulfed in self-doubt. As I followed, his slumped shoulders made me feel like he was leading his best friend to the gallows.

'Oh, it's a surprise,' I thought, 'and they don't want to give it away.' Then, we turned into the principal's office and I caught sight of a mortified Bridie standing in the corner. Garbed in her usual house dress (she never wore pants) her look was reminiscent of the durty picture episode and ripped right into me. The corner of her mouth had the Bridie cock. She said nothing; she didn't need to. I was too stunned to speak, knowing that Bridie's presence and her look meant doom.

"Have a seat," Falla ordered. Feeling tentative, I raised my right arm and gave Bridie a weak wave. Her pose and stance didn't budge. There was silence save for the clatter of the secretary's typewriter...and then that stopped too, and now, complete silence. I looked away from Bridie, needing a distraction and stared straight down at my scuffed shoes. It didn't work. I could still feel her wrath, her stance, her folded arms, her cocked head, all uniting in one strafing surge to rip a hole in my heart.

"What was I putting this poor woman through? What was the hierarchy going to put *me* through?"

The secretary couldn't resist taking a stab too, and peered over her bifocals with an extended look of revulsion. I was surrounded by disgust. The office secretaries were as omniscient as Alfred back at St. Edmund; they knew everyone's business, always thought you were guilty and only took the job because they got to see all of the executions...like the one at hand. It wasn't for the money, with the way the Cardinal paid.

I twitched in my seat waiting for the next axe to fall as the principal's door opened, breaking the silence. I kept my eyes glued to the floor. I could barely breathe. The principal's clanging rosary beads broke the silence as he came lumbering out of his office. He stood in the doorway as his imposing figure cast a shadow from the light beyond upon my constricted and cowering countenance.

"Would you all please step in," he asked with his usual impersonal tone. I stood, still looking anywhere but toward Bridie and shuffled my way through the door. I was walking into another inquisition without anything for a bail-out and quickly began to design an escape. The blasphemy in my essay was sure cause for damnation. But that would be the penance from God. I still had a lifetime to atone for that, but how was I going to get around the hammer that was coming down from the priest? The punishment from the priest was the cause for real concern. These guys could make your life on earth very unpleasant so I got my wheels turning in order to mitigate matters. There was no saint to bail me out this time because now he hated me, too. You couldn't blast the canons like I had in the essay without alienating everyone, all saints included. I looked up to see my essay, the one I had been so certain would catapult me to stardom and fame, face up on the desk and slashed with red pen markings.

The principal began, "Most of what you have written in your essay qualifies as heresy, young man." He looked at me with disdain. "There is no tolerance for such balderdash at this school," he continued. "And it wasn't long ago that the penalty was a lot more severe than what you're getting today."

'Oh,' I thought, my heretic beliefs rising like a fever, 'Are you out of firewood, then, and you won't be able burn me at the stake for heresy?' I was recalling the Spanish Inquisition and the torture and burnings *at the stake* that had taken the lives of millions at the Church's hands. The Catholic priests hadn't included that bit of history. I had happened upon it, perusing an old encyclopedia.

The principal didn't enumerate.

"Well, he learned none of that in our home," Bridie chirped, throwing me the ole' dagger look and trying to clear her conscience.

The Father continued, "I know he didn't, Bridie, coming from a good Irish Catholic home, like the one you run. We get this sort of thing when they start to think they're smarter than two thousand years of Christianity. It's a common failing that needs to be nipped in the bud." He again cast his glance on me. "Young man, do you believe anything that you've written here?"

"Every blasphemous word," I thought. However, I could see being truthful would not serve me here, and it was time to slither. "Father," I said, "I don't believe anything I've written, I was only trying to illustrate how difficult it was to understand the mysteries of faith because there are so many of them and they reach so deep for our puny intelligence to grasp. I intended only that it requires great and unbridled faith to accept the mysteries."

The priests loved calling them "mysteries" as if they would figure them out some day.

Bridie softened her glare. I was selling my soul again but I didn't care. I only wanted to get the Hell out of there, hop on my bike, fill my basket with newspapers and inform the world. I wanted to be free.

"Will we have future problems with these errant thoughts, Sean?" The principal asked.

"Oh, no Father!" I said. "Over the next four years I'm going to regurgitate the whole litany anytime they ask for it,' I thought. 'You'll get it staid and straight.' Aloud, I said, "Father I need to learn to write with more clarity; it wasn't my intention to create this much confusion."

The principal seemed to buy my explanation but seemed unable to grant acquittal. They never could just let you go. He placed his hand over his mouth as if to symbolize my silencing and mulled over his next move and then succumbed to his executioner instincts.

"I'd like an essay on the great mysteries young man, just to make sure that your part of the flock and not straying away...you know a black sheep. And a stop at the confessional, make sure you apologize to God the Father when you're there."

"I certainly will, Father...and to Mary, too," I finished.

There was silence as he nodded, which gave us our exit. Bridie escorted me down the hall and out the door without twisting my ear, and at the bike rack grabbed my arm and asked me where I had gotten such ideas?

"Ma," I said, "I know that there is no magic and that God is probably too busy to bother with our paltry lives, but I've prayed and hoped for a miracle many times, just like the ones in the Bible and it's never worked. Prayer has a high rate of failure. I know that material things are not important, but there are so many things that we need. And I always thought that if I believed strongly enough someone, somewhere, somehow would throw us a bone. I do my school work, earn my route money and most importantly, think for myself, just like you've taught us. And I've had some thoughts that a lot of the teachings are malarkey. Not yours, the Church's. You've taught me for years that there aren't any short cuts and anything that's worth while takes hard work and determination. The miracles are all too fantastic for me because I've never seen one and don't think I ever will." I listed them: "Jesus rises from the dead, Mary's a virgin after giving birth, the Red Sea parts and five loaves turn into five hundred." "I don't buy it, Ma, because I don't need to and believing that stuff doesn't make the man. I'm sticking with you, Ma, and everything that *you've* taught me, especially the part about keeping an open mind. And I'm going to leave the miracles for the really needy, the ones that can't think for themselves."

I left her agape and aghast. I hopped on my bike not waiting for the response that she couldn't give, and rode off, waving without looking and feeling the freedom of the wind and the catharsis of my words, leaving Bridie stunned that she had a son with such thoughts.

"Watch for traffic!" "Be careful!" Then the prophetic, "Look both ways!"

She was all the prayers I would ever need.

My First Kiss

The rest of my freshman year was marked by conformity and a staid attitude. I left the trailblazing alone after failing to mount much momentum with my heretical paper on Catholic ideologies. They tried to squash my creativity like an ant hill at a picnic but just like an ant hill, you can't ever kill them all. My ideas were on life support but not completely snuffed out. I got the message and started feeding them the company doctrine, regurgitating the status quo and as a result aced most everything. I gave them nothing more to worry about which is the way they wanted it; abject compliance and total allegiance were the formulas. I kept my desire for creative ideas and heretical thoughts, simmering but reticent. As the school year neared an end and summer approached, the year of blind conformity fostered a need for adventure. It didn't matter where or what kind, just some adventure. Up until now, my adventures were of the fantasy sort, the ones I fostered by scanning the tattered atlas.

Some thoughts of the opposite sex began to emerge as summer dawned, but they were rather nascent and certainly unfulfilled. Bridie's philosophy was to keep her lads far from the girls. When Bridie landed from Ireland in '29, she brought with her all the archaic Catholic tenets about sex. The attitude was summed up in one word: "Forbidden!" The core belief was that sex was for procreation only...you know, make more Catholics but don't have a good time doing it. That's how most things were, being a Catholic, if it felt good it probably was on the 'Don't Do' list.

Bridie kept my older brothers on tight leashes and away from the fillies by constricting their social involvement. There were no dances or dates or mixers or any events that involved girls. The extent of our heterosexual activities was reading the "durty" magazines in the alley and maybe a smooch or two with the O'Brian girls in the darkened garages during games of *hide and seek*. We knew nothing of what came after the smooches but we did know that there was more exploration needed.

The two oldest Brennan boys, Tom and Padraig, accepted and never challenged Bridie's Draconian ways but the third, Michael, rebelled and upset the apple cart. Tom had eyes for a cute little French girl named Claire who lived down the block but his admiration never got him closer than half of a block away. Padraig was the same – admiring many from afar. Michael, two years older than me, was a different story and bolder than a thief at the blind man's newsstand.

He broke the ice that imprisoned our interest in girls and started the rebellion from which the three youngest lads would benefit. A redhead, Michael hated the rules even more than I did and was determined to get smooched and touch the girls; it didn't matter where. He hooked into a Prod who lived a few blocks away and who would sit on her front steps waiting for Mike to deliver her newspaper. She was not interested in the newspaper. She confessed later that she would set her alarm early just to see Mike deliver the morning newspaper from her bedroom window.

Once Mike had established his initial and main squeeze he wouldn't be denied. The smooching mattered a bit, but it was the rebellion that really mattered. Mike was taking on a formidable foe in Bridie. Many a night, standing up to the autocracy, he stormed from Cloonmore as we watched in awe. At first Mike would sneak out. But Bridie caught on to that pretty quickly when she couldn't find him in the alley.

"Where have you been?"

"Out."

"Where?"

"Out!"

He would never say where he had been and it infuriated Bridie. And then he took the next step to total disregard and would announce his departures.

"I'm going out."

"No you're not. Don't leave this house."

And off Mike would go, down the backstairs, jumping on his bike and riding off down the alley and to some smooch session behind some dimly lit staircase. The screen door never slammed because Bridie was always in hot pursuit and would catch it just in time. But she never caught Mike.

Bridie would recruit my oldest sister who could drive, and scour the alleys in pursuit of Mike and his damsel but it did no good. Sometimes she'd track him down and order him home and he'd run and run, leaving many a broken-hearted lass with empty arms and closed eyes waiting for the next kiss. Her efforts failed, Michael had a head harder than Bridie's and a will to match. Over time he wore Bridie down and she gave up the battle and surrendered. Perhaps she reasoned that a few adolescent smooches weren't so bad after all, but 'don't go any farther!'

We were all amazed at Mike's bluster and determination and thankful that he had worn down Bridie and opened the door for the last three lads. I got to watch Bridie's dragnets from the cheap seats and knew there must be something out there more than just basketball and routes if Mike dared to defy Bridie. Mike was no dummy and was on to something.

I searched my mind one day, trying to come up with a target for my newly discovered pursuit...someone to smooch. What could Michael be on to? I was going to find out. Names flew through my thoughts, Spagattini? Nah, too skinny.

Charlotte? Nah, too tall.

Masters? Nah, too chunky.

Sally? Nah, mean older brother.

Haggerty? Too ritzy, but maybe, *Ummm*, Yea, let's try Haggerty.

There were challenges but she was just the right size, cute and my hero. Haggerty was the one in the yellow sundress whom I had met at the park. I had dismissed my chances with her, thinking that she was out of my league. But then again as I reviewed the scene back at the arbor, she had been happy to see me, I had made her laugh and she did invite me to sit next to her. And Murphy was out of the picture.

I kept building a case. In school she always knew the answer, always had done her homework and was always the picture of confidence. Jayne was the Doctor's daughter; she was accomplished, smart, spunky and just enough out of reach to make this a challenge. She lived on the rich side of Lake Street and I'm sure her socks always matched. It was time to give her a taste of a South Side ruffian like myself. I ran the idea past Michael and he rolled his eyes saying that she was out of our league. "That's the whole point," I said. "If I can get a smooch from her, I'm on my way." Make no small plans.

It took me awhile to muster up enough courage to embark on my quest and a few times I got to the pay phone over at the Arms Hotel and choked. But one summer night I got to the phone disgusted with my past foibles, paused and dropped the coins in the slot. Every *ding, ding,* as the coins descended the slot, heightened my angst.

"You know I see an angel in the leaves today," Bridie said. "Is there something you want to tell me?"

"No ma."

The phone began to ring and my heart began to thump and I began to hang up and before I could I heard, "Hello."

It was Jayne's angelic voice. Jayne – my heroine in grade school whom I secretly admired from afar was on the other end of the line.

"Hello?" She said again, this time asking. She was one of those museum pieces, nattily dressed and organized and at the top of the class and from the ritzy side of town and unattainable. She was out of reach – that's how I felt about every girl; all the good ones were out of reach. What interest could they have in a skinny little mick whose wardrobe was his brothers and social status undefined? My life was in the alley, swinging and shooting, running and getting dirty and...I needed to change and I wanted my world to expand and bring me to new things and ideas that had always been beyond my reach. I was ready to sail and I didn't care how high the waves were. I stammered and stuttered, "Jaaayne?"

"Hello?" she sounded firm, waiting for an answer. I had my finger on the receiver ready to end my adventure but my frozen state kept me from pressing it down.

"Who is this?" she demanded.

"Uhhh, Sean," I finally gasped.

"Oh, hiiiiii Sean,"

I couldn't go back after that welcome. The ice broke a bit and my tippy toes felt the cold waters, which were starting to warm. It sounded like there was some mutual interest, so I continued.

"I saw you coming out of Dee's on my route yesterday and just wondered how your summer was going?"

"Oh, I saw you too and heard that noisy spoke on your bike. Why didn't you say Hello?"

"Oh, when I'm doing my route, nothing can get in the way."

Are you kidding, I'm too goddamn scared.

"Well it's nice that you called and I always wondered why you never called after our day in the park."

"But that's over and we can talk now."

"I sure would like to see you this summer."

What? This was supposed to be harder than this. She's supposed to hang up on me and be insulted that I even called. Was Bridie *right?*

"Girls that know what they want can be dangerous," she'd warn.

Should I hang up and run? There's risk in this world. I paused and decided to explore further.

"Still dating Murphy?" I asked. I knew the answer because I had heard the slap and later seen Murphy arm and arm with a busty blonde who was a head taller than the shrimp, but I wanted to hear it from Jayne.

"Oh, no, he was a little fast for me and couldn't get those times tables when I tried to help him. I don't want to have anything to do with a dumbo like him. He didn't know, "Nine times nine.""

"Eighty-one!" I blurted out, passing the test and leaving Murphy in my dust. The conversation flowed from there until she proposed a rendezvous Saturday night at her baby-sitting job. Mike had taught me that the best opportunity for some smooches was on a babysitting job, on a nice comfortable couch and not trying to make moves in some dusty stairwell. I was startled, even scared, by Jayne's suggestion but knew that I couldn't turn back now, not if I wanted to get to the big leagues.

"See you on Saturday," I committed.

I hung up the phone and fell into a trance at what had just happened. This wasn't supposed to happen like this. How could a girl be so unafraid and confident? What was I getting myself into? Here was someone who wanted to be with me. And Jayne was smart and rich and lived in a nice house and probably had a bike with all the spokes. You just never know, do you?

There was no turning back now, full throttle forward big guy. I dipped into my savings account, pillaging my tuition money and snuck off to the department store on my ragtag bike, the spoke was still broken and clicking on the frame with each revolution. Intending to appear as a complete makeover, I bought a crisp madras shirt and some khakis that fit my style, and then stashed my purchase in the garage rafters so no one could find them and guess what I was up to.

Not by choice, I was part of the dupers, the kids who combed their hair over and wore penny loafers. Our nemeses were the greasers like Murphy, who combed their hair back after soaking it in Vaseline, wore Cuban heels and leather jackets. We were way cuter. They looked more dangerous.

Saturday was inching closer and would bring me north of Lake Street into the high rent district and I had to look the part. As far as the north people were concerned, south of Lake St. was where the ruffians lived, where you had to be careful, on the wrong side of the tracks.

Everything about my Saturday night plan had to be done on the hush-hush. Publicity would bring out my hound dog brothers. "What's her name," and "Where ya going?"

This venture required secrecy. I planned on dressing in the garage after sneaking out. Even though Mike had broken the ice with Bridie's inquisitions, Bridie still had her antennae out for the youngest three lads. I was not going to ask her for permission and risk not getting the smooch. I was willing to suffer any punishment that getting caught would bring. I knew the feeling.

I figured that on Saturday night, Bridie's war with Michael would create enough distraction to give me an escape route, and I was right. I slid out the back door while Bridie was at the front door screaming at Michael as he ran down the front stairs, ignoring her pleas to stop.

In the garage, I slipped into my new duds and walked over to the grimy window that served as a mirror. I wiped away the grime, in circular motions with the butt of my hand and took an admiring long gander. Wow, is Jayne in for a treat. I gave myself the nod, started for my bike, turned back for one last inspection…pretty cute…nice upgrade, I thought and fled down the alley in a burst of speed before I could be discovered and stopped. The *clink clink clink* of the spoke came faster with each rotation matching the speeding beats of my heart.

The excitement was electrifying. I pedaled my arse off and was out of earshot and eyesight within seconds. *So far, so good.* I was on my way with the wind rushing through my hair and freedom and excitement flowing through my bones.

About two blocks from my house it started to dawn on me again that I was cruising into a big unknown, and my old fears of 'what the Hell are you doing?' set in. My urge to break from the bosom of Cloonmore, overcome my phobias and discover the outside world was too strong. With each turn of the pedals my resolve grew.

I journeyed on in a state of exuberance, north of Lake Street, to invade this upscale neighborhood with its mowed and manicured lawns, expansive homes and people of another ilk. I was lost but ecstatic – searching each house for its address and then I saw the numbers that Jayne had given me…321. The countdown had started.

I circled around the block a couple of times, mired in abating self-doubt, building up some courage and fighting temptations to turning back. 'Oh no you don't buddy, you've come this far and you're going through with it.' I looked for a spot to hide my homemade wheels and keep my birthplace a secret. Sight of my ride would be the first sign that there was a ruffian invader, so I tucked the old relic well behind the first hedgerow I saw. I took a deep breath and scanned the area for Bridie and her chauffeur. The coast was clear. I dusted off my threads, pulled up my belt buckle, took a deep breath and started for the house.

It was a mansion, the likes I had never seen or been in and my walk up the stairs felt like a trip to the altar. I tiptoed just like I would do at church, not making a sound. Ahead of me was another tabernacle, only Jesus wasn't inside this one...Jayne, and my first smooch was. Intimidated, I went to ring the doorbell, hesitated with thoughts of escape and closed my eyes and pushed. "*Ding Dong*" went the bell and "*Ding Dong*" went my heart. I gazed around the grounds trying to act like I had been there before and began to hope that maybe I got stood up. No such luck as the door opened and a titillating Jayne blushed, "Oh Hi, Sean."

She was in her yellow sundress. "Remember?" as she spread the hem wide with each hand and curtsied, like a debutante on stage. Oh, boy.

I stepped into the foyer and into one of those mansion type homes that seemed so far from my humble Cloonmore. My head rotated in awe from ceiling to floor. Chairs and sofas matched, they all had four legs, there were no dust balls and the walls were painted and without handprints and there were no missing balustrades.

"Where's your bike?" she asked. My mouth had gone dry and I swallowed deep and moistened my cheeks with my tongue.

"Oh, I put it behind the hedge so no one would steal it." No one would steal that thing unless they had life insurance, I thought. She grabbed me by the hand and led me into the living room.

"Come on in there's a good movie on and I have some pop and potato chips," she said.

"Oh, I like them."

So far I didn't have to do a thing; Jayne was in control. She sat on the sofa with her knees at a slight angle and patted the spot right next to her with her left hand, just like she did on the park bench. I sat down with plenty of room between us, not wanting to crush her fingers. Pop and chips, I thought, already the evening was worth every ounce of angst that I went through to get here, only a Western would make the night complete.

"Where are the kids?" I asked.

"Oh, I put them to bed early. I wanted us to be alone." She slid closer to me on the couch, exhausting any open space. The temperature was rising.

I tensed up and the nerves set in. I had gone and done it again. Gotten myself into a real fix, only this time I couldn't run. I thought about asking for something in the kitchen and slipping out when she left, but valor seized my wimpy thoughts and I decided to persevere.

'What the Hell comes next?' I thought. Are there bail out saints for this one? Hell, how would the saints know what to do? They grew up in a seminary.

John Wayne and a good saloon brawl got me to relax a little and forget the moment. The rest of the evening was steeped in silence with occasional small talk and then the final scene beamed out of the TV with Wayne grabbing the girl and laying a good one on her as the sun set. This was my moment. Haggerty was vulnerable, her face gone soft and melting with Wayne's kiss.

I turned, held her arms and planted one on her trembling lips. She closed her eyes calling for more but one was all I had. I pulled away, triumphant. I had done it. Kissed Haggerty and on the north side to boot. It wasn't about sex, just triumph.

"Can you stay a little longer," she beseeched.

"I'd love to, but I've got my route in the morning" I said. "And the news can't wait." Routes were getting in the way again.

Jayne walked me to the door claiming to have had a wonderful evening. As I stepped through the doorway, I turned to bid goodnight and she grabbed my arms and kissed me. "There, we're even," she said. "Let's keep the count going next week."

I waved as I pulled my bike from behind the hedges and rode off, the spoke still clanging and tire rubbing. I didn't hear either one, my mind deep in a haze of glory. I couldn't believe that I had just dressed like a dude, kissed Jayne Haggerty, asserted myself on the high side of town and that she wanted more. But reaching this summit scared me and as the days passed, my verve shriveled like hot plastic in a fire pit and I never called back. There never was a next week. It wasn't Haggerty. It was me and my fear of what might follow...

Summer of Love: The Frisco Frolic

It was the summer of '68 and often I'd spend nights paging through our atlas. The covers had been ripped off long ago and the United States was shrinking, half the states were missing. But California somehow survived, and that's where my sister Riley lived and my brother Tom was playing Hippie.

Maybe...just maybe?

I knew Bridie would never let me go alone so I hatched a plan with Reno to go with me. He had an aunt out there and I knew that would make Bridie rest a bit easier.

"Yeah, I'll go," Reno said. He had saved some dough from sweeping up the sawdust at his old man's butcher shop. It never dawned on me that I would actually get on a plane and go but my plan started to hatch when I realized that my sister Riley was living near Frisco and my big brother Tom who had bugged out was missing but probably nearby.

Bridie had a soft spot for Tom and was broken-hearted because we hadn't heard from him in a while. Bridie might just give a green light to my plan if I could sell it as a retreat to save Tom from himself.

"Hey Ma, I've been saving my route money and thinking about visiting Riley in Cal and putting out a dragnet for Tom? Whadda'ya think?"

"Only if you stay with your sister and put your foot up Tom's arse when you see him."

I was outta here.

Riley was cute, smart and liberal, had fallen in love, married and moved to California seeking all of the adventure and new ideas that were just sprouting in Chicago but well blossomed in

Cal. Riley had always been an inspiration to me because of her wonderment. She was a striking contrast to our regular world of 'don't ask questions and follow the prescribed protocol'. And when she bolted for California seeking a new, fresh, and exciting world, my thoughts went to someday having a place to visit. One of those spots in the atlas that I had circled and dreamt of.

Tom was the oldest boy and a complete malcontent, but a silent one. He never voiced a word of displeasure or protest. He just kept right on doing whatever he wanted to. It was his way or the highway and if you ever saw some of his work...well, he should have been listening a little. He baffled the nuns and tortured them and I've often thanked him for his methods because Tom just plain ole' drove them nuts. No punishment or threat ever worked on him and he had a tormenting way of smiling through any sentence that they could give him.

Bridie worried about Tom, the oldest boy who had defied Catholic protocol for years and finally bugged out after a year of college and a short stint in the Air Force. Short, because he drove the sergeant's nuts too. They wanted him to make his bed so you could bounce a quarter off the stretched sheets, only Tom didn't have a quarter and had never made his bed in his life. When Tom entered boot camp in Texas it wasn't but a few days before he knew he was in the wrong place. Tom had two choices; one was to run and the other was to play on the soft heart of the camp administrator, who happened to be a mick from Chicago; McGillicuddy. Tom thought that running would mean a never ending chase so he took a shot at soft soaping McGilllicuddy. Every day he camped out at Mac's door and complained of a different malady and when he would get a one-on-one with Mac, who didn't want to be there either, he went into heavy detail about how bad he felt for Mac and how he would change places with him if he could. It took Tom one month to soften Mac up and on the day that Mac signed Tom's honorable discharge he proclaimed, "One of us has to get outta here." Despite needing fresh carnage for Viet Nam, Tom was free.

Thanks Mac.

Tom had taken on the nuns and the military and he had beaten both. He was back to being his own man and still quite single-minded and vowed that that was the last time anyone would ever get a hold of him.

After he had left home we didn't know where he was because he never bothered to write…except when he was hungry or needed a tenner.

When he did write and send us an address, Bridie would bundle up a care package full of sausage, crackers, and toilet paper and whatever else could make it through the mail without rotting. Tom never stayed in one place very long so the chase to find him was interminable.

After his stint fighting for his country, he went back to Oregon where he went back to singing, raising chickens and running laps around a track. Riley called one day and said that she thought she saw Tom getting off a bus in Frisco. It was rush hour and too crowded so Riley couldn't catch up to him. But she was pretty sure it was Tom. And then Bridie got a note in the mail from Tom with a return address in Frisco. It had been Tom. Bridie sent the usual care package and the search for Tom was on. It was '68, The Summer of Love…sounded like Tom was trying to get smooched too.

Tom was our hero back in the day and quite a pioneer. He stole the plates off of the EL-train gates at Lake Street and wired them to pilfered pipes from the neighbor, making our first weight lifting set. It didn't do us much good cause we couldn't lift them, only Tom could do that.

Often when Tom was missing we'd find him by just listening for the sound of the clanging plates coming from the basement. He was the first body builder in the neighborhood and the first at a lot of other things too. When we were little fellas and couldn't push the basketball to ten feet and make a basket, he cut the seat out of a chair and nailed it to the side of the house at 8 feet, just so we could taste success. His inventions were never pretty, Tom wasn't interested in aesthetics, but they were always effective.

On Sunday nights long before it was popular, he took us to the running track at the high school where he pried apart the bars in the wrought iron fence so we could get our heads through and made us do laps. Tom was always doing things before anyone else even thought of them.

He built a steam room in the basement with plastic sheets taped to the overhead pipes that ran down to the floor. Inside his plastic cove was a baby pool with a chair in the middle. He ran a hose from the hot water spigot in the basement, filled the pool and then sat in a chair in the middle. When the water cooled he had a kettle boiling on the kitchen stove. The whistle would go off and Tom would race up the stairs, getting a little exercise on the way, retrieve the kettle and replenish the hot water. His steams never lasted long cause the water would cool off too fast. But he tried. I still wish I had a picture of that one.

He raised chickens and ducks at Easter time until they croaked from disease or found a home in the heating ducts. Daddy would have to open the duct work and extricate Tom's flock, just so we could get some sleep. One day someone asked Tom who his favorite animal was and he responded, "I'd have to say the chicken." And he meant it.

He'd send away for all kinds of stuff that was advertised on the backs of the comic books and then sit at the top of the stairs and smirk when the salesmen were at the door asking for Tom

Brennan and get Daddy, his namesake. Daddy would curse out the salesmen and threaten them if they ever came back. Tom would just smile from the top of the stairs and fill out another coupon.

And he never obeyed the nuns or the priests. They'd beat him senseless and exact every punishment and he'd sit there and smile, further infuriating them. He was promoted from grade to grade only because no nun could take two years of him. He never read a manual or followed a rule or did anything that he was supposed to, or anything they wanted. He should have been put in a barn alongside a river, Tom's favorite natural place, with assorted tools and left alone. But no one ever realized that until it was too late. He'd still be there today, propped against a pile of wood, but like as not, the barn wouldn't.

Tom could work harder than anyone and took pride in his endurance. When you heard a distant saw or the beat of a hammer, you knew it was Tom busy at his newest invention. Yeah, Tom was Tom and would always be Tom and still is Tom. He lives near the Mississippi, rides his bike with a basket on the front and one on the back, just in case he finds a treasure and helps his buddy raise ducks for an animal preserve. Tom makes friends with everyone and has friends everywhere. The philosophy came from Bridie. "There's goodness in everyone."

The hippie movement came along and Tom succumbed, deserting inventing for communes, pot and free love. He left behind school, Catholicism, a forlorn Bridie, Daddy, routes and his little brothers. West was his general direction and he remained missing for months until a note with a San Francisco address showed up at Cloonmore. Bridie immediately sent her usual care package filled with salami, Irish bread, underwear, socks, a sweatshirt for the night chill and toilet paper. Bridie was famous for bringing toilet paper...right when you ran out.

Tom's new address was all I needed to convince Bridie to let me head west and make sure her first born son was coddled.

I had saved up some dough over the summer that was intended for tuition but I could always make more later and I'd rather spend my scratch on adventure than tuition and if I had to, just give the cardinal an IOU.

So with my own plane ticket, a shopping bag for a suitcase and 100 bucks cash, Reno and I left for Frisco, our maiden adventure. Neither of us knew what we were getting into. It was just go and whatever happened, happened. We would stay with Riley and let the rest just fall into place.

On the flight out I felt like a big shot sipping the free cokes and snacking on the free peanuts. "May I have another bag Miss?"

"You can have all the peanuts you want, cutie," the stewardess chirped bending over and thrusting her cleavage in my face. Lordy! I started ordering more peanuts just to get another view of her bosom and she happily complied. She was having fun too, watching my eyes grow wider and wider. Eight bags of peanuts later my stomach ached and my eyes were sore. I was digging the trip already. As we left the plane I thanked the stewardess for her lovely hospitality and salty chest...I mean peanuts.

"Catch you on the return trip," she warned.

"Order some more peanuts," I begged.

After we landed in Frisco and left the plane we walked down the terminal to the tambourine chants of some bald-headed guys dressed in orange chiffon, clogging the halls.

Never saw these guys in Chi. We stopped to stare, wondering what the exercise was all about. They ignored us except to ask for some cash and my membership but I only gave them some loose coins, keeping my independence my own. I felt like a big shot ignoring their pleas and walking on. The orange chiffon was a bit much.

The chants grew dimmer as we walked on and the shopping bag I had for luggage drew stares. Hey! All my socks match, my underwear's clean, I've got a handkerchief and my shirts ironed. It's progress.

Steered only by my tattered atlas, we hopped a bus and headed for Riley's pad in Santa Rosa taking in the Golden Gate Bridge, the hills, Victorian architecture and lots of hippies.

It was August 1968 and the Summer of Love. Our necks got sore turning with every new sight, street musicians and protesters and every crazy hipster, half-dressed and with glazed eyes.

"What's that smell," I asked Reno when we stepped off the bus. "Burnt hippie," he cracked. The cigarettes the hipsters were sharing were wrapped in wrinkly paper and smelled funny. We were in awe of every new thing we saw. It was awesome and scary, to two young crew cut lads from the Midwest descending into the eclectic world of California where every established thought was getting its ears blown away. Long hair, free sex, marijuana, no religion, braless women, women's lib, war protesters, pollution protesters, gay people and freedom from regular ordained existence; It was all here.

Riley was glad to see us and had forgotten what a crew cut altar boy face looked like. She had gotten a bit hip too, wearing a tie-dye blouse and fingering the beads that were draped around her neck.

"I have to work this week so you boys are on your own," she said. "Be careful, it's a bit zany out there."

The next morning we were on our way, hopping a bus at the station, riding through the mountains of Marin County, crossing the Golden Gate Bridge and setting out to discover Frisco for the first time.

We climbed every hill, saw every sight, smelled that funny smell everywhere but couldn't find Tom. At first we shied away from dipping into the culture that surrounded us, it was just too foreign. All we did was look. But on our third day, I said to Reno, "Let's just ask someone, what the Hell are we afraid of?"

We approached a hipster, playing his guitar and chanting a tune, who looked a bit sleepy.

"Can you help us find this address?" And I held the crumpled note up assuming that he could read. He moved his watery eyes over to the note, broke away from his song and said, "Wow, man, it's right around the corner."

We had had Tom's place surrounded and didn't know it. The dilapidated tenement was just blocks from Haight-Ashbury and the center of everything that was going on during the summer of love.

I knocked on the door and an oozy hippie girl with one breast exposed, answered. I tried to look her in the eye but didn't get far from the breast.

"Is Tom around," I nonchalantly asked sneaking one last peek at her nipple.

"You mean the guy from Chi?" she asked. "Wow, that rhymed," she surprised herself.

"Yea, good one," I praised, wondering if her other breast might peek out.

"You look a little outta place junior with that crew cut and buttoned down collar." she said.

"I'm an altar boy from Chicago and I'm on a mission."

"Not to convert me, I hope" she shot back and went into a hard giggle. "Hail Mary, fullo' grace," she sang.

"He's in the basement cutie, stop up when you can." And she closed the door.

I turned to Reno, "Did you see what I saw?" He couldn't get a word out as he gasped but flipped me the thumbs up.

I rapped on the basement door and greeted a yawning, half-naked Tom as it opened. Doesn't anyone wear clothes around here? Tom didn't have a spot for his hankie.

"What the"…he uttered in complete surprise when he saw me.

"The steam room's got a leak," I quipped. Tom got the joke and nodded with a smirk.

As I pointed over his shoulder I said, "Hey, what's that." Tom fell for it and as he turned to see what was there I planted my foot in his arse.

"That's from Bridie, write more often."

He smirked again knowing he had it coming.

"Come on in," he warned. We walked into a dark, brick-walled, dank basement with a mattress on the floor, one blanket and Bridie's sweatshirt draped over the radiator. There was no bathroom, kitchen, closet or anything.

"Where do you keep the salami" I asked.

"Tied with a shoelace and strung from the rafter so the mice don't get at it, got a few roommates you know," he said.

"Can you put us up? Just kidding, we're staying with Riley." Tom gave us an account of his trip west and the drop out and his newfound freedom. He emphasized the freedom part. He worked in a pub cleaning and washing dishes. It didn't pay much but was all you could eat. "Bridie's worried about you," I said. "Tell her I'm fine since I got the priests and nuns and that asshole sergeant off my ass."

"Duly noted" I said. "She'd love to hear from you now and again."

After a quick spin around the basement, it didn't take long, Tom offered for us to sit down and then remembered that he didn't have any chairs.

"Let's go upstairs," he said. And, eager to see more of Breasty, we agreed.

Tom knocked on the door and Breasty answered. "We need a place to sit," Tom asked.

And Breasty invited us in still displaying the same loose breast.

"These guys are cute, Tom," she said.

"How about a nice hot cup of tea," Tom offered.

Breasty had a mop and a broom and washing machine and sink and stove, sheets for curtains and most of the comforts of home.

"Wow, nice place," I cracked. Tom and Reno went into the kitchen to fire up some tea, the kind you drink, leaving me and Breasty to get acquainted. I plopped myself down in the two seater and scoped the flat stopping at a poster of a skinny black guy playing the guitar.

"Who's that," I asked, pointing at the poster.

"Wow, you don't know? Hendrix, man."

Like I was supposed to know.

"Wanna smoke some pot" she dared.

"Oh, no, I don't think so," I quivered, not knowing what the Hell she was talking about and not wanting to become a heroin addict. She made a box with her index fingers and declared, "Wow man, you are square."

"Oh c'mon just one hit," she begged.

"What's a hit," I asked.

"Just a puff, don't let me smoke this by myself."

"Will it hurt," I asked.

"Does it look like there's anything wrong with me?"

"Not anything I've seen so far, but I don't have much to compare you with," I joked. She didn't get it.

Feigning compliance, I figured, oh what the heck and took a puff, coughed and got dizzy.

"One more," she begged and I toked my second…my mind began to float. I looked over to see if the maverick mammary had slipped out again and got an eyeful. She looked up and busted my curious glance.

"Do you like that," she said.

"Couldn't tell you, mam, I never saw one until today," and then I remembered Pinky in the alley. "Well, maybe once."

"You're cute." She opened her blouse grabbed my hand and placed it on her breast. I don't remember if it was the right or left breast, they both looked the same. I pulled back my hand and she pulled back my hand harder and I gave in and gave it a rub. She moaned and I gave her one more caress and then another, softly brushing her nipple and then she closed her eyes, threw back her head, dropped her arms and gave an even deeper moan. Did she like it? It was like I knew what I was doing. She wanted more. And then the kitchen door swung open. It was Tom with the tea.

I pulled my hand back, brushing her nipple one more time…one more groan and turned to Tom, "Did you bring the honey?" Tom went back for the honey and I placed my hands on my knees with my heart beating like a drum at halftime.

"Wow, I've never had an altar boy," she said.

"We're supposed to be special lads, but I think you just bought this one a ticket to Hell."

"Oh, Jesus wouldn't send *you* to Hell."

"Would you like to see more?"

"Welllll, were not staying that long," acting like I was really thinking about it.

"Oh, it doesn't take long."

"What doesn't take long?"

"You know a little…"

The bang of the door ended her thought. Tom and Reno came back in the room with the tea, the honey and some cups, oblivious to my sexual encounter.

"I think we're past the tea, Tom," I said, still in a state of shock over the breast but surprisingly without any Catholic guilt. Breasty was covered up by now, making me feel special, like I was the only one.

"We'll miss our bus if we don't hurry," I said and slid over to the door. I slipped Tom a tenner that Bridie had given me and left wishing him luck and extending Cloonmore's unconditional love.

"You finally found your Claire, don't overdo it Tom," I admonished. "You look like you've got your hands full." And mine too, I thought.

"I'll tell Bridie how well you're doing," I said, and we hurried off to the bus depot in a stunned state.

"Reno, I touched her breast while you were in the kitchen. For real!" He knew I wasn't lying.

"How was it?"

"I think it hurt her a little because she kept groaning. "But then she asked for more, so it couldn't have hurt that much. Wait'll the boys hear about this!"

"And that odor we've been smelling…It's marijuana."

"Wow!"

I got the munchies and had an urge for some Oreos on the ride home and fell into some deep thought, thinking that I should never wash my hand, ever again. Maybe I should have taken another puff or another rub, but you can't overdo things. The whole experience was more than enough. You can't get greedy.

The guilt that I should have felt wasn't there. Drugs and sex and I didn't feel guilty. The yoke was loosening and with it, the cheeks of my lily white, Irish Catholic ass.

Riley fired up a classic Mexican dinner that night and I gobbled it up. 'Why am I so hungry?'

"Boy, you sure can eat," she admired, not knowing about Breasty and the pot.

We spent the rest of the week absorbing the entire scene in Frisco. We saw it all like two little birds on a fence post; freedom, drugs, music and a big world full of everything and no one telling us what to do or what not to do.

I was happy Tom had found his spot and his Claire. Our trip was an experience of a lifetime and it changed my life forever – tolerance for all.

Reno and I flew home exhausted and educated. In one short week, I had seen a new world, touched a breast, smoked pot and ate lots of peanuts. The same stewardess served the flight home and her cleavage somehow looked ordinary. It's funny how things can become old hat in such a short time.

"Don't you like the peanuts cutie?" when I didn't ask for a refill.

"Oh, Hell one more won't hurt," I said, regaining my admiration.

Bridie was full of excitement when I walked through the door with my tattered shopping bag, and a slight sunburn. She mentioned how grown up I looked. 'You have no idea,' I thought. She couldn't wait to hear about Tom.

"Well Ma, he's got his own heated apartment, his own bed, a job and a lovely community minded girl upstairs that looks after his every need. You know, laundry and housecleaning and some spirituality. The girl knew all about the Hail Mary and how to share all the things that God blessed her with."

"I feel much better Sean, knowing he's doing well, safe and in good hands."

"As well you should Ma, she's a fine, sharing girl."

Descent

When I got back from Frisco and huddled in the alley with the boys, I couldn't wait to broadcast the news about my trip and the kind of women that were on the coast, women so far from our imaginations, as to be almost aliens. My account found willing ears and complete disbelief. Tales of getting stoned and reaching inside someone's blouse to find an erect, supple nipple at the end of a perfectly rounded breast were complete malarkey.

"Yeah,right"

"No way,"

Every time, "C'mon," was the dubious response I got for my grand adventure and having descended into the middle of the "Summer of Love" and lustily risking my every virtue. No one bought my first brush with debauchery and had I not experienced it myself, probably wouldn't have either. Girls like Breasty couldn't possibly exist, didn't have a place even in our imaginations and certainly wouldn't be attracted to crew cut altar boys such as myself.

After a few tries, I didn't tell anyone else; it was no use, but maybe that wasn't so bad. Now I could store my adventure in my own private mental library, let it collect some dust over the years, watch it grow in stature and dimension and unveil it again in my golden years, in my first book when it surely will have added attraction. They'll listen then.

The trip to Frisco raised the curtain on a new act within the drama of my life and introduced me to a world that I had no idea existed. The ice was broken, the secrets revealed, the cows were out of the barn. There was no going back now… not that I would ever want to return to the full-out repression that preceded the

Summer of Love. Frisco was full of people doing exactly what they wanted to do and chasing pleasures that they never thought they would, unfettered by faith or any other constraint. Artists, poets, long hairs, short hairs, braless women, shirtless men and every one of them trying to shake the shackles of pre-60's life, to pursue exactly what they, not what society or the church wanted. Could life really be this free?

People were designing their own thoughts and exploring them without caveats or conditions. Had I just witnessed an imaginary, completely foreign world that could never work or last, or was my trip as real as I wanted it to be? I knew that I was too young to cut the reins from my Midwest upbringing and bug out, but I now had been exposed to something beyond walking the straight Irish Catholic line of patterned, pious existence. Now, there were options. From the outside it looked appealing – to glide with the wind, surf the sexual tide – and all without a single nun or priest checking you at the door. I wanted more.

I started my next year of high school with a carefree and careless, west coast attitude. School became an impediment and an unfortunate daily stop in my quest to find real answers, the ones that they were hiding from me and the ones that would become my own. I had reached the threshold of a different world, with the door ajar and taken a long look inside. I was intrigued and emboldened and ready to take the next step. The company line that had guided my life up until now had been rubbed out, like a crease in the sand. I could always return to it, but why would I ever want to?

Until now, the way I'd lived was at the behest of others and what they thought was the formula for success and happiness. My own thoughts and desires were never tolerated or even considered as part of the life scenario. Catholic education and faith were all laid out for you and all that you had to do was follow it and all would be well, even after you died. And that's how it was laid out; "Do this and that and Eternity will be yours." Eternity...how about today?

Until now, I had bought the manual because I didn't know or even consider that there was anything else out there. Suddenly and quite unexpectedly, with that one short sojourn, I discovered that there were other choices and my inner spirit liked what I had seen and wanted more. It wasn't just the dame or the reefer or the hippies or anything else… it was choice. I wanted to start to make my own choices.

As my adventurous spirit rose and my distaste for prescribed life waned, my interests and focus on school strayed and my grades began to fall. I started defying protocol with inane and puerile pursuits: I was late, didn't do my homework, talked in class and didn't listen…. it went on and on. Whatever they wanted me to do, I didn't do it. I went from aceing almost every class to being the bad boy and recalcitrant and getting C's and D's. The manual got tossed and I began to like anything that wasn't their dogma, only because it wasn't theirs. I was nibbling at my nose to spite my face… for now just nibbling. I began to reject the pompousness of my school and the whole idea that somehow I was elevated because I went there. I had just discovered a huge world, filled with people who didn't go to my school; people who had lots of different ideas, thoughts and pursuits and I wanted to hear them, see them and touch them. It didn't matter if they were good for me or not. That wasn't important. All that was important was that I tasted what I wanted. I knew now that not everyone had a crew cut, a buttoned down collar shirt, loafers and Latin to study.

This new chapter in my life proved Bridie right again. My trip had exposed me to many different kinds, with many different interests and ideas. Bridie was tolerant of all and professed it. Her bromides were short and sweet…and always true. She offered me a valid faith, based on fairness, equality.

"Don't ever think that you are better than anyone else," she'd say —"Even the poorest, or the saddest, or the hungriest knows something that you don't." She loved the less fortunate and the underdog, because she had been one of them. Everyone was to be respected and listened to. And when you acted superior or were mean, you'd incite her wrath and she'd cast her Celtic glare -- Her smirk was her sword. But pursuing her creed didn't imply self-destruction and that's where I went off track…

No one noticed my decline. The school was too big and impersonal and too elite to have help for the penurious troubled; Bridie and Daddy were too overwhelmed with the other ten sibs and providing for them, to notice my changed behavior. The more I was ignored the more I self-destructed and the farther I fell. With each stumble, it got harder to recover and I dug deeper into my chasm with the climb out getting steeper… not that I wanted to climb back up to my old self. I was enjoying my plunge and total rejection of the company line. I intercepted the mail and the report cards that would have bared my destructive plight. My grades were falling, my demerits rising and all the while I was thinking that I was outsmarting Big Brother. Naively, I forgot that Bridie could miss a few things every now and then, but that sooner or later she'd spot the big stuff, sniff you out and apply a cure.

Mischief led to detentions and more mischief and more detentions. Jug – which was sitting with a priest and copying religious canon kept me after school and delayed my afternoon routes and got me home after dark.

"How come you're late?" Bridie would ask, and I'd lie and say I stayed after school for extra help. Well, maybe they were trying to help with all the punishment, but it wasn't doing much good as

I began to enjoy the pain and self-destruction and life on the other side, the side that didn't include them or their formula. No one noticed, and I liked it just fine.

Corporal punishment was the norm at the school, back when it was legal and most infractions were met with a quick slap across the face. When they weren't feeling physically abusive they'd just give you jug. The whole process only fueled my animosity more, which led to more jug and more detentions.

Occasionally you were called to a teacher's office which always meant some elevated level of discipline or organizational stab at complete intimidation...or both. After missing a math assignment, Mr. Buffer summoned me to his office. He headed the Math department and directed the school plays and was known for his famous line, "I can hear you," in response to our side stage giggles at play practice. Mr. B was big and strong, crew cut, and had hands like an axe man but he carried his books like a girl and still lived with his mother. There were rumors about Mr. B, stories I guessed might be true. Everyone suspected his little secret but no one ever said anything conclusive.

Filled with trepidation, and trying to delay the inevitable, I slowly approached his office. School had just ended and the halls were silent and empty; I walked slowly, deep in contemplation. What forms of punishment would I receive; jug, a twist of the ear, more homework, a lecture on unrealized potential or would it be some form of physical punishment?

I felt like I was walking into some form of torture chamber as he opened the door in response to my tentative knock. I looked up and nodded as he placed his axe-man hand on my right shoulder

"Hello Mr. Buffer," I stammered.

"Mr. Brennan," he replied and pulled me into the room. My diminutive self was no match for his obvious strength. As I stumbled in he lost his grip. As I stared into the room with my back to the door, I was slapped with a musty scent of cheap cologne, or was it his mother's perfume, or old newspapers and leather books, or something indefinable? Mr. B stood six feet tall and towered over me. Without saying a word, he turned and closed the door behind me and locked me in. In one short moment he established total control and heightened my dread. I was shaking.

"Mr. Brennan," he began, "Have a seat."

The room was tiny and cramped and housed only a desk, his chair, a love seat and a bookcase filled with leather bound editions. On his desk were piles of papers, neatly stacked and a statue of an angel with open wings. The blind that dressed the window was open just a bit, letting in a sliver of light.

I shuffled over to the love seat, large enough just for two, or one and a half, the way that this was sizing up. I sat down on the edge of the sofa and as close to the arm as I could get with my weight resting on the balls of my feet in case I needed to spring toward the door. Mr. B sat down next to me, brushing my leg with his ham-sized thigh and placed his large hand on my knee.

Uneasy and engulfed, my breathing became erratic. Not wanting to look at him, I focused my eyes across the room on the portrait of a recent Pope garbed in all of his red silk finery with a huge glittering gold cross hanging from a chain around his neck. The Pope stared but didn't see. He was probably on Buffer's side anyway. I needed a saint, any saint. Were Pope's saints?

It was starting to look like a crisis was about to occur and *I was going to have to go it alone, when suddenly* the sun peeked out from behind a cloud and came rushing into the room through that slit in the dusty venetian blinds. Dust particles danced in the ray. The ray of light came shooting across the room, ricocheted off the Pope's gold cross and pierced Mr. Buffer's determined look, blinding him for just a moment. 'You don't have any idea who you're up against,' I thought, as Mr. B began.

"I've noticed a decline in your performance and attitude," he started in a deep, concerned and intimidating tone, squeezing my thigh with his powerful grip. "You've been missing assignments and you sit in class with a smug look, staring out the window, ignoring my lesson. Do you have anything to say for yourself?"

I thought of Bradley and all those years of window watching and now knew his motivations…freedom from them.

I shrugged and gave him a "Nah," knowing that I was inciting his ire and casting my fate. He didn't know that I wasn't alone and that help was imminent.

His face turned red and his massive frame began to tremble. He lost his grip on my thigh and his fists clenched.

"You little smart ass," he barked, finally getting something right. I anticipated some devious attack and I was right. He grabbed me by the shoulders and lifted my 120 pound body up, threw me over his knees and began to spank me with a rapacious glee. After a few good whacks, I decided that it was enough punishment for one day and struggled to extricate myself from his grasp. I lurched back, brushing against his stiffened appendage.

"I'll not miss another one Mr. B," I begged, as I fell backward and straight into his bookcase, knocking Copernicus and Newton onto the floor. I reeled again and with my arm, propelled the statue of the Angel off of his desk, and sent it crashing into pieces on the floor. One of the wings was spinning like a top, as I grasped my reddened posterior with both hands and turned and raced for the door. The guardian angel's career was over, but I was sure that, with my recent performance, he hadn't been assigned to me. Some other poor bastard was now out of luck. The angel would never fly again, or protect his assigned sinner, but I had my legs and could still run.

"I've learned my lesson; you have no more worries," I proclaimed, stumbling to the door and fumbling to turn the handle.

"Goddamnit!" It was locked. When I'd come in, I had noted how he locked the door. Perhaps there were miracles after all – I took a chance at how that might unlock, and twisted the latch releasing the hasp as he strode toward me looking for one more whack or...something. The door opened and I dashed out, tripping on the threshold and landing spread-eagle on the marble floor. Realizing my vulnerability and his desires, I stumbled to my feet and crashed into the lockers on the other side of the hallway, spun, saw him at the doorway coming after me and dashed down the hall with both hands cupping my reddened arse, all the while proclaiming my salvation:

"Your message has been well received. I'll be a good lad," I called over my shoulder.

Down the hall I raced, taking the marble steps two at a time and then at last running out the oak doors, leaving behind most of my books, coat and most of what I had when I entered the school that day, but still owning my virility or virginity or something like that. I headed straight home and the second I was inside the door, I opened the math book. My work became punctual and my test scores soared, keeping Mr. B's lust for me at bay. In the days ahead, I could feel Mr. B's angst or was it attraction, as he stared down at me during class, waiting for my next stumble and his next assault, but it never came as I added and subtracted my way past his fantasies.

My brush with Mr.B started me working but only at math. My attitude toward everything else stayed sour. I was still too defiant to completely recover in my other subjects and continued to maintain some of my aura of dissension. The only good news, besides the math upswing was a new pulse that I began to feel inside my own trousers.

My underwear began to snug up and readjustments became more necessary and regular. One day I noticed a sprig of nascent manhood. Could it really be here? A hair? Could two years of hiding my boyhood and agonizing each time I took my clothes off, be over? I plucked the first one to see if it was attached and a part of me.

"Owww."

'Yahoo!' It was... manhood.

The growth spurt accelerated: each day, a new sprig, another millimeter. I had waited for years, agonizing over this hair's untimely arrival, cursing my Irish heritage and its encumbered evolution, wondering why the Greeks, Italians and Poles evolved quicker? I'd been surrounded in the locker room by these strapping hirsute, endowed alien ethnicities. I had stuffed my pants with rags, covered myself with the crossed hand over the groin guise and cowered by corner lockers, all to keep my immature boyhood a secret, but it was all over now. I could bare myself to all. Sal, no longer had anything on me.

With my newly pronounced manhood and love-laced trip to Frisco, I was now ready to put the new Sean to the test. I had the tools. Experience in Frisco and now the weapons of love were all I needed to plunge into the sea of teen romance. High on the rocks perched above the glimmering water, like Elvis in *Blue Hawaii*, I was ready to dive into a new chapter and the stage was set when Reno announced a party in his basement: live, with girls. This would be it, my coming out, my grand opening. It was time to start rehearsing.

Nadir

To the scratchy waves of our transistor radio, I practiced some dance moves before the bathroom mirror, combed my blonde curls, ironed and pressed my duds and announced myself ready for my big audition in Reno's basement.

I arrived fashionably late at Reno's big bash to the sounds of the Four Tops and Supremes filling the smoky basement. Mike had taught me that trick, "Don't be the first one at the party, you'll look like a needy nerd." The smoke was just tobacco, there wasn't a scent of that California gold or whatever Breasty called it. No, I was back in the Midwest, where they weren't ready for the real stuff. I didn't care, knowing that I would need all of my senses for my next move on some innocent lass.

Hometown girls, drenched with Catholic rearing and faced with confession every Friday would be a much tougher test than that floozy in Frisco. I bounced my way in, full of cockiness and resolve. At the bottom of the stairs, I slapped Reno a high five and thanked him for his hospitality, coyly scanning the crowd. The lighting was dim.

"Nice touch, Reno." I kept my cocky countenance front and center as I parsed Reno's digs looking for someone who met my standards. I started to rhythmically bounce as "*I Heard it through the Grapevine*," filled the room.

Coiffed and confident, just back from Frisco, I inched through the crowd checking and being checked. A couple of the girls turned their heads to check me out as I walked by. Both maintained their gaze but I turned away disinterested. Mike taught me that one:

"Don't let 'em think you're interested, it lights a fire inside them,"

Without discouragement, my scan continued. Too tall, too chunky, not cute enough, where did she get that dress? and finally... voila! She was a cute, curvy, brunette and...she was alone, just my type, or so I thought. I really didn't know my type, but I had a feeling.

My target was set as I contemplated my strategy. 'Don't give yourself away,' I remembered and I looked right past her, not indicating one iota of interest.

"Don't show your cards," Mike would admonish and I now had an inner Mike directing my every move.

I ambled my way over still bopping to the Temps, feigning interest in the Jagger poster on the wall and gave her a short nod. Nothing... and then she smiled and flipped her hair back across her shoulder, a sure sign of interest... or so Mike would teach.

"When they play with their hair, you have a chance," he would say.

The Temps broke into *Poppa was a Rollin' Stone* as I continued to feign my interest in Jagger's image; a phallic strut, perched on the panel wall. My peripheral vision took in her dimensions; round and plump, tight jeans, tight sweater and curves like a Monaco roadway. Surely my type or so I thought. Who was I fooling? I didn't even have a type even though I had been to Frisco, but I suspected that if I had one this damsel fit the prescription. I felt a slight tug from her presence and figured all systems were go as I inhaled deeply and turned from the poster to make my move. Sorry Mick, my interest lies elsewhere.

"He who hesitates"... Mike would warn. As I turned, Reno brushed by me and grabbed her by the hand and led her to the dance floor. Damn! Reno had pilfered her right from under my nose and I was filled with regret. Oh, those moments lost to indecision! My best laid plans had just been dashed.

I looked around for better fish to fry, but there weren't any. Reno's dance partner was *The One*. How could I get a second chance? Before the thought had left my brain, I heard an older woman's crackling voice: "Raymond, come here for a moment." It was Reno's mom calling down the basement stairs.

"Goddamnit," he said to the one, "I'll be right back."

This was my chance. Reno, dutiful lad that he wasn't but not wanting Mom coming down, took a pause and left to answer his mom's request. As my girl started her next spin, apparently deciding that dancing alone was better than not at all, I mustered my courage and stepped in and took Reno's place greeting her as she finished her turn.

"Reno got called away," I sputtered and whirled into a spin of my own igniting a smile from her.

"I'm Sean," I said, dispelling any shyness and plunging myself headfirst into the new world of girls and that stuff that Breasty had showed me. Hell, it was the next step. I was a dude man, just back from the coast.

"I'm Jo," she said, seeming to not mind the switch from Reno and she wiggled her hips and flung her long brunette hair from side to side. Reno's time was over and mine had just begun. The moment felt easy. There was nothing strained or clumsy. Could love be this easy? Could my heart melt this fast? Could I be whipped this quick... without even a little resistance?

I was engulfed with rapture. I feigned a little disinterest, not wanting to show all my cards, but my ruse was transparent, even to me. I was cooked, knew it and abandoned any schemes that Mike had taught me. I danced with total interest and even more passion. This felt better than any game Mike could teach. My attention was obvious and focused. Nothing else mattered.

Gradually, the room emptied except for the two of us, at least in my mind. Only Jo and I existed, and the now, muffled tones of the Temptations... Euphoria. My senses were numb and my heart smitten. I wanted the moment to last forever. I sensed my life would never be the same. On this first night of looking for girls, I had hunted, stalked, and chosen my prey with guile and in a couple of short minutes had become *her* victim. The trapper was trapped; the hunter, the prey, the master, the slave.

Each dance, we engaged, oblivious to our surroundings as her interest seemed to match my complete capitulation. Nothing else existed anymore for me, not my routes or school or basketball or Bridie or anybody, and then Reno supercharged the evening with the Chi-Lites and *Oh Girl*.

I slowly pulled her body close to mine, placing my hand on her curvaceous hip as I inhaled her luscious and addicting scent.

"I'd be in trouble if you left me now," the singer crooned...And I was indeed in trouble, not wanting this moment or evening to end and feeling like my bumpy path was somehow hitting a straight-away. Emboldened by the moment, and putting the pedal to the metal, I slyly sidled our way toward a darkened corner and brushed her lips with mine as I slid my cheek from one side to the other. I returned and brushed again and stopped, caressing her moist lips with mine. There was no resistance as she succumbed to the moment and let her own desires steer a long and sensuous kiss. The song had long ended before the kiss did and then another and another.

And then... in all my self-destructive infinite wisdom, Mr. Frisco raised his right hand and clutched at her left breast.

Her left hand came crashing across my face quicker than Ali in his prime. I was stunned. My arms dropped to my side and my face reddened.

"Pig!"

All I can remember was holding my chastised cheek and the sight of her backside as she grabbed her coat and stormed out the back door. Just then the ice gave way and I fell through into the frigid dampness of the dark basement, drowning the most sensuous moment of my life and with it, any hopes for my first love.

"What happened?" Reno called out, and in total embarrassment, without saying a word, I shuffled my way to the stairs and stumbled out the door and into the chilled evening without my coat or my dignity. I had just pissed into the wind and tugged on Superman's cape all in the same instant and ruined my greatest moment with another stupid antic. Mr. Cool Guy had just been put straight with a solid left. I shuffled home, massaging my reddened cheek, wondering when I'd wake up and how I'd dig myself out of this one.

Phone calls to apologize went unanswered, and rightfully so. I had violated Jo's integrity and dignity and that deserved no reprieve. My only hope was that time would assuage her hurt and somehow, somewhere, I could again cross her path, apologize for my devious assault and try to resurrect our natural connection.

Stunned and feeling like I was in a hole that I couldn't climb out of, I spent the rest of the weekend in a stupor.

"You seem a little down on yourself," Bridie diagnosed.

"Oh just a stomach ache, Ma," I lied. I did my math, though.

My comatose state came to an abrupt end on Monday morning in Economics class, when Mr. T. announced the start of the midterm exam.

"Goddamnit," I thought, as the exam was placed on my desk.

"Time, good luck, gentlemen," the teacher barked. I had forgotten all about this one and hadn't studied, not that I would have, if I had remembered and as I read the first question, I knew that I was in trouble.

I glanced over at my neighbor's paper and noted his first choice: "C." It's funny how desperation can make one agreeable.

"C" it was. And then "D" and "A" and for the next hour my classmate and I were becoming fast buddies, even though he didn't know it.

I could scam my way through this one and then… I promised myself: 'I'll turn over a new leaf.' Using my roving eye, I duplicated every one of my neighbor's answers. It was so easy I even stopped reading the questions. I was too dumb and desperate to change a few of the answers and cloak my loathsome larceny.

The next day, I got my test back with a big "A" pasted across the top.

'Nice job, you rat', I thought, slouched in my chair feeling as empty as I've ever felt.

"Mr. Brennan, could you see me after class?" Mr. T asked. Why would he want to see me? Either hearty congratulations on my sudden improvement or I faced another bout with total embarrassment. After class ended and only when the room was empty, with my head down, I shuffled up to the teacher and stood in front of him. I tried to distract myself from the miasmic moment, counting the square tiles beneath my feet. I wanted no accolades if he was misinformed enough to think my grade was my own effort.

He looked up from his work and came right to the point:

"Sean, is your grade your own work?" This guy was nice enough to not call me an out an out cheater…which is what I deserved. I thought about adding to my disgusting behavior and lying and then thought better of it, feeling like I needed to come clean and scrub my soul. I nodded an embarrassed 'yes,' and followed it with, "I cheated."

"You're dismissed," he said and nothing else. There was total silence, no slap, no jug and no spanking, only his look of disappointment. My punishment was hearing me call myself a cheat and it echoed wide and deep into my soul. Covered in chalk and disappointed, Mr. T stuffed his papers in his briefcase as I stood motionless, too humiliated to even move and he left the room. I watched him leave, some of his papers sticking out of his sealed case. I didn't move for several moments, actually enjoying the solitude of the empty room, alone with my thoughts. His look and that empty room were all that I needed to realize what I now was. The dread of the moment seeped into my heart and stained any goodness that was left. This was rock bottom. A lad with intelligence and a family that loved him had turned every positive ounce of grace he owned into disgrace. And that was what it was: *Disgrace*.

I walked home in a comatose and dazed state only to find Bridie waiting at the door holding my most recent report card, her mouth cocked and a bit of steam rolling off her head. My scheme to intercept the mail was exposed and so too, was I.

I took the lead, saving Bridie the torment of castigating her wayward son.

"There's no need to say a word, Ma. I know you want to plant your foot in me arse, but you'd only be kicking a dead horse. I'm guilty and there's not much more that you can do to me that I haven't already done to myself. I've been an embarrassment to the whole family and everything you ever taught me." She raised the hand that clutched the report card and crumpled it into a ball.

"Tomorrow's a new day, Laddy."

The Ascension

I had sunk so deeply into an abyss of shame it seemed that my climb out would be insurmountable. I felt like I had the days after Turk and I pilfered the cash from his attic. At first it was great and exciting walking on the danger side but then the realization that I was a thief enjoying someone else's efforts ended it. My decline and self-destruction in school, the liberties I had taken with Jo, wasting every ability I had, ignoring everything Bridie had taught me, all combined to bring me to the bottom. I felt a morass of disgust for myself. My soul needed a scrubbin'.

Out of respect for Bridie and the values that she had tried to drum into me, I decided that ascent from my pit of rot was in order. I knew the values were buried somewhere, but they needed to be rediscovered. I established a plan to take it one day at a time and hope that eventually my reformation would accelerate and I would land on the sunny side with some renewed self-respect.

One chilly winter morning as I shoved my paper cart across the boulevard and neared the end of my route, I saw the high school bus approaching. For a moment I froze, not from the cold but from the humiliation of still being a rag tag paper boy. I looked for refuge and spotted a large oak tree and ducked behind it.

The foul diesel exhaust and my embarrassment wafted over me. That was when I caught myself and asked, "What do I have to be ashamed of?"

Here I was working my way through high school by rising every morning at five bells and carting the news to the South End of Oak Park, through snow, rain, cold and anything else that might get in the way. Why should I feel embarrassed? I came from a family that valued what mattered: caring and sharing. What the Hell was wrong with me?

At my high school I was surrounded by upper- middle-class rich boys who had far more than I did, at least materially. For three years I had let myself be intimidated, not by anyone in particular but by the gap between them and me.

As the bus faded into the eastern sunrise, it dawned on me, that I was doing a lot of things right and had the foundation to be better than I was. I rose at five bells and did my routes; saved my money and paid my own tuition; defended the weak and respected those who had less than I did. A smile came to my face and a feeling to my soul.

The seed had been sown long ago by Bridie and all that she was. Now it needed to blossom and that was up to me. Effort, desire, determination, respect and a dash of creativity was all the seed needed to be a bloom. I knew that it was within me.

As I turned from the tree, exposing my new self, back to the world, my nose brushed against a carved-out heart from the trees bark. The letters and the message, etched deep in the bark: "SB loves JM." The piercing arrow was a bit askew.

"That's me and Jo." I gasped.

The Chase

Was it just coincidence that the initials matched mine and my curvaceous lost love from Reno's basement? Had Reno etched the design knowing that my route brought me by this antique oak, or was it Sam Baker and Jayne Mills spreading the news of their romance? Whatever it was, the sight of those entwined initials ignited my thoughts of that magical night when I first felt desire and love for a girl who truly mattered to me. Now, my need to atone and the feelings that I longed to have again...and again... and again, surfaced as more than regret: I had to take action and recover the girl...the love that I lost.

Jo was back on the radar and I needed to track her down and give it one more shot. Reliving the feeling that I had that night in the basement was worth any effort and any risk.

As I pushed my paper cart home, in a trance at my epiphany and mesmerized by the rumble of the wheels across the cobblestone street, I felt full of resolve: I would rise from my gopher hole. I began to think that maybe it was time to bag the paper routes and graduate to a more mainstream career. It had been a long journey, actually since I was eight, bearing the morning darkness in cold and heat and rain and snow, alone most of the time except for the odors of the mornings and the twitter of the birds. I had seen enough of Pinky and the hairy ape and all the other creatures of the dawn.

Yeah, it was time to move on and as I passed the gas station on the way home, I noticed a Help Wanted sign in the window. 'Part Time Grease Monkey Wanted,' it beckoned. I figured if getting dirty was a requirement, I was their man. My inked stained hands would at least get me the interview. And it did as I knocked on the door that said 'Manager.'

The door slowly opened and a rotund hillbuck peaked out and said, "Can I help you," in a long drawn out southern patois. "You're up awful early."

"Everyday, sir. My route can't wait."

"I'd like to apply for the grease monkey job, Mr. Gene"

His name was sown across his left breast.

"How'd you know"…and then he remembered the name plate.

"Let me see your hands."

I held out my ink stained hands and flipped them palms up.

I could see Gene was impressed.

"Do you know where a dip stick is?"

"Right under the hood and they use it for the oil."

"Can you scrub a windshield and make change?"

"A's in math (thank you Mr. B) and I can make a window squeak."

"You know any Elvis tunes?"

"Love me Tender, Sir."

"When can you start?"

"Today after school."

"How's 3 bucks an hour sound to y'all?"

"I'm your man."

That afternoon, I donned my Mobil answer man uniform and got ready to pump some gas. In short time Gene had taught me the basics. "Greet the customer, be courteous, check the oil and wash the windows." It didn't take me long to see that Gene wasn't one for work as he let me wait on all the cars as he played manager in his office. It didn't matter because I was going to live up to my standards not his. As the next customer pulled up in a black sedan, I leaped to service him.

"May I help you sir…err I mean, Father." Well, damned if it wasn't the parish priest puffing on a smoke. He put the cigarette out quickly and said, "Are you done with the routes my lad?" he asked.

"I've moved on Father to bigger and better things, I hope."

"Well, I'll miss seeing you in the mornings son, I was always impressed with the way you worked so hard."

"I'll miss you too father, sorry I was never able to help you in the sacristy; the morning news needed to get out, and it looks like I'll be just as busy with this employment."

"I would have loved to have had your help, but I was always able to find someone else." I thought of whoever he cornered…poor bastard.

"Good luck son and stop in at the rectory some time without your ear in your Mother's hand," he said, chuckling a bit. Good one.

He eased down the drive in his black sedan and black suit, waving as he faded into the afternoon. I never knew he had a sense of humor as I cracked a smile.

As I watched him drive away, my smile and wave faded; I felt a tinge of empathy for his lonely life. The black sedan disappeared round the next corner. I began to wonder how these colorless men of the cloth handled being perched atop their pedestal, always out of reach, always above the masses, like lonesome birds clinging to a bare, brittle branch? That's where the Church put them, up high and above anything human. They had a lonely life up there grasping the gnarled limb they were perched on and looking down and only looking, because they weren't allowed to touch. It was *not touching* that made them so Godlike…. and solitary.

A week into my new gig, as I rode into the station on my battered bike pedaling to the constant tick of the broken spoke, hurrying to beat the clock, I brushed against a car as it pulled out from one of the pumps. As the car left the drive and turned onto the street I realized that the driver looked like Jo.

I pulled a quick 'U-eey' to get a better look and pumped the pedals hard trying to catch up. It was Jo. Her brunette mane swirled out of the window and billowed in the breeze. She was unmistakable. I don't know what I would have said if I had caught up, but it was too late, the distance between us widened, and I realized the moment passed. I slowed my pedaling, knowing that I couldn't catch up.

She sped down the street leaving a trail of exhaust for me to swallow. Pay back for the loose hand, I thought. I sensed that getting to the point of forgiveness wouldn't be easy…but seeing her meant she was nearby and that meant I would get a chance. It's all I wanted. I was sad that I had missed her but encouraged that we would meet again. Now that she was on my radar screen I knew we would meet again…but how? As the days passed I began to convince myself that there was something about the incident that wasn't just coincidence. Had her disgust with me waned? Did she want to relive that night of bliss? Was she admiring me from afar?

Despite my boorish behavior there had to be something about our magical night that Jo held dear. She couldn't have known about my problems at school, the punishments and bad grades; she had to think that I was worth a second chance…I hoped. Was it the bad boy attraction? Mike would say, "They like the bad boys, don't be too nice." But I wasn't that bad and Jo was more sophisticated than that.

There had to be something that brought her back snooping around and all I could come up with was the magic of that night.

My grades were starting to improve and I noticed that the girls were taking a bit of notice too. What was different? I still looked like I was five years younger than my age. All the other boys were bigger and stronger and still hairier than I. It must have been future development they saw… and maybe the big bucks that I was now making as my pay had doubled at the gas station job.

I started to notice a lot of the local girls were now buying their gas at my station.

"You know you've been good for business," Gene croaked one day, "There's a lot more female customers."

"Hi, Sean." No one had ever known my name before.

My bubble burst when I realized that my name was sewn on my Mobil shirt, just over my heart.

I was still flattered a bit because I knew that something about me was changing but the interest from the other girls didn't matter…only Jo did. The rest of the girls didn't have what Jo did and would have to wait to see if our connection didn't work out. Jo was the one who imprisoned my heart and held my fancy. She's the one that set my bar. And it was a bit higher than the others could reach. I wasn't going to be happy until I got a second chance with this alluring colleen.

One evening shift, as Gene left to go home and I pulled in, he mentioned that someone had been in and asked for me.

"Boy or girl?" I asked.

"There's no mistaken those curves," he bellowed, and shook his hand like he was cooling it off.

"Yellow car?" I asked.

"I think a Buick," he guessed.

"That's the one Geno," I said and my heart began to pulse. Gene was admiring her too… the dirty animal.

That was twice she had circled *my* garage. It was… her. There was interest and now she was asking for me. She was watching from afar. My heart began to beat faster and my mind began to hatch a plan. This siren of Madison Avenue needed her whirr of temptation snatched from the sky and tucked inside my arms.

The days passed and so did the yellow Buick, always out of reach, always a moment after I had just started work. She would zip by, knowing that I was helpless to follow. And I felt helpless, seeing those silken brunette tresses blow in the breeze from the car window. This was not fair. It was like trying to catch the wind in my arms. I needed help, and Reno came to mind.

I asked Gene if I could be fifteen minutes late one day and he agreed, telling me it would cost a full hour of pay. I didn't care about the three bucks, as long as my plan worked. It would be money well spent.

I signed on Reno as an accomplice and on the crucial afternoon, stationed him four blocks down from the station. "It's a yellow Buick and if she passes, you have to pedal your ass off and see where she goes or comes from," I ordered. I was stashed behind a mailbox, perched atop my bike waiting for her daily pass-by, when I saw the yellow Buick approach and the brunette mane flowing from the window. Quite unknowingly, the little allure was falling into my trap but maybe she wanted to be caught? As she passed I noticed that she took a gander inside the station but I was across the street perched behind a mailbox and ready to peddle my ass off. I needed to know where she came from. Just to make sure, I ducked so she wouldn't see me, and then took off, pedaling for my life after the yellow Buick. She started to put distance between us but I knew that it was just a matter of time until I closed the gap. As I panted and pedaled, I realized that I didn't hear the spoke. The light ahead was red and gave me hope and then suddenly turned green and I knew I was cooked as she sped up and zipped through the intersection. The sirens from a fire truck slowed her down again, but not for long as I began to catch up and then...a loud pop and I really knew I was cooked as the air escaped from my back tire and with it my hopes of pinning down this elusive damsel. Kerplunk, kerplunk, kerplunk, was all I heard as the bike slowed and rubber separated from the rim.

All hope was not lost, there's still a chance. Reno was perched four blocks ahead and could pick up her trail and continue the chase. 'C'mon, Reno,' I willed, 'pump those sticks and come through for me.'

I walked my disabled bike back to the station and signed in for work. "Don't forget the docked hour," Gene barked. 'Piss off you lard ass,' I thought, 'I have more important things to worry about than your measly three bucks. This is some life changing stuff, Big Boy'. By then, all I could hope for was that Reno picked up her trail and followed her to some destination that would reveal her haunts.

The clock ticked by and no Reno. 'I hope he's not under a bus,' I thought. And then, amidst the glare of the setting sun, up the driveway, returned the redhead, smirking and pumping his fist.

"She's ours," he yelled.

"No, she's mine," I reestablished. He saw the look in my eyes and knew that he was playing second fiddle. Reno would have to find love elsewhere.

"What's the lowdown?"

"She's a checker at the *Jewel* food store," he announced. "I pumped my ass off and almost lost her when an ambulance came whizzing by and she had to stop. If she's as fast as she drives, you might be into something," he warned.

I promised Reno that if it didn't work out I'd give my blessings to him and he could try his luck, knowing that there was no chance.

"Thanks for your help," I said, as Reno rode off proud to be a part of my latest caper.

The rest was up to me. I cased the *Jewel* for many a day and spotted her through the picture window, just to the right of the "Plump Grapefruits" poster. It was her alright, garbed in a pink taffeta uniform with saddle shoes to match. All I could see was her shapely backside and silky pony tail, but that was good enough for now.

I agonized how to approach her and started my quest many times, always to withdraw in total fear. And then one day, I declared – 'It's now or never. Buckle up, big boy and hit the pedal.' I entered the grocery store on foot and slipped down the dairy aisle, grabbed a choco and got in her checkout line.

I had rehearsed my lines many times and had them down pat. There were three people in front of me, the last a big fat guy whom I could hide behind. As Jo finished ringing up his order, bagged his groceries and counted his change, I broke into a whistle of *Oh, Girl*. I was still concealed by the fat guy; she looked around to see where the whistle was coming from and cracked a smile knowing that the tune was ominous. The fat guy squeezed out of the aisle and she turned to find me staring into her hazel eyes.

"You're a hard one to pin down," I said as she turned and flinched at my confident but apologetic glare.

"Have you learned some manners yet, or should I call for the manager?" she warned.

"I can only offer my deepest apologies. I've agonized daily over my boorish behavior and can only hope that you can find it within yourself to forgive me. I'm sure you've wondered about how someone could be so stupid and ruin something so nice?"

"Are you really that dumb?"

"Not anymore."

"25 cents for the choco," she said.

"Will the coupon on the carton get me a date?" I begged.

She laughed and gave me a nod. "383-6741," she whispered.

"Now beat it before the manager comes."

My heart began to pound hard and my sails filled with expectation as I floated out the door. I didn't come down for some time and only landed because I couldn't stay like that forever. I wanted to but couldn't.

I repeated the number again and again as I touched off the automatic doors. 'No shoes, No shirt, No service,' the poster on the door warned. The sign was for the hippies and I wondered if the management thought they would dance across the meat counters.

When I got outside, I inked the number on my forearm, not wanting to take any chances.

"Always have a pen," Mike warned, "In case you run into something and get a hot number." Now, his advice paid off. When I got home there would be no shower, this badge of honor was staying etched across my forearm.

There was no praying or bowed head at dinner that night, only an ethereal air that engulfed me.

"You seem a bit dreamy tonight," Bridie noticed. "The tea leaves looked like a heart this morning."

"Is there something that you want to tell me?"

"Maybe, if you promise not to laugh."

"Promise."

"There's this girl that I met and I have a feeling inside me that I've never had before."

"Not even for me?"

"Oh, Ma, it's different, but just as strong."

"Well, laddy when you feel like that you're supposed to go for it."

I couldn't believe what I just heard, coming from a lady who had padlocked her lads love trains. We were all transforming.

Ecstasy at the Drive-In

"Keep 'em at bay," Mike taught. And for the next few endless days I resisted calling. It was pure torment. "Don't you dare pick up that phone," he warned. "You can't let them think they got you or it'll be over before it starts."

"To Hell with it," I said the third day. I couldn't wait any longer. I was pure mush, mash potatoes, oatmeal and smitten – I dialed. By then I knew the number by heart, but mysteriously the etching on my arm hadn't faded.

"Hello," it was the voice of a whipper snapper. "May I please speak with Curv...err...I mean Jo."

I almost blew it.

"Who is this?" a girl's voice commanded.

"It's Sean."

"Who?"

"Sean," I repeated. The whole family was going to make me pay. 'All right you little brat, get your sister,' I thought.

"Joan, it's some guy named Sean, I'm telling Marin," I heard the little brat warn. Marin must have been the now, old boyfriend. I knew him and his bad teeth, from baseball. I wasn't worried, there was better competition.

"Hello," it was a demure tone, alluring yet full of uncertainty.

"It's Sean," I said, "the choco guy," I reminded her.

"Oh, Mr. Manners," she quipped.

"I said I was sorry."

"Some things take a little longer to get over than others," she advised.

"Well I'm hoping it's at least near the end," I shot back.

"It's close," she said, giving me hope.

"Everyone deserves a second chance," she said, "Even you," and the conversation eased into mid gear and floated.

"There's a good movie at the Granada this weekend, would you like to go?"

"I'll buy the popcorn," she said, reminding me that she was something special. What girl offered to buy the popcorn?

"Hey Daddy, can I have the car Saturday night?" I had never asked for the car, if you wanted to call it that; I was always being about fourth in line and most times without gas money.

"And what might this be for," he asked. "It might be a new addition to the family," I said. "Aren't there enough of us already?"

"This one's special, Daddy"

"I've heard that one before, but good luck, it's yours."

I couldn't believe my good fortune. I wasn't even going to ask. That'll teach you to always give it a stab, they just might say yes. Jo was in, and now, so was Daddy.

Daddy was not one to acquiesce very easily. The car...well let's just say it ran. This one was a '62 Olds, brown, rusted and in need of a good scrub. Daddy never put much resource into his work wheels and changed them every other year when the mufflers rusted out and the tobacco build up on the mat got too thick. Sometimes the cars were cheaper than new mats. Daddy chewed tobacco and in the winter months with the windows up, he had nowhere to spit other than the passenger floor mat. During the summer when he could open the window, there was a stream of stain from the back door to the taillight. It was never about appearances to Daddy, just substance. With Daddy you had to read, write, do and dare. Life was all about active living and not passive observance. That's why we had the great TV wars. "Get out there and be a part of it."

All day Saturday, I scrubbed away any trace of his tobacco habit just to raise the respectability a few notches. With an old sheet pinned over the seat, the tobacco mat removed until Monday morning and the tobacco chips scrubbed from the dash board, it was just about like new. Well… not quite. A few stray shots of Jovan musk oil in the corners and real elegance was at hand. This was as good as it would get. The wheels were ready and now I had to work on myself.

I didn't need to dress in the garage any more, as Mike had broken down Bridie's resistance to chasing the girls. I could primp and preen in full view, even telling Bridie it was for a date with a real live girl.

"Make sure you're a gentleman, if you know what I mean, Laddy," she admonished. She'd never directly tell you what she meant because she'd have to mention sex and we never talked about that.

After my session in front of the cracked, silverless mirror, a quick brush of the ivories with baking soda, I headed out with coiffed curls, pressed pants, a bit of wax on my shoes and all the healthy expectations in the world. We hadn't discovered toothpaste yet, so all we had was a box of baking soda that would sit on the side of the sink and eventually become a hill of soda when the bottom of the box would give way from the moisture. Somehow we made it work even sharing the brushes when it was too hard to identify your own. Sharing our germs never hurt…hell we had the same last name.

The engine roared when I turned the key, I added two bucks worth of gas and was ready for the excursion of my life. I had a quarter of a tank for the entire evening, Jovan musk filled the air; a clean white sheet covered the seats and love and excitement were on my mind. I didn't much care what came after tonight – this would be the big leagues for the next few hours… a clean car, some cash and Jo on the horizon.

My next hurdle was getting past the screening her parents would give me. I knew thirty years before, her old man had been a swim star at my high school because his picture hung among the honored on the walls at the school. We had some common ground, even though I hadn't done much to be proud of over at the old alma mater. Most alums held the school in a special place and I knew that all I had to do was mention my membership and I'd at least get past the first screening. Her Mom would be a different story; women knew that where you went to high school was no guarantee that you had any character. I polished my best Eddie Haskell impression in hopes of winning her over. "Oh, good evening Mrs. M, whatever you're cooking, it sure smells good."

I was ready and rehearsed, as I pulled up in front of the beige stucco house just south of Madison Avenue. This was 'the hood' filled with Irish Catholic families all suffering the same problem – not enough money, and too many mouths to feed.

As I climbed the front stairs that could have used a little paint, I still felt that I was out of my league, entering a world where things matched, walls were painted and both sides of the toaster worked. And I was. As the door opened after my polite knock, I looked in to see a newly polished foyer of checkerboard pattern, a carpeted staircase with all the balustrades still in place. A little squirt in a page boy haircut, greeted me. "I'm Birdie," she said, "And we've been waiting all day to see what you looked like." Her voice matched the one on the phone.

"Well I hope you're not disappointed," I joked.

"Probably a little, the way Jo has built you up," she cracked and turned and ran up the stairs and perched herself at the top and yelled over her shoulder, "Mr. Wonderful is here, Jo," blowing her big sister's cover.

Ahhh, Jo had been talking about me. This was my big chance to step up to the next level, a new world, one a little outside my life at Cloonmore.

I heard a newspaper crumble and the spring from a cushion ring out and then Mr. M came around the corner clutching the sport section.

"I'm Jo's father," he announced, and a big affable man extended his hand, giving me a squeeze to let me know who was boss.

"Sean Brennan," I shot back. 'Look 'em in the eye and squeeze back,' Daddy had taught. I lost the squeeze contest but didn't wince. From the far reaches of the kitchen, Mrs. M appeared, garbed in a house dress and fronting apron. She extended her small, soft hand. Mrs. M had faded blue eyes that matched her apron and a ripened version of Jo's prettiness.

"Sure smells good, whatever you're cooking," I said.

"Nothing," she replied. "We ordered out."

Oops, I thought no more Haskell's after that whiff.

Before I could utter another word and not a moment too soon, my siren appeared at the top of the steps, right behind Birdie who still had her elbows on her knees and chin in the palm of her hands. Jo stepped down around the turn in the stairs and stopped, like a beauty queen making her decent from a cloud. We all obeyed her silent command and looked up, the Mr. and Mrs. and Birdie too.

She was a sight to behold. I gasped. Even her parents had a stunned look on their face. Garbed in powder blue hip huggers and a white sweater, the curvaceous lass slowly descended each step like a winning pageant contestant coming to accept her prize. There was no reason to rush this as I became more enamored with each step. My mind went blank, suddenly not one thing about the rest of my life mattered. I watched each step and thought about how there might not be any turning back from this moment. This was serious and I knew it.

"Hi," she said, flicking back her streaming brunette tresses with her left hand, as if to announce that I never need to look any further.

"Hi," I choked. My mouth went suddenly dry.

"You won't be late," Mrs. M warned.

"Oh no," I said hoping that the evening would last forever and we'd never come back.

"Nice to meet you both," I Haskelled again, forgetting my promise, and I held the door open for the queen to exit.

We left without saying a word, as Birdie came running to the front window and pasted her nose on the glass. I couldn't get a word out.

"Where are we going?" she asked.

"There's a good western at the Granada theatre," I stuttered.

"I have a better idea," asserting her control. "How about, *Gone with the Wind* at the drive-in. John Wayne can wait…"

"Sure," I wasn't going to argue, the movie was of no consequence. She was driving the bus, and what a ride this was shaping up to be. I opened the car door for her and looked back to see Mrs. M peeking out the window, checking on my manners, and Birdie too, with her nose still smashed against the window.

My whole being had a buzz that I had never felt before as I slammed her door shut and skipped around the car like Kookie Burns did on *77 Sunset Strip*. Here I was, outside my cloistered world, with a set of wheels, pressed and preened threads, some cash, two bucks worth of gas and Miss Universe sitting at my arm.

"Smells good in here," she said.

"It's a French scent," I said, assuming Jovan was a frog.

"Well, you look glorious," I started. I couldn't help myself. Mike told me not to show my cards to soon but he had never been in this position before. Not with the dames he was chasing.

"Thank you," she said, "it's not really anything," stealing a line from Violet in *Wonderful Life* and grossly understating her look.

My high continued as we engaged in small talk on the way to the Drive-in but she kept her distance on the far side of the front seat. As we pulled into the Drive-in and got set up to watch Clark Gable and Vivien Leigh, clouds filled the sky, a crack of lightning zigzagged and a burst of thunder ignited a torrent of rain. I flicked the windshield wiper lever and watched as the driver side wiper was the single wiper to respond.

We turned to each other.

"I'm not that smart," I begged. "I didn't know."

"Well, we have a choice. I can slide over if you promise to be a gentleman, or we can try the western at the Granada."

"I'm all for the slide and trying to be a gentleman if you'll give me the chance."

I gave her the answer that she wanted. She slid across the seat and got close filling me with her scent. It further numbed my heightened state. I still couldn't believe I was actually sitting where I was.

The movie started and grabbed my interest immediately. Well, not all of it. "This is as good as a western," I critiqued, "At least there's a few horses in it."

She laughed.

Our heads moved back and forth in perfect synchronization, to the constant rhythm of the wiper. Each swipe built greater rhythm. And just as Clark was leaving Scarlett at the front doorway, the wiper stopped and we bumped heads, ever so slightly. We turned and looked at each other and laughed, and stopped. Then we looked into each other's eyes and inched our mouths closer and kissed. And kissed again, and again and...

The next thing we heard was a rap at the window. "It's time Romeo," the security man in the orange jacket bellowed without looking inside. We parted lips, wiped down the foggy windows and looked outside to see a blank screen, and an empty parking lot. The movie speaker crackled static.

There was no sense of time, only bliss. We both leaned back, not sure of what had just happened but we both knew that it was something special. By mutual consent, the connection, as right as the rain that had created it.

"Well," I gasped as I took a deep breath. We were encapsulated; fogged into the car as if in a space ship. I flipped the fan switch and popped the windshield with the back of my hand and sent the disabled wiper back rotating.

"Glad you didn't do that before," she said.

I turned and smiled and cast a disbelieving look...and kissed her one more time.

When the windows cleared, I dropped the car in gear and inched my way out of the Drive-in. The only sound was the tires crushing the stones beneath them.

Jo reached over and grabbed my hand and pulled it onto her lap. No one spoke. It was OK. I was a gentleman and she a lady.

Our evening together was more than anyone could have asked for and established a deep connection. Each subsequent date held the magic of the first one and more. Each encounter, more desire. Senior year was now nearing an end and I was still pushing hard with the school work and pumping gas at the Mobil station. Motivated by my new love and distaste for the old Sean, I was transforming myself into the person I wanted to be, and possibly could become. Time and resolve would erase the blights on my character and well...make me worthy.

Last Call

One Saturday evening, Jo called and my father answered.

"Is Sean there?" she said. "Yeah, he's here," and Pops hung up.

"Sean, just someone who wanted to know if you were here," he yelled up the stairs. That was Pops, always the semantic. If you wanted to speak with someone you had to ask to do that, not ask "Are they there?"

The phone rang again. "Daddy, lemme get it..." I cried out but Pops picked it up again before I could.

"May I please speak with Sean?" Jo Inquired.

"He's right here," Tom Brennan said, proud that his English lesson worked. I grabbed the phone from him as he turned and walked away. Those words would be the only ones that Jo and my father would ever share.

"He's kinda rough," she said.

"You gotta get it right or you won't pass with Daddy."

"Party at Duffy's tonight," she announced.

"I'll be there when I get off from the gas station," I promised.

I was a little rusty Sunday morning after a wild one on Saturday night. It was all good fun, a couple of malt liquors, only cause you got tipsy a little quicker and a long night of dancing to disco and James Brown.

On Sunday, Daddy announced that he wasn't feeling well which was like a Cubs World Series title, very rare. He was never sick and never complained. It was always straight ahead for him until you couldn't stand anymore. He was all about music and words and creativity and doing, not watching and never turning on the TV. Life was to be lived and you were to get smarter every day. Nothing passive would do.

On Monday, everything was normal as we all went to school. Daddy went to work and Bridie boiled the oatmeal and slapped together the cheese sandwiches for lunch at school. Tom left the usual five dollars on the kitchen table for Bridie to buy groceries at Krupa's for dinner.

By the time we returned from routes, Daddy was gone and would be gone forever…the single trace of him was the fiver sitting on the table nestled next to the sugar bowl. It was there every morning, but this morning, for the last time.

Bridie read the tea leaves before we went to school and declared complete confusion, "I've never seen a formation like this one, probably something unexpected, can't even tell if it's good or bad. Be careful lads."

After a good day at school, I checked in at the gas station for my night shift. I had to do all the work, as the rotund hillbuck Gene sat on his fat arse and watched…as usual. As I was giving change to a customer and starting to head back into the hut to get warm, I heard the phone ring from inside and saw Gene struggle to get off the stool and answer it. There was an old phone booth inside the hut with a folding door and dimpled siding that Gene couldn't squeeze into but could still reach inside to answer the phone.

I saw him put the receiver to his ear and nod.

"Just a second," he said. He called out to me "It's for you," as I crossed into the kiosk. I knew it was for me because if it wasn't for him there was only me left. It had to be for me. My antennae went straight up because I never got phone calls at work.

"Make it quick," Gene warned, afraid that he might have to wait on a car.

"Sean," it was my little brother, Phelim. My antennae extended higher. He never called.

"Yes."

"Tom is dead," was all he said. I dropped the phone and left it dangling and banging against the dimpled siding and raced out the door.

"Hey, you can't leeeaaa," Gene screamed. I never heard him finish. I was already on my bike and peddling hard, oblivious to his request. I flew across the boulevard and the avenue without looking, only thinking that maybe Phelim had gotten it wrong. Maybe, just maybe there was a second chance or breath or anything to keep his call from being the truth.

When I got home, I hopped off the bike without stopping, sending the relic into the bridal veils that were just starting to bloom. I raced up the wooden stairs two at a time and burst inside the front door to the sight of a tearful Bridie just inside. Her look said it all. It was true.

She threw her arms open and I ran to them and squeezed her as hard as she squeezed me.

"Shhh," was all she said and she squeezed harder. After an eternal moment, I let go and stepped back and tilted my head as if to say, "What happened?"

"His heart," was all she said. Tom Brennan was fifty-five.

"Ma, what are we going to do?" I begged.

"We're going to live on, just like he'd want us to."

"We're going to breathe and seek and create and try and whistle and...all without the "tellie". That'll make him happy."

"But Ma...couldn't I have just had one chance to say good-bye or tell him how much he meant to us or just something to ease the pain of it all being over in just one short moment?"

"Life doesn't have a script or a watch or an alarm." Bridie said. "That's why we have to live everyday like it's our last and why we have to love each and every soul, because it might be their last or yours."

"He did leave one little gift, though." She reached inside her dress and pulled out a card.

"This was inside his wallet, Sean." She handed it to me and squeezed my hand with both of hers. As she let go, I looked down and opened the folded card. It was my last report card with my grades underlined in red, as if he was correcting my latest essay. It was better but still not perfect. Daddy had been quietly watching. Bridie reached out with both arms and I followed, embracing each other, both knowing that he hadn't just left.

Tom Brennan was with us and always would be.

The Wake

Tom Brennan's passing draped a pall over Cloonmore. He had died at the age of fifty-five without warning. The thought that he would never walk through the front door and cut the plug off of the "tellie" put us all in shock. There was never again going to be a float for the Nurses' Day Parade, Easter outfits for the whole clan or Daddy demanding that we write an essay after a family outing.

Most of Chicago turned out for the wake and funeral because Tom Brennan was a big deal in the business and Irish communities. The Easter outfits had made the Brennan's famous and Pop's obituary in the *Trib* on March 10, 1969 sent out a call for many to mourn.

Ahern, another mick from the old sod who seized on the Irish love for a good send off and owned a funeral parlor, rolled out the red carpet for the wake. I don't remember if he extended a discount to Bridie but I had my doubts as a call went out for, "help with the funeral."

Daddy didn't have an insurance policy because that would have meant some foresight and the Irish in general and the Brennan's in particular, weren't going to ruin any grim surprise that was coming tomorrow, by planning for it today. Serendipity was the essence of our madness and without it...well...would we ever laugh?

The wake was typical in form but unique in character. All the ladies cooked and contributed all kinds of food, corned beef, soda bread, roasted potatoes. If it hadn't been Tom lying there in the box, we would've wanted to go to one every night. The tables were loaded with all the Irish fare we'd get at home on a special occasion. A whiskey room was designated for all of the old country lads who, as much as they loved Daddy, wouldn't have come if there wasn't one. The lines for the friends and relatives to extend their sympathies extended out the door and around the block. And each one of us stood tall alongside Bridie and accepted every well wish from every sympathizer in between trips to the snack room.

The next day's funeral mass was grand and filled the church to the brim. Bridie eschewed the typical black bonnet and black lace veil, choosing instead to don her own version of sorrow with colors that looked death in the eye and expressed her fierce determination. A flute filled the Basilica with airs of Irish lilt.

For me, the deep moments were the most sincere and surprising: walking up the aisle alongside the coffin with one hand softly placed on top, I saw people who I never would have expected to attend – through my tears I spotted Mr. T, my high school teacher who had caught me short changing his test. He winked as I passed. The silent rich guy who drove down our alley and once a month, tossed a new softball out of the window was in the back row. I still never got his name. Chris Dates, the puddle jumper and Ollie the Kraut all had a seat. And Hank, the mailman who, when I was in first grade, let me help deliver the mail; he now stood erect like the soldier that he was.

And Jayne and Jo both wishing they could give me a hug…and for more than one reason.

Passing every row as we slowly made our way up the main aisle toward the altar, each filled with mourners trying to soothe our pain with their gaze. And as I saw each face, I was warmed by how giving and thoughtful people could be during your time of need.

And then the Father, amid a plume of incense, eulogizing the merits of Tom Brennan and all of his wonders and greatness and hearing Bridie whisper to one of the girls, "Do they have the right man in the coffin?"

No, Bridie never lost her humor or ever forgot the eternal need for it. It was always the one thing that we always had no matter what we needed, how bad something hurt, or sad you might be.

And then the three lads, Michael, Sean and Tom in *a capella*, filling the basilica with their own version of "Galway Bay." I can still hear it and I'm sure Daddy can too, "And if there is going to be a life hereafter, and I'm sure there's going to be…"

Then, one last trip for Tom Brennan, for the first time quiet and still in the back of the hearse, down Euclid Avenue past the yellow and green Cloonmore. The wooden shingle that hung above the front stairs and welcomed all that came, swinging and squeaking gently in the breeze. We'll oil it tomorrow.

I remembered again the moment we all first saw the shingle, and the look on Bridie's face. How Daddy had quietly painted it and hung it just above the front steps, welcoming her to her new world by remembering the old.

At the cemetery as Tom Brennan was lowered into his eternal resting spot, we each tossed a handful of dirt and the red roses from our lapels and bid a final farewell…to Daddy and an era the likes of which we'll never see again.

When we got back to Cloonmore, most in a stupor of what tomorrow would bring, just inside the front door, the piano started to bang and the chorus started to sing, "Sure a little bit of heaven fell from out the skies one day and it nestled in the ocean in a spot so far away," and sure a bit of Eire and the lass who was full of its charm and had left, was all that we needed to forge the future.

The party was welcomed… the pain was eased…but just a bit. And for the next few hours we jammed around the piano in a style that would have made Tom Brennan proud. All that was missing was his accordion. His style didn't demand talent, only heart.

The night wore on, the bottles emptied, the stories paled, the tears flowed and finally I broke away and tripped my way up the stairs and into the bathroom that had the single mirror in the house. How fitting, that in a house that was steeped in Bridie's selflessness there was only one mirror, a spotted, cracked, smokey piece of silverless glass, unwilling to let anyone feast on their looks.

I grabbed each side of the sink with my now steadied hands, sidestepping the hill of baking soda and looked hard and deep into the mirror and what it could echo back. I weaved through the smirched glass and found my own eyes, took a breath and made a solemn promise to my own self that although Daddy had been torn from my young life I would continue on with all the resolve that he had sewn into each and every essay, Easter outfit and Sunday night musical. His insistence and invention was now, my new light.

The next day, there wasn't a moment to grieve, Bridie herded us around the kitchen table with the silent tea pot steaming the wall and the oatmeal bubbling away like the volcano of life.

"Lads, we've been dealt a bad hand. There's a challenge in front of us, the likes of which would wilt most. Now I want you to hold your head high, try as you've never tried before and remember that your thoughts should caress, not what we lost, but what we had."

The next day, despite the void that would take years to even partially fill, we all trudged on with our regular lives. Bridie decided to join the work force and landed a job at the local department store, and with that Irish gait that had plodded through the fields of Eire, made the two mile walk each way every day.

"Can we get you a ride?"

"I wouldn't think of it." Her straight, proud figure could be seen morning and night, as she strode to and from her new job.

Every night I laid in bed and stared at the ceiling hoping that somehow this was all a dream and that in the morning I would hear a call from the bottom of the stairs, "The photographers are waiting!" It would be Easter morning again...the girls curling one more tress...the lads in the front yard modeling their new suits as they crossed the goal line...Bridie pressing the wrinkles out of one last suit...and Tom Brennan awash in pride and expectation at his brood leading Chicago's Easter Parade.

Daddy's next chant may never come but I still listen for it.

Epilogue

Return to Cloonmore

"It'll give you a taste of the Old Sod," he said.

I'd been to the doctor for a bad strep throat and sitting in the waiting room, was an old man, enrapt in a thick tome. His reddened face and cocked head lead me to think he was Irish. Most Irishman had a wee bit tilt to their heads; it came from the soft nod that they often greeted you with. "A bit of the gleck," Bridie called it.

The book was big and fat – not my type but it was bound in the colors of the Irish flag and had "Trinity" splashed across the front. Another church book, I thought and didn't give it a second consideration.

After a few minutes and surveying the stately gentleman's deep interest, I took the bait and asked about the book.

"How are you enjoying the book?" I asked, ignoring the obvious.

"Grand, just grand, almost done," he replied in a deep heavy Irish brogue.

"I'm learning things about my home that I'm ashamed to admit I never knew. It's taken a passionate Jewish author to expose our tragic history to me."

"Huh?"

"Leon Uris is the author and he goes to Temple instead of Church, but we won't hold that against him."

"Oh."

"It's a must read if you have Irish roots."

"Ummm."

"Next," came from the buxom nurse. And that meant me.

I left, wondering about Ireland and why I never had any interest in its history. For years when it was naptime or bedtime, Bridie would tell us stories of the "Black and Tans," mercenaries that terrorized the Irish rebels at the turn of the century or Nora Corrigan, the widow who would play her fiddle on a hilltop under a bright moon, overlooking the Kiltimagh River.

The doctor flinched when he looked down my throat and saw the golf ball sized tonsils.

"It's time to pull the plug on those things," he advised.

And after a prescription for some medicine and a scheduled date with the surgeon, I slipped out of the office, taking one last look inside the waiting room to thank the old-timer. The bloke was gone but the book was lying on the seat of his now empty chair. The book beckoned me and I strutted over to examine it further. Inside the front cover was a note: "I hope you enjoy this as much as I did. "Erin Go Braugh"

There was something fateful about our meeting.

That night I started the book and in a week finished. I immediately laid plans to visit the old sod. It wasn't the abuse of the English or the dominance of the Church that seized my interest, it was the mystic aura of that grand land that seemed to seep through the pages and into my first generation blood.

I was twenty-five and in need of some adventure and change. I had never been overseas and was employed by a government agency, chasing alleged "tax cheats" who weren't doing anything that everybody else wasn't doing. When I first signed on, I thought that I would be investigating big timers, the modern day equivalents of Capone or Dillinger. But today's tax cheats had learned the ropes and had gone underground with their larceny. It made it harder for the Feds and they never liked a challenge. Instead of Capone-like weasels, I was going after Ma and Pa's like my own folks. The motto was "get the people who could afford the least resistance" and it discouraged me. Every day I went to work, I pushed my pencil having no desire to put anyone in jail, least of all guys like my own father. I was surrounded by middle-aged agents counting their days to retirement and adding up the sick days they hadn't used that would give them an early out.

Ironically it was my own sick day that sparked my interest in Eire. Bridie may well have seen it in her morning tea leaves.

"Hey, Ma, how about you and I visit the old sod?"

"The map of Ireland was at the bottom of the cup this morning," she said.

We never really knew if Bridie had the gift of clairvoyance or that her oracles were prophetic, but their timing and frequency made it just too hard to believe that there wasn't something magical about her glorious soul.

Bridie's stories and my newfound thirst for adventure melded into a plan that would take Bridie and me across the pond and to my heritage. Bridie had been easy to convince:

"I'll take you home to Cloonmore and show you the rest of Ireland for the first time."

"I'm in," she said.

I knew what she was thinking – what would she find? She had left home for America when she was just a seventeen-year-old schoolgirl who had never seen any of Ireland but her own home village Cloonmore and the nearest town, Kiltimagh. She'd left behind her family, all her friends and neighbors. Who and what would be left?

They told me that Ireland was a shade of green that existed only on the Emerald Isle and they were right. From the airplane window as we descended into Shannon airport, the land I saw glistened like one big emerald pillow just waiting for me to roll down the hill and lie in the plush grass.

When evening descended on our first night in Ireland, we arrived at our first bed and breakfast, the only places to stay in Eire, we pulled back the comforters in the chilly room only to find a hot water bottle warming our welcome.

"Jesus, Ma, just like back home at Cloonmore," I quipped.

"Weren't the wool blankets good enough for you," and she tossed the pillow at me.

The next morning was breakfast with the residents and lots of conversation. And when they heard Bridie's brogue and that we were Yanks, the welcome carpet got redder, the tea sweeter and the aura warmer. I could see Bridie in the host of the B&B and how her only quest was to make us as welcome and comfortable as possible. It brought back the kitchen table at Cloonmore, the cornerstone of my life.

After Donegal, Dublin, Derry and Dunloe it was time for Bridie's home – Kiltimagh town and at last, the village of Cloonmore.

We parked the car at the far end of Cloonmore and decided to stroll into town unannounced. It was lunch time and all the town was out and about in the warm Erin sun. Seeing the sun didn't happen often in Ireland and the town folk didn't miss any opportunity to bask in the clear day.

"It stopped raining,"

"You're noots"

"It did!"

Down the road we strolled looking for the first countryman who would have the shock of seeing Bridie as a specter from the past. It didn't take long.

"Bejasus, is that you, Bridie. I can tell that gait anywhere."

It was Nora, the violinist. Back in the day, when Bridie was a wee lass, she would sit with Nora as she played her violin on the hill that overlooked Cloonmore. Nora was older now and walked with a slight limp. Dressed in a monk-like robe, she put down her bundle, wrapped in brown paper and string and threw her arms out and wide open and came to Bridie with a smile as wide as the River Shannon. After hugs and kisses and wails and gasps the parade started. The cry went out: "Bridie's back, Bridie's back!"

"Who's the lad," Nora inquired.

"That's my Sean." Bridie introduced.

"BeJasus, doesn't he look like Eamonn." Nora said, referring to Bridie's deceased brother. To every Irishman, everyone looks like somebody.

The street filled. The joy spread. The screams echoed.

And finally at the doorstep of Bridie's thatched roof old farmhouse, I gave a rap at the gold knocker and Bridie's youngest sister Molly opened the door.

Molly gave out a gasp, hands over her mouth and then threw her arms wide open and clutched her big sister who at last, found her way back after so many years. Molly was mute from emotion, stunned by surprise and her face wet with tears...Bridie, the same.

The next day, after much hoopla and just good ol' simple happiness, Bridie, Aunt Molly, Uncle Tom and I took a walk to the graveyard. In Ireland you don't have to look hard to find a graveyard. They put them everywhere just in case you need to say a prayer for someone. We said a prayer above Bridie's brothers, Anthony and Eamonn who had died in accidents in England. Back in the day, if you didn't emigrate to America you chose the quick jaunt across the Irish Sea to England where there was work, because in Ireland, there was none.

Finally, we made the pilgrimage to the Kiltimagh train station from which Bridie had departed so many years before. At the train station, that was now abandoned and overgrown with grass and weeds, Bridie started sniveling and said, "I can still remember the day."

"Me too," said Molly.

And then Bridie told the whole story as we stared at the empty tracks, the rutted earth and weeds that waved where once the train wheels turned.

"It was 1929 then and I had to choose between stepping onto that rickety train as it sat belching out steam and ding ding dings, leaving the *streeshing* relatives on the platform, maybe for life, or staying and living the desolate life that Ireland was offering. At the time it seemed like an easy decision – the prosperity of America or the penury of Ireland. Little did I know that if I got on that train I was heading straight into the stock market crash and Great Depression. Oh, for a little timing."

"I can remember the torture of my heart and soul as I raised my quivering leg and placed my foot on the first step of the train. I couldn't look back…not yet anyway. I could only stand to hear the sobs and wails coming from the souls behind me, the souls who had been a part of my every breath…until now. I lifted my leaden legs two more times, got to the top of the train landing and mustered the strength to look back. Despite the pain, I had to. And then the train gave one more glorious, final belch of steam, three more 'ding, ding, dings' and broke into motion, southwest, toward the Irish coast and the *Scythia,* the ship that would carry me to America.

"I remember stepping back down the stairs, not to change my mind but to get one last look at Ma and Pa and Molly and Aiden and Sonny and anyone else from town who had the fortitude to see a loved one leave for the new country. Your only thought was that it was the last time you would see them…and many times it was.

Irish good-byes are never easy, even if you're heading home after an evening with a neighbor. For the Irish, each time you leave someone it might be for life so you better get all the hugging and holding and conversation that you could possibly fit into the precious final moments. If it was the final time, you had a treasure of sentiment to last your lifetime and ease you through any forlorn memories.

"I gripped the rail with my right hand just to steady myself and waved and waved with my left, looking back with my eyes full of tears, blurring the world that I was leaving behind. With each turn of the massive metal wheels and each new bellow of steam, my last vision of Kiltimagh narrowed and faded and was finally gone as the train turned the first curve."

And then Molly broke in:

"It was like seeing someone take their last breath. Seeing that train turn the curve and watching your image get smaller and smaller and finally I saw only your waving hand…and then nothing."

By now Molly was holding Bridie's hand and then they turned and embraced, erasing the years and miles that had come between them.

Acknowledgements

The writing of *Bridie's Boy* began some three years ago partly as a challenge from Mary Lou Edwards, author, of *"Look Back, But Don't Stare"*.

"You have a story to tell, get to it." she said. And I did.

Bridie's Boy started as a series of short stories about life in a big Irish family with few resources, chronic mayhem, but a sense of humor that served as an omniscient panacea. The stories grew into a full memoir.

None of the joy, laughter, and predicament on these pages would be possible without the legacy of my mother's great Irish wit. It permeated every moment of our lives, knew no off switch, salving all of the sores that existence can bring. Nothing was off limits and at my father Tom's funeral when the priest extolled his virtues, Bridie asked, "Do they have the right man in the coffin?"

I would like to extend my sincerest and deepest heartfelt gratitude to that wit, the essence and uniqueness of that distant island, the ancestry of all of the Brennans and Colemans, our friend Nora Corrigan and her family, and my ten brothers and sisters who helped weave every twist and turn in this story and finally to Bridie and Tom, who made our life possible and grand. Thank you to all of my editors, supporters and contributors whose input has a place on every page.

– *Sean Brennan*

About the Author

The tenth of the eleven Brennan children, Sean began his writing career at the dining room table in Pop's sewing room. His stories of growing up in Chicago and Oak Park have grown into this memoir of his Irish American boyhood in the 50's and 60's.

Sean Brennan has been married to Joan Brennan for 35 years and they are the parents of Eamonn and Devon. Sean Brennan lives in Long Beach, Indiana.

Cead Mile Failte

Cover design by Julie Nitz, JLN Studio, Three Oaks Mi.

Front cover photo:
It's Easter Sunday 1961 just three months after John Kennedy's inauguration. Our new President was the first Chief Executive to wear a top hat to his inauguration since Woodrow Wilson in 1913. Tom Brennan took notice, finally having an Irish Catholic in the oval office and was never one to miss a cue or opportunity. Off the Brennan clan marched to another Chicago landmark, McCormick Place clad in the 'Classic' look as Pops referred to it. The Chicago Tribune did the photographing.

Back cover photo:
Sean and Bridie in front of Dominican High School, graduation day 1969.

33960602R00173

Made in the USA
San Bernardino, CA
16 May 2016